The Suriname Writings of John Gabriel Stedman

The Suriname Writings of John Gabriel Stedman

Edited, with an Introduction, by

Jared Ross Hardesty

Hackett Publishing Company, Inc.
Indianapolis/Cambridge

Copyright © 2024 by Hackett Publishing Company, Inc.

All rights reserved
Printed in the United States of America

27 26 25 24   1 2 3 4 5 6 7

For further information, please address
    Hackett Publishing Company, Inc.
    P.O. Box 44937
    Indianapolis, Indiana 46244-0937

    www.hackettpublishing.com

Composition by Aptara, Inc.

Library of Congress Control Number: 2023943366

ISBN-13: 978-1-64792-154-5 (pbk.)
ISBN-13: 978-1-64792-155-2 (PDF ebook)
ISBN-13: 978-1-64792-156-9 (epub)

The paper used in this publication meets the minimum requirements of American National Standard for Information Sciences—Permanence of Paper for Printed Library Materials, ANSI Z39.48–1984.

∞

Contents

Maps	*vi*
Preface and Acknowledgments	*ix*
Introduction	*xi*
Reading This Edition	*xxxvii*

The Suriname Diary of John Gabriel Stedman

Volume I: February 1773–April 1774	3
Volume II: October 1775–December 1776	45

The Narrative of a Five Years Expedition against the Revolted Negroes of Surinam (1796)

Volume I	95
The Preface	95
Chapter I	97
Chapter V	109
Chapter VIII	121
Chapter XIII	129
Volume II	141
Chapter XX	141
Chapter XXIV	153
Chapter XXVII	162
Chapter XXIX	170
Appendix: The Diary and the Narrative	*183*
Further Reading	*197*
Index	*199*

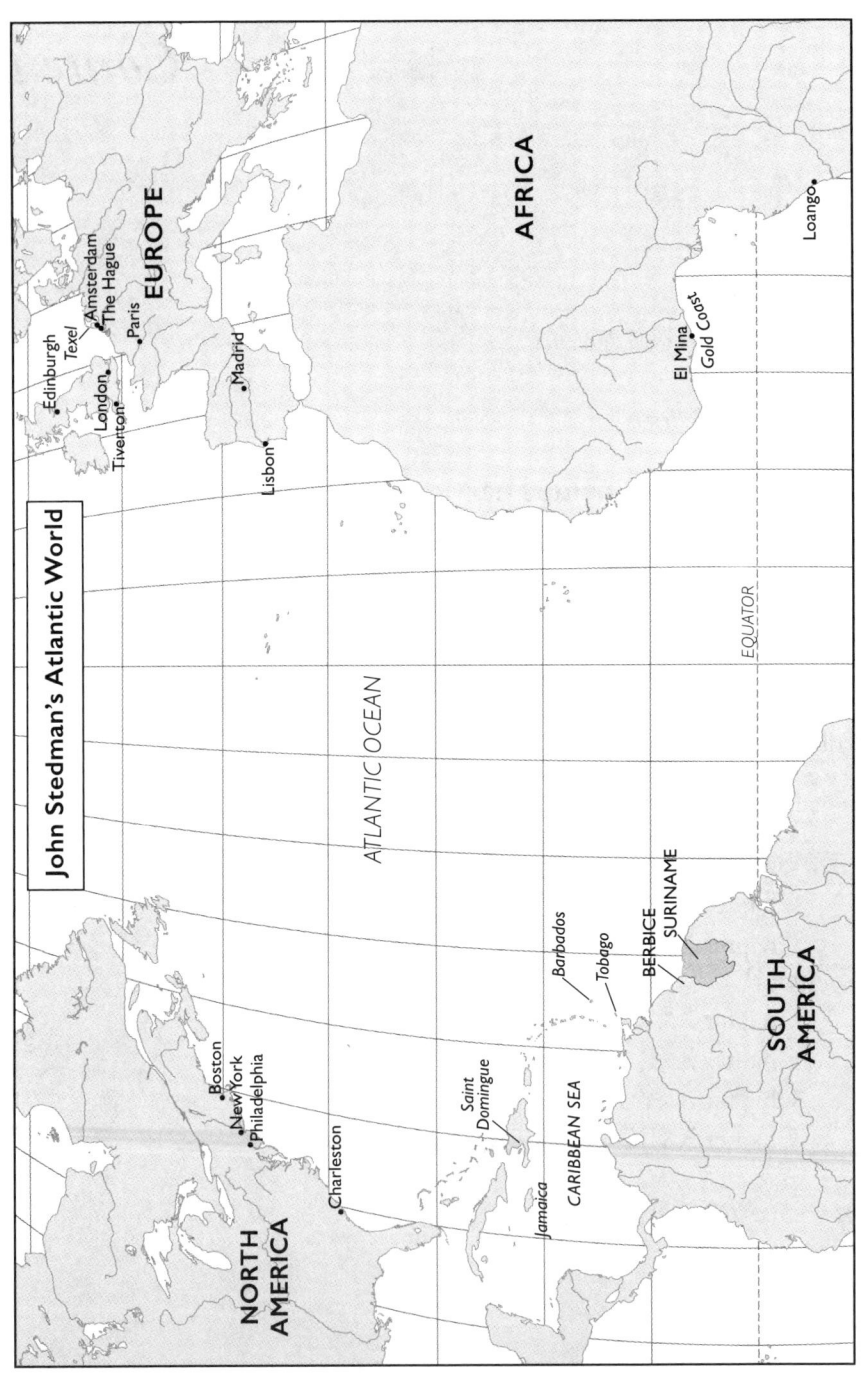

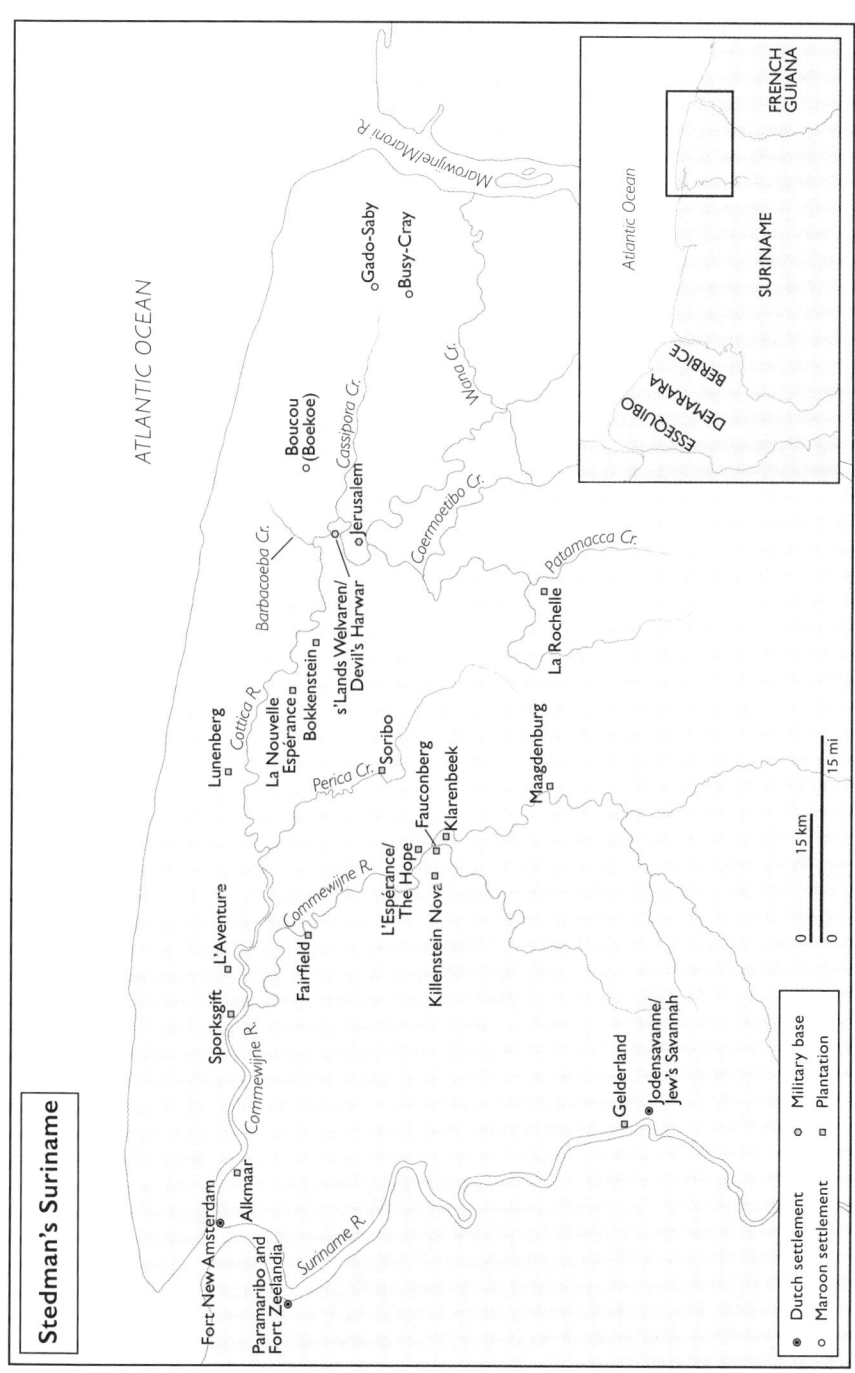

Preface and Acknowledgments

The Suriname Writings of John Gabriel Stedman introduces readers to soldier and author John Gabriel Stedman (1744–1797). Today, Stedman is remembered for his time fighting against maroons—runaway slaves—in the Dutch colony of Suriname between 1772 and 1777 and his later book about that experience, *The Narrative of a Five Years Expedition against the Revolted Negroes of Surinam* (1796). From the publication of the *Narrative* until the present day, activists, literary scholars, military strategists, anthropologists, and historians have taken a keen interest in Stedman and his work. As such, various versions of Stedman's writings have remained in print since 1796.

This edition takes a different approach to understanding Stedman and his world. Whereas previous editions emphasized Stedman's 1796 *Narrative* or the 1790 draft version, this book centers on the diary that Stedman kept during his time in Suriname. As Stedman's primary source for the *Narrative*, the diary offers Stedman's immediate, unfiltered observations of his experiences in Suriname. Throughout the diary, Stedman revealed much of his character, his behavior as a white man living in a slave society, his thoughts about the world he encountered, and the subjects he took a deep interest in. Some of these, such as his fascination with Suriname's natural history, later appeared in the *Narrative*, but he obfuscated or removed many entirely. The diary reveals Stedman's propensity for violence; ambiguous attitudes toward slavery and racism; dutiful, if entitled, military service; and indulgence—and overindulgence— in Suriname's debauched high society.

In the two decades between Stedman's service in Suriname and the publication of the *Narrative*, he reimagined, sometimes dramatically, the meaning and purpose of his time there. Thus, this edition also includes chapters from the 1796 *Narrative*, modernized and annotated, for the reader to understand better the transformation in Stedman's attitudes regarding his time in Suriname. He—and his editors and publisher—sanitized much of his unsavory behavior, expanded his thoughts about Suriname's history, and articulated a reformist vision of slavery and the slave trade. By 1796, Stedman argued that while slavery was morally repugnant, it was also a necessary labor system that could be effectively reformed into a more humane institution.

Taken together, Stedman's Suriname diary and selections of the *Narrative* offer a new way of reading Stedman and his importance in the literary canon of slavery. Reading both texts in unison, readers can see how Stedman's thoughts on slavery, race, and the maroon war evolved and how he censored himself for allegedly respectable audiences. Ultimately, however, Stedman chronicled a dynamic plantation society and made a habit of greeting and getting to know everyone in Suriname society—European colonists and enslaved people, Indigenous peoples, maroons, as well as mixed-race, white, and Black creoles (native-born colonists), and the colony's Jewish population. Such detail, insight, and empathy make John Stedman's writings important sources for studying and understanding slavery in the Atlantic world and New World slave societies.

Many people assisted with my understanding of John Gabriel Stedman and the preparation of this edition. Karwan Fatah-Black is the authority on all things Suriname, and his knowledge, conversation, and scholarship were all important. Craig Gallagher served as my "MacGregor translator," helping me work through Stedman's language in the journal and teaching me about the Scots dialect in the process. Emi Foulk-Bushelle and Owen Stanwood talked to me about editing documents and how to best format this edition. Annie Avila helped format and prepare the diary and *Narrative* for editing. Marguerite Ragnow, curator at the University of Minnesota's James Ford Bell Library, answered a number of queries about the manuscript diary, how it came into the possession of the Bell Library, and the digitization process. Finally, I would like to thank Rick Todhunter, senior editor at Hackett Publishing Company, for his steadfast support and encouragement of all things Stedman. Elana Rosenthal and the rest of the team at Hackett deserve praise for shepherding the volume through production. All mistakes remain mine alone.

Introduction

John Gabriel Stedman (1744–1797) was a career soldier, the oldest child of Robert Stedman, a Scottish military officer, and a Dutch mother, Antoinetta Christina van Ceulen. Like his father, Stedman was an officer in the Scots Brigade, a long-standing foreign unit in the Dutch army. He enlisted as an ensign in 1760 and eventually became a major before resigning in 1783. Looking to escape debt and personal troubles, he joined a mission in 1772 to aid planters and officials in the Dutch plantation colony of Suriname in a war against the colony's maroon, or runaway slave, population. Over nearly five years, Stedman endured disease, a challenging political climate, and brutal guerilla warfare as he helped to destroy the maroon threat systematically. He fully imbibed in plantation society, engaging in great feats of drinking and using enslaved women to satiate a seemingly unlimited sexual appetite. Early in his sojourn, Stedman bought access to and raped a fifteen-year-old mixed-race enslaved girl named Joanna, eventually falling in love, "marrying," and having a son with her. Always positioning himself as an outside observer, he meticulously recorded everything he witnessed and experienced in a diary he kept during his stay in the colony. Eventually, in the late 1780s, after returning to the Netherlands and being exiled to England during the Fourth Anglo-Dutch War (1780–1784), Stedman wrote a narrative of his experiences in Suriname.

Today, John Gabriel Stedman is most famous for writing *The Narrative of a Five Years Expedition against the Revolted Negroes of Surinam*. While not published until 1796, he used his diary to compose a draft that he finished in 1790. About a year after the publication of the *Narrative*, Stedman died on March 7, 1797, in Tiverton, England. Although he did not live to see it, Stedman's book took on a life of its own, going through more than twenty-five editions since publication, being translated into many languages, and having excerpts published as stand-alone books. Popular with literary scholars interested in abolitionism and colonialism, anthropologists studying maroon communities, historians of slavery, counterinsurgency experts, and readers looking for a great adventure story for more than two centuries, Stedman's *Narrative* has earned a place in the literary canon.

Early Life

Much of what we know about Stedman's early life comes from an autobiographical narrative he wrote shortly after his retirement to England in the late 1780s. Imitating popular eighteenth-century fictional works such as Tobias Smollett's *The Adventures of Roderick Random* (1748), one of Stedman's favorite books, his own recollection creates the image of a rowdy, frivolous, and ultimately harmful (to others and himself) young man. Even if parts of the story are fictionalized and dramatized, Stedman does offer important factual details.

After being born in what is today Belgium while his father, Robert Stedman, a captain in the Scots Brigade, was on campaign, Stedman spent his early boyhood in various Dutch garrisons on the southern frontier of the Netherlands. Around the age of eleven in 1755, Stedman's father sent him to live with his uncle, John Stedman, a medical doctor, in Dumferline, a Scottish town just north of Edinburgh. The elder Stedman, who John Gabriel derisively referred to as "the *Philosopher*," sought to provide a formal education to the boy, but his cool and aloof demeanor largely alienated his nephew. Instead, young John Gabriel made friends with local boys and found ways to get into mischief, such as breaking into the local parsonage, swindling local farmers, and scaring elderly women by firing pistols behind their backs. Such behavior garnered Stedman a bad reputation. After Stedman had a number of run-ins with local magistrates and—perhaps an indication of his budding misogyny—"attempting to shoot [his] uncle's old maid," the elder John sent his nephew back to his father in Holland. Given the "antipathy" between the two John Stedmans, when Robert agreed to take John Gabriel back, it gave "the *Philosopher* inexpressible joy, but not more than it did poor Johnny Stedman."[1]

Upon his return to the Netherlands, Stedman's parents explored the possibility for John Gabriel to become a painter, a hobby he pursued for the rest of his life, but he ultimately became a soldier. In 1760, Stedman mustered as an ensign, the lowest-ranked commissioned officer in European militaries at the time, in Colonel Stuart's Regiment of the Scots Brigade. Organized as a foreign expeditionary force or, perhaps more honestly, a mercenary corps, in 1586 to assist the Dutch Republic in its long war of independence from Hapsburg Spain, the Scots Brigade was still a robust military force in the Netherlands in the mid-eighteenth century. During Stedman's youth, the Brigade consisted of between three and six infantry regiments and upward of 7,000 soldiers and officers.[2] Many of these men had family connections to the Brigade. Stedman's

---

1. Stanbury Thompson, ed., *The Journal of John Gabriel Stedman, 1744–1797, Soldier and Author: Including an Authentic Account of His Expedition to Surinam in 1772* (London: The Mitre Press, 1962), 12–13.

2. Stephen Conway, "The Scots Brigade in the Eighteenth Century," *Northern Scotland* 1 (2010): 30.

father eventually became a lieutenant colonel in Stuart's Regiment, while his younger brother, William George, also enlisted as an officer.

By the mid-eighteenth century, however, the Scots Brigade had changed. A major concern was that most of the Brigade's officer corps were, unsurprisingly, Scots, creating tension between the Netherlands and Great Britain. For that reason, after 1678, all officers in the Scots Brigade had to pledge loyalty to the British monarch in addition to the Dutch Republic and could be called into British military service at any time, meaning the Scots Brigade was technically on loan from Britain to the Netherlands.[3] Indeed, during his time in Suriname, Stedman recorded news in his diary that King George III considered recalling the Scots Brigade to Britain and deploying it to North America to suppress the king's rebellious American subjects.[4] Despite the tension, however, Scots military men continued to enlist in the Brigade, often out of economic necessity. Scotland, very poor yet possessing an excellent educational system, overproduced well-educated, ambitious young men who disproportionately looked to military service to improve their condition.[5] Robert Stedman, John Gabriel's father, very much fit this mold, leaving Scotland to join the Brigade in 1730. Having seen the poverty and lack of opportunity in Scotland in his adolescence, John Gabriel followed in his father's footsteps.

After receiving his ensign's commission, Stedman spent the next decade traveling around the Dutch Republic, serving garrison duty in several frontier areas. Although eventually receiving a commission as a lieutenant, Stedman described himself during these years (and during much of his time in Suriname) as a victim of authority. Somehow, he always found himself caught in the political machinations of his senior officers. Often in a bind, Stedman bounced from situation to situation, place to place, his fate largely, at least by his own description, out of his control. Stedman certainly did not do himself any favors, however. Quick-tempered and itching for a fight, he threw himself into the Scots Brigade's factional infighting with little regard for the consequences.

Stedman's description of his youth also reveals him as a man of voracious appetites. He loved to socialize, drink, gamble, and fornicate. Not only did these trap Stedman in a significant amount of debt by the time he was in his mid-twenties, but they also created serious social frictions. As previous editors of Stedman's work have commented, he envisioned himself as a "Lothario" that could not escape the attention of women.[6] Whether in the Netherlands or Suriname, Stedman constantly found himself in the bedrooms of magistrates' daughters, being seduced by married women, or being pursued by domestic

---

3. Conway, "Scots Brigade," 31.
4. See diary entry for May 21, 1776.
5. Conway, "Scots Brigade," 33–34.
6. Richard Price and Sally Price, *Stedman's Surinam: Life in an Eighteenth-Century Slave Society* (Baltimore, MD: Johns Hopkins University, 1992), xvi.

servants and maids. Rarely in these encounters does Stedman describe himself as the agent or initiator but rather a passive vessel for the sexual urges of women. Nevertheless, as his Suriname diary often reveals, Stedman was a womanizer and found many ways, consensually and nonconsensually, to obtain sex.

Before discussing his time in Suriname, it is important to recognize two additional hallmarks of Stedman's life that shaped his experience there. First, Stedman was a soldier who also envisioned himself as a humanitarian. Throughout his life, he vocally criticized the mistreatment of downtrodden people and defenseless animals, often committing himself to their aid. Yet, as a soldier, Stedman's business was violence. When provoked, he could threaten and inflict great harm on others and always believed there was a place for disciplinary violence. This paradox—a humanitarian ethos underpinned by violence—may make parts of the diary and *Narrative* seem contradictory, but Stedman lived in the eighteenth century, a time and place far different from our own. He would have seen no contradiction between doing his job as a soldier while also embracing the humanitarian impulse that was a key part of the European Enlightenment.

Second, by his own admission, Stedman was an unusual person. He strove to be unique and, as he later recorded, was always "studying to be singular" as much as he could.[7] Marching to the beat of his own drum, Stedman developed his own ideas about the world and how it worked. In some cases, this impulse causes Stedman to seem naïve or ignorant, such as his idea that slavery was a necessary evil that could be reformed to be more humane. Nevertheless, Stedman could also offer unique, perceptive insights into his own condition and the situations he found himself in.

Suriname

Stedman's voyage to Suriname ultimately defined the rest of his life and legacy. While it was not the first time he contemplated serving abroad, when the States General, the legislative body that governed the Dutch Republic, ordered the creation of a regiment of volunteers to serve in the "West Indies" in 1772, Stedman answered the call.[8] By that time Stedman's debts and sexual foibles had started catching up to him. He had already absconded to London once to evade his creditors, and his personal behavior burned the connections necessary for advancement in the Scots Brigade.

---

7. Quoted in Price and Price, *Stedman's Surinam*, xvii. For full original quote, see entry for November 29, 1785 in Thompson, *Journal*, 269.

8. Thompson, *Journal*, 112.

By signing up for foreign service, he not only found a way to make enough money to settle his debts but also advanced in rank, receiving a commission as a captain in the expeditionary force.

Unfortunately, the narrative Stedman wrote of his early life ends before he joined the volunteer regiment, and he only left a brief outline of his decision to join, noting sometime in 1772 that he "resolve[d] to accompany" the expedition.[9] It is unclear how much Stedman knew of the situation, but he had signed up to help quash a maroon war instigated by officials in the Dutch colony of Suriname. Since 1765, the government in Suriname had waged war on the Boni/Aluku band of maroons—the descendants of runaway slaves living autonomously in Suriname's rain forest. After suffering a string of embarrassing defeats at the hands of the maroons and proving themselves incapable of waging an effective military campaign, Suriname's officials asked the States General for assistance. Little did Stedman know that he agreed to spend over four years conducting counterinsurgency operations in the remote jungles of South America.

By the time of Stedman's February 1773 arrival in Suriname, it had become a profitable plantation colony that produced large quantities of sugar, coffee, cacao, and cotton. Perched on the northeastern coast of South America, the settlement was socially, economically, and demographically similar to colonies in the Caribbean—its entire existence was predicated upon the exploitation of a large enslaved African majority to produce valuable tropical commodities.

Being on the mainland and not confined to a small Caribbean island, however, provided seemingly endless growth possibilities. Indeed, that area of South America, known as the Guianas or the Wild Coast, had long been an area of interest for European colonizers. Well drained by a series of north-flowing rivers enveloped in a lush tropical jungle, the region was easy to explore and invited the wildest colonial dreams of early modern Europeans. In the late sixteenth century, explorers such as Walter Raleigh identified the potential riches that could be harvested from the region, even speculating it was the site of El Dorado, a legendary city of gold. Around 1600, Dutch, French, English, and Spanish settlers began attempting to colonize the region. However, dreams of vast, easy wealth vanished quickly, and the few settlements that survived did so by carrying on a robust trade with local Amerindian peoples.

At the same time Europeans colonized the Guianas, they also began establishing settlements on the smaller islands of the Caribbean. The most significant of these was the English colony of Barbados, first settled in 1625. Through extensive economic experimentation over the next two decades, English settlers developed a highly productive—and highly exploitative—plantation model. Using large groups of unfree labor, at first a mix of white indentured servants

---

9. Thompson, *Journal*, 112.

and enslaved Africans and later exclusively enslaved Africans, and expensive, state-of-the-art machinery, they started to grow large quantities of sugar cane. Sugar, known as "white gold" in the seventeenth century because of its value, provided vast riches to Barbados's planter class, and the integrated plantation model developed on the island provided a template for other colonies in the Caribbean.

It should be no surprise, then, that European nations sought to export that model to the Guianas. The first Europeans to seriously colonize Suriname proper were the English. In 1650, English settlers from Barbados established a colony on the Suriname River around what is today Paramaribo. Over the next seventeen years, Suriname, copying the economic model created in Barbados, developed into a dynamic plantation society that included fifty operational sugar plantations and more than 3,000 enslaved Africans.

Having uncovered the secret to finding riches in the Guianas, the English colony of Suriname became a target. In 1664, during the Second Anglo-Dutch War (1665–1667), a small Dutch fleet sailed up the Suriname River and forced the English garrison to surrender. During negotiations that ended the war, the Treaty of Breda, the English agreed to surrender Suriname to the Dutch in exchange for the Dutch North American colony of New Netherland (today's New York).

After assuming control of Suriname in 1667, the Dutch stumbled at first but quickly began further developing and profiting from the colony. The Dutch eventually outsourced governance and administration of the colony to the Society of Suriname, a private company. This company, a joint venture between the city of Amsterdam, the Dutch West India Company, and the Van Aerssen van Sommelsdijck family, would manage the colony until 1795. Although subordinate to the States General, the Society of Suriname had broad powers within the colony, including maintaining an army and levying taxes. Despite some issues, this model of private governance proved successful, and plantation agriculture flourished in Suriname.

By the time of Stedman's arrival in Suriname, the colony had developed into one of the wealthiest and most productive plantation societies in the Americas. The colony hosted more than 400 plantations in the second half of the eighteenth century, illustrating its dramatic growth since the Society of Suriname assumed control.[10] Using Dutch water control methods—the *polder* system—that included drainage canals and elaborate dam and sluice networks, planters in Suriname were able to keep land well watered and fertile. These waterworks

---

10. Cornelis Ch. Goslinga, *A Short History of the Netherlands Antilles and Surinam* (The Hague: Martinus Nijhoff, 1979), 100.

could also be used to power mills.¹¹ The rivers and creeks that crisscrossed the colony proved to be an effective transportation network allowing for the easy shipment of heavy loads of sugar, molasses, coffee, and cacao.

As the plantation complex expanded, so did Suriname's population. In 1774, as Stedman observed, the colony was home to more than 60,000 people. The vast majority of the population was made up of enslaved Africans. Fewer than 3,000 people in Suriname were free in the mid-1770s, and that figure includes Suriname's whites, Jews, and free people of color. Enslaved people outnumbered free people twenty to one and outnumbered whites closer to thirty to one. In rural plantation districts outside the capital Paramaribo, enslaved people could outnumber whites by more than one hundred to one.¹²

Despite its economic success, Suriname can only be described as a demographic disaster. Suriname's equatorial rainforest climate created a veritable breeding ground for mosquito-borne and tropical illnesses, and every demographic group, European, African, and Amerindian, suffered from their afflictions. It was not just the environment, however. Whites in Suriname, as the master class, had, as Stedman chronicled and participated in, a cultural proclivity for overindulgence in liquor, leading to early death from accidents and alcoholism.

Enslaved people, however, suffered the most dramatically. Exposed to the climate while working in the cane fields, coffee groves, and cacao walks with little protection, enslaved people caught and died from disease. Moreover, planters, overseers, and colonial officials used extreme violence and torture on Suriname's enslaved population. Without this violence, whites feared enslaved people would refuse to work or, worse, rebel and undermine the colony's productivity. Enslaved people also worked long hours with little rest. Day after day, month after month, year after year, such heavy labor took its toll "gradually and incrementally." Such so-called "violence of the mundane" murdered enslaved people and was one of the chief, if not the leading, cause of the high mortality rates on plantations. The average lifespan for an enslaved person working under these conditions was five to seven years.¹³

The human toll of such a system was staggering. The colony imported over 124,000 African captives between 1730 and 1780, but its total slave population in the 1780s was only 50,000.¹⁴ The causes of this great mortality were

---

11. For more on the *polder* system and its importance for making Suriname productive, see Wim Klooster and Gert Oostindie, *Realm between Empires: The Second Dutch Atlantic, 1680–1815* (Ithaca, NY: Cornell University Press, 2018), 126–28.

12. Klooster and Oostindie, *Realm between Empires*, 131–32.

13. Justin Roberts, "The Development of Slavery in the British Americas," in *The World of Colonial America: An Atlantic Handbook*, ed. Ignacio Diaz-Gallup (New York: Routledge, 2017), 135.

14. Natalie Zemon Davis, "Judges, Masters, Diviners: Slaves' Experience of Criminal Justice in Colonial Suriname," *Law and History Review* 29, no. 4 (October 2011): 930.

disease, brutality, and overwork. In short, colonial Suriname is best understood as a society driven by collective sadism and sociopathy, which placed economic productivity above everything else. It was a world of calculated terror, violence, and horror aimed to keep enslaved Africans producing valuable tropical commodities.

Thus, it should not be surprising that enslaved people resisted this system whenever possible. Slave resistance in Suriname was a spectrum of large and small acts aimed at protecting autonomy, undermining the colonial system, and, more often than not, survival. Enslaved people broke tools, committed acts of arson, poisoned livestock, and feigned illness and ignorance to lessen their workload. These were everyday acts of resistance that worked mostly for individuals and did little to harm the plantation machine. They also committed dramatic acts of violence against enslavers, overseers, and *bassia*, the enslaved drivers who kept them working. Violent resistance, especially open rebellion, however, was rare and, as Stedman related time and again, was met disproportionately by colonial authorities, who exterminated rebels with malice and gratuitous violence.

Perhaps the most common long-term slave resistance strategy in Suriname was running away. Flight from slavery occurred everywhere slavery existed in the Americas but took on a special significance in Suriname. Situated in a tropical rainforest, Suriname offered plenty of places for runaways to hide. Colonial authorities lacked the resources to track every escapee through the jungle and were themselves often ignorant of the terrain beyond plantation borders. Such ignorance created possibilities for enslaved people. Some would hide out in the forest for a short amount of time, perhaps waiting for a conflict with an overseer or *bassia* to blow over.

Others, however, committed to long-term fugitivity, called *maroonage*. They carved out a life in the jungle, banding with other runaways to form communities. Those who committed to this lifestyle were known as maroons. They organized their societies around a blend of African and Native American traditions, eking out a living on plots of land beyond the plantation frontier. Maroon communities appeared in almost every slave society in the Americas, but in Suriname grew quite large and persisted. Indeed, these communities still exist today.

While many of the maroon communities began during the English period, they grew with the expansion of slavery under the Dutch. By 1750, it is estimated there were nearly 3,000 maroons living near Suriname. Many had existed for so long that there were adults who had been born in these communities, assuming leadership positions and defining each community's identity. Four distinct groups emerged, including the two largest, Saamaka (also known as Saramaka or Saramacca) and Okanisi (also known as Ndyuka), and two smaller, Boni/Aluku and Kwinti. Although partially self-sufficient, as these communities grew, they required more resources and labor. To obtain these, they raided plantations and stole necessities. Most importantly, since those who ran away to the maroon communities were largely men, when raiding plantations, they offered enslaved women the opportunity to join and, if they would not come willingly, often stole them away.

Between their survival strategies and swelling numbers, the maroons caused considerable alarm among colonial authorities in Suriname. Different factions emerged about how to deal with the maroons. Some wanted to wage war on the maroons, while others favored appeasement. War, however, ultimately proved futile and expensive, and beginning in 1760, after a particularly devastating loss for the colony, Suriname's government settled on a different strategy. Looking to how the British dealt with maroons in Jamaica, the Dutch negotiated peace treaties first with Okanisi in 1760 and Saamaka in 1762. These treaties stipulated that the maroon communities had a right to exist, and the Dutch recognized them as legitimate, free communities. In return for that recognition, the maroons had to agree to stop raiding plantations and kidnapping women. They were also required to return any new runaways to their communities and potentially assist the colony in the case of a slave rebellion.[15]

Halting treaty negotiations in the early 1760s was another event important for understanding Stedman's time in Suriname. In February 1763, enslaved people in Berbice, a Dutch colony neighboring Suriname to the west, rose in rebellion and seized control of the colony for more than a year. The Berbice Slave Rebellion sent shockwaves across slave-holding areas in the Americas and would deeply influence Stedman's time in Suriname.[16] Stedman himself had contemplated joining the expeditionary force that helped recapture the colony from the rebels, although his "application came too late."[17] Many of the figures involved in ending the Berbice Rebellion later found themselves in Suriname. Stedman's commanding officer, the Swiss-born Louis Henri Fourgeoud, served in Berbice, where he gained experience fighting in the Guianas. In his diary, Stedman mentioned two Black men, Gausarie and Accara, who were also instrumental in recapturing the colony. Guasaric, who had been a rebel leader, worked with the Dutch in Berbice and later served Stedman's unit as a spy. Accara, also a rebel leader in Berbice before turning on them to aid the Dutch, was the manager of the enslaved porters in Stedman's baggage train.

More immediately, in the aftermath of the Berbice Rebellion, colonial authorities in Suriname worried about the rebellion spilling over into their own colony or serving as inspiration for enslaved people there. They were especially concerned about several small maroon bands that had formed in the

---

15. For more on the history of maroons in Suriname and the population figures, see Klooster and Oostindie, *Realm between Empires*, 146–48.
16. For more on the Berbice rebellion, see Marjoleine Kars, *Blood on the River: A Chronicle of Mutiny and Freedom on the Wild Coast* (New York: New Press, 2020).
17. Thompson, *Journal*, 48.

eastern part of the colony north of the Cottica River and near the Maroni/Marowijne River, the border with French Guiana. Around the time of the Berbice revolt, these groups increased their raids on plantations located on the Cottica River. As the bands grew, they needed tools, food, and women to build their communities. Alarmed by the increased raids and fearing the maroons would capture and/or sack all the plantations on the Cottica, Suriname officials decided to act quickly, attacking the maroons in fall 1765. This conflict eventually became known as the First Boni War (1765–1777), and Stedman was a later participant in it.

The conflict received its name from one of the principal maroon groups involved in the war, Boni/Aluku. This band, consisting of a few hundred people, lived in the forests of northeastern Suriname and had a village located between the north bank of the Cottica River and the coast. The group took its name from their leaders, Aluku, of which very little is known, and Bokilifu Boni (1730–1793). Boni had been born a maroon and was of mixed race, either African and Amerindian or African and European, depending on the source. By the mid-1760s, he, along with Aluku, had emerged as a leader of the group. Boni led the war effort, while Aluku managed the home front in the conflict with the Dutch.

Although the war started as a series of raids and counterraids by maroons and colonial forces, in 1768, the Dutch captured Boni's village, a dramatic escalation of the conflict. At first, the move seemed decisive, but in reality, it triggered a change of course. First and foremost, the number of raids conducted by each side increased dramatically. Second, the capture of Boni's village helped the maroons overcome a major hurdle to waging war on a larger scale. Limiting the scope of conflict in the first years of the war was the presence of so many small, diverse maroon groups that had little reason to cooperate. When the European soldiers sacked Boni's village, however, it created a common cause, and by 1770, at least two other maroon bands had joined Boni. Meanwhile, deep in the jungles of eastern Suriname, Boni established a new village, a heavily fortified settlement deep in a swamp named Boucou.

From Boucou, Boni and his new allies conducted raids on plantations all along the Cottica River. By early 1772, the raids halted the plantation economy in eastern Suriname. Boni's devastating effectiveness caused Suriname authorities to appeal to the States General and implore them to raise an expeditionary force to end the war once and for all.

As the States General recruited soldiers, Suriname's authorities attempted to capture Boucou. In April 1772, they discovered the village's location and began preparing for a siege. Despite near-constant patrols around the settlement, however, Boni was able to continue sending raiding parties to strike plantations. Patience wearing thin, colonial officials resorted to recruiting enslaved men, many former soldiers in Africa, who would serve as the colony's elite counterinsurgency forces. In return, they received their freedom. Stedman called these soldiers "Rangers." They were highly effective, successfully preventing further maroon raids. By the end of August 1772, Suriname's government had purchased and freed over 300 men to serve as Rangers. Feeling confident, in September 1772, colonial authorities raised a large force of Society of Suriname soldiers, colonial militia, and Rangers to capture Boucou. Their last assault was successful, eventually leading to the capture and/or deaths of nearly 200 maroons. Nevertheless, Boni escaped and began to regroup. The successful capture of Boucou and Boni's escape set the scene for the next stage of conflict—the stage where Stedman played a key role.[18]

Stedman's Suriname

Ostensibly, Stedman arrived in Suriname as part of the army sent to defeat and suppress Boni and his followers. Stedman joined the force to escape his mounting debts, personal and family turmoil, and an opportunity for promotion. He received a captain's commission for joining the expeditionary force, making him the commander of an entire company of soldiers and one of the expedition's leading officers. He and his men departed the Netherlands and, after a rough sea journey, arrived in February 1773. From the moment he arrived, however, Stedman found himself constantly distracted and delayed from achieving the mission at hand. Between his personal vices, politics, and attempting to wage war in a foreign and strange land, Stedman's time in Suriname dragged on for nearly five years.

For Stedman, Suriname was an alien, alluring, and, ultimately, dangerous place. As a white man and military officer in a slave society, he arrived with standing. Less than a week after his arrival, he began receiving invitations from the colony's leading planters and merchants, all hoping to cultivate Stedman as an ally and get in his good graces. Constantly feted at balls, dinners, and soirees, Stedman fully indulged in the privileges slave societies offered powerful white men.

In the *Narrative*, Stedman positioned himself as an outside observer of Suriname and slavery, but the diary reveals otherwise. Within weeks of his arrival, he was fully socialized into the conventions of Suriname's white population. He drank excessively and had sex with many different Black and mixed-race women. On February 9, 1773, a week after stepping foot in Suriname, Stedman described getting "fuddled" (drunk) and "fuck[ing]" a planter's enslaved maid.[19] One of the many enslaved women Stedman raped during these early debaucheries was Joanna. Stedman, like other white men

---

18. For more on the early Boni War and the fall of Boucou, see Price and Price, *Stedman's Surinam*, xx–xxii; and Wim Hoogbergen, *The Boni Maroon Wars in Suriname* (Leiden: Brill, 1990), chap. 3.

19. See diary entry for February 9, 1773.

visiting Suriname, bought, rented, and borrowed women like Joanna to "serve as sexual and domestic partners for the duration of their stay."[20] To Stedman, enslaved women became playthings to satiate his sexual appetite and pass the time. Likewise, ever the military officer, Stedman thought little of inflicting violence on social inferiors whether enslaved or soldiers. Over time, especially once out in the field, Stedman reined in these excesses and, it seems, came to regret some of his earlier behavior.

Part of Stedman's socialization was his personal ownership of enslaved people. Shortly after arriving, Stedman received an enslaved boy named Quaco as a gift. Stedman eventually purchased him outright. Quaco would serve Stedman as a valet and assistant during his entire stay in Suriname and even returned to the Netherlands with him. He was Stedman's constant companion, something repeatedly acknowledged in the diary and *Narrative*.[21] In addition to owning Quaco, Stedman also engaged in the slave trade and used enslaved labor. Both of these are harder to discern, especially in the *Narrative*, but are nonetheless present. Every time Stedman wanted to build a hut or cabin out in the field, for example, he used enslaved people to build it. Likewise, in a discussion of an enslaved family, the reader learns the husband had the initials "JGS" branded on his chest, revealing that Stedman owned the family. Finally, at multiple points during his time in Suriname, Stedman entertained the idea of purchasing land and starting a plantation for himself. Such embrace of slavery and slave labor suggests why, when writing the *Narrative*, Stedman equivocated on the question of abolition and instead advocated for a more benevolent slavery.

As Stedman fully imbibed Suriname's slave society, he became embroiled in military politics. The officer commanding the expedition was Colonel Louis Henri Fourgeoud, a Swiss military officer and veteran of the Berbice Rebellion. Familiar with the nature of warfare in the Guianas, the States General selected Fourgeoud to lead the expeditionary force against Boni. Yet, Fourgeoud proved to be unpopular with both Suriname's civil government and his own soldiers. Stedman—and many colonial officials, including the governor, Jan Nepveu—found him unfair, prickly, corrupt, cheap, and indecisive.

Out of pettiness, Stedman took to calling Fourgeoud a variety of nicknames such as "Old Shaver," an eighteenth-century slang term for a conman or cheater.[22] Of course, rather than any sort of malice, much of this behavior had to do with Fourgeoud's distrust of and lack of confidence in Stedman. Nevertheless,

---

20. Mary Louise Pratt, *Imperial Eyes: Travel Writing and Transculturation* (New York: Routledge, 1992), 95.
21. For a graphic novel imagining Quaco's life, based in part on John Gabriel Stedman's writings, see Ineke Mok and Eric Heuvel, *Quaco: My Life in Slavery* (Oosterhout, Netherlands: Uitgeverij L, 2022).
22. See, for example, the diary entry for December 12, 1773.

because of the shared dislike of Fourgeoud, Stedman formed close working relationships and friendships with colonial officials, including Governor Nepveu. Over time, at least according to the *Narrative*, Stedman reconciled with Fourgeoud—as did the governor.

The political squabbling between different military factions and Colonel Fourgeoud and the governor did nothing to help the military mission, an endeavor that can only be described as failing until colonial forces achieved a limited victory. To wage war on Boni, the colony deployed three distinct forces. First were the soldiers who served the Society of Suriname, who Stedman called "Society" soldiers or troops, comprised of free white men, both local and foreign. These soldiers were often poorly disciplined and even more poorly equipped, although they were useful for garrisoning fortified positions. Second were the expeditionary force soldiers that included Stedman. In theory, these were trained, disciplined soldiers capable of fighting anywhere in the world. The reality, especially the ravages of tropical disease, proved otherwise. Finally, there were the Rangers, still employed by the colony and the best counterinsurgency forces at its disposal. Stedman came to have great regard for these soldiers, reflecting at one point that "one of these [Rangers] is preferable to half a dozen white men in the forest of Guiana."[23]

Much of Stedman's affection for the Rangers stemmed from his and his soldiers' harrowing experience of jungle warfare. Actual fighting was rare and open combat was even less frequent. Rather, the soldiers mostly traveled from post to post on heavily armed barges or marched between different points in the jungle. Spending long periods of time in the field with little action may have been boring, but it was nevertheless deadly. Full of dangerous flora and fauna, such as prickly bushes, fire ants, caimans, monkeys, wild pigs, and piranhas, the jungle became Stedman and his men's main foe. The humid climate took its toll on clothing, leaving soldiers barefoot and in rags. Weapons failed. Replacements were in short supply and could take weeks to arrive in the field from Paramaribo. And tropical diseases and parasites, such as malaria, yellow fever, and hookworm, haunted the soldiers wherever they went. Rarely did a day pass when Stedman did not suffer from some affliction and/or record the deaths of his men, regular troops and officers, in his diary. All told, scholars estimate that more than 80 percent of the expeditionary force soldiers died in Suriname, mostly from disease and privation.[24]

Jungle combat was also a terrifying experience. Many of the maroons were veterans of West African wars, engaged in guerilla tactics, and were deeply familiar with the forest terrain. Save the Rangers, colonial forces could not match maroon military expertise. That said, they did have a major firepower advantage as the maroons struggled to acquire enough guns and gunpowder

---

23. See Chapter XX of the *Narrative*.
24. Pratt, *Imperial Eyes*, 90.

to fight effectively. Indeed, Stedman often noted how the maroons would arm some of their men with sticks made to appear as if they had muskets. Thus, European soldiers sought direct confrontations and pitched battles where their superior firepower could overwhelm the enemy. The maroons tried to prevent these as much as possible, and Stedman engaged in only one open battle (recounted in Chapter XX of the *Narrative*) during his entire time in Suriname.

The inability to provoke Boni and his followers into open warfare changed the nature and objectives of Stedman's military mission. Instead of defeating the maroons in a dramatic confrontation, the expeditionary force, Society soldiers, and Rangers had to erode the maroons' resolve and willingness to fight. Colonial forces took to seeking and destroying maroon settlements, targeting food supplies, and upending village life. By constantly marching, Stedman and his soldiers kept Boni's people on the run. While rarely resulting in confrontation, over time, these counterinsurgency tactics whittled down the maroons' determination, and they scattered. Ultimately, Boni and his followers, reduced to no more than 300 people, fled Suriname entirely and settled in neighboring French Guiana in 1777. Boni's actions allowed Colonel Fourgeoud to claim victory and order the withdrawal of most of his veteran soldiers, including Stedman. Fighting, however, continued on and off until Boni died in 1793.[25]

Although Stedman was in Suriname to wage war, he also formed a long-term relationship with a mixed-race enslaved woman named Joanna. Of all Stedman's experiences in Suriname, his relationship with Joanna is the most recounted and retold, largely because of the way Stedman described her and framed their companionship in the *Narrative*. He initially portrayed her as a "charming creature" who "could not but attract" his "particular attention" and was "so much distinguished above all others of her species in the colony."[26] According to Stedman, he was immediately smitten with Joanna, an attraction that quickly turned to affection and love. He then arranged a "Suriname marriage," a term denoting a long-term, affectionate relationship with a woman of color since interracial marriage was illegal. They then continued their companionship, started a family, and even lived in the field together while Stedman was on campaign. Their relationship only ended when Stedman had to depart Suriname in 1777. Stedman could not secure Joanna's freedom, and, even when she had the opportunity, Joanna, according to the *Narrative*, refused to leave with him for fear of causing Stedman embarrassment in Europe. Stedman, dutybound to the military, had a tearful departure with Joanna and never saw her again.

---

25. Price and Price, *Stedman's Surinam*, xxiv.
26. See Chapter V in this edition.

Of course, Stedman's description of his relationship with Joanna in the *Narrative* was highly romanticized and meant to play on the emotions of his audience. The reality was much messier. The narrative Stedman crafted about their relationship was, in the words of one scholar, a "romantic transformation of a particular form of colonial sexual exploitation" that many white men in Suriname engaged in.[27] White men, especially those there for business like Stedman, sought companionship and sex while in the colony. They needed women's labor to keep their houses, cook, and do laundry. Thus, men often sought the services of enslaved women, making deals with their enslavers and families for these domestic and sexual services. As for the enslaved women like Joanna, they were property, had little say in the arrangements, and could not decline the advances of men like Stedman seeking sex and labor.

And calling Joanna a woman would be generous. When Stedman first encountered her, she was a fifteen-year-old girl caught in a property dispute between her enslaver and his creditors. According to Stedman, she was the daughter of an enslaved woman named Seerie (spelled "Cery" in the *Narrative*). Seerie was the property of a Mr. D. B., the proprietor of Plantation Fauconberg. Joanna's father was a white Dutchman and Fauconberg's manager, Anthony Tielenius Kruythoff. As manager, Kruythoff placed Seerie, Joanna, and their other children in the house to work as domestics, where Joanna learned sewing and housekeeping as a young girl. Kruythoff also taught Joanna how to read and write, although she was never baptized. In the late 1760s, Kruythoff attempted to buy Joanna and his four other children out of slavery, but the deal fell through. When Kruythoff fell ill shortly after, he returned to the Netherlands and died in 1769 or 1770 without purchasing his family's freedom. Meanwhile, Plantation Fauconberg, now under new management, fell deeply into debt. The owner, Mr. D. B., was bankrupt by 1772 and fled Suriname to escape his creditors. To help pay the debt, Mr. D. B.'s wife sent Joanna, her mother, and her siblings to Paramaribo to work in the households of wealthy townspeople.

This was the context in which the twenty-eight-year-old Stedman met the enslaved girl. Almost immediately upon arrival, Stedman began seeking enslaved Black and mixed-race women to serve as his companion. In exchange for companionship, sexual services, and housekeeping, Stedman offered patronage and protection. As mentioned, these social arrangements were common in Suriname. However, in the *Narrative*, Stedman described Joanna coming to his attention because he felt a strong sympathy for her plight at the hands of her enslaver's creditors.

The diary offers a different version of events. Joanna was one of at least three females Stedman sought a "marriage" with, but he chose her. But not because of Stedman's beneficence or even her own initiative. Rather, it was Joanna's

---

27. Pratt, *Imperial Eyes*, 95.

mother Seerie, who Stedman vaguely alludes to as Joanna's "female relation" in the *Narrative*, that brokered the relationship. When Stedman began showering Joanna with gifts in April 1773, Seerie visited him and "close[d] a bargain" with the captain that included eventually purchasing Joanna's freedom and paying a small fee to Seerie too. On April 23, 1773, Joanna moved in with Stedman; he gave her presents and described himself as "perfectly happy." Two weeks later, Stedman "gave [his] wedding" to Joanna and formally sealed their partnership. How Joanna felt about the situation is unclear, although she seemed apprehensive, an understandable feeling given how little say she had in the whole affair.[28]

Characterizing Stedman and Joanna's relationship is difficult, not only because we know so little about how Joanna felt about it. Any words used to describe it, besides neutral terms such as "relationship," as noted by one historian, "imply conclusions about the extent and significance of inequality, choice, and coercion" that are near impossible to verify. Thus, when discussing their connection, it is best to read Stedman's description of their relationship critically. Joanna had little ability to consent but also sought to exert control over the relationship where and when she could.[29] For example, when first trying to arrange Joanna's services, Stedman sent her gifts that she subsequently returned to him. Stedman framed this act as a sign of Joanna's honor and honesty. Looking at it from Joanna's perspective, however, it could be interpreted as a way of rebuffing Stedman's advances or stating that her body, labor, and personhood were more valuable than whatever trinkets Stedman, only an upstart military captain, after all, could send her. Likewise, having been taught by her father to read and write, Joanna was literate, something implicitly acknowledged when Stedman noted writing letters to and receiving letters from Joanna in the diary. It is safe to assume that Joanna was much more informed, knowledgeable, and world wise than the sincere and pure, yet ignorant and benighted caricature of her created by Stedman in the *Narrative*.

Until Stedman's departure in spring 1777, Joanna was, based on the agreement struck with Seerie, Stedman's constant companion. When not on campaign, they lived together, and she even joined him on a plantation used as a military base for months. There, Stedman, using slave labor, had a cabin constructed as their family home. Although the relationship started as an arrangement for sex and labor, and Stedman continued to have sex with other women, he did develop a deep love and affection for Joanna. In the diary, he referred to Joanna as the "girl I love" and "my sweet Joanna."[30] Once again, how she felt is unknown, although she cared for him when he was ill, sent him gifts and

---

28. For Stedman brokering a deal with Seerie, see the diary entries for April 10, 11, 13, and 23, 1773 and May 8, 1773.
29. Diana Paton, "Mary Williamson's Letter, or, Seeing Women and Sisters in the Archives of Atlantic Slavery," *Transactions of the Royal Historical Society* 29 (2019): 163–64.
30. See December 18, 1773 and March 1, 1774 diary entries.

provisions when he was out in the field, and helped him make connections in Suriname's enslaved and free Black communities.

In addition to serving as Stedman's sexual partner and housekeeper, Joanna also gave birth to Stedman's child, a son named John after his father and affectionally called Jack or Johnny. Born on November 27, 1774, Johnny became a constant presence in Stedman's life and occupies quite a bit of space in the diary. Fatherhood softened Stedman, a hardened, cynical military man before, and he doted on the boy, sending Johnny gifts and looking after all his needs. Nevertheless, since Johnny's mother was enslaved, Johnny was too. After his birth, Stedman became increasingly concerned about the fate of his family and sought a way to free them.

Ultimately, Stedman decided to purchase Joanna and Johnny out of slavery. Military officers, however, were not wealthy, and Stedman did not have the money necessary to purchase Joanna and their son. To arrange the sale, Stedman borrowed 1,800 Suriname guilders from Elizabeth Godefroy, a wealthy widow and plantation owner, to purchase them from Mr. D. B. in August 1775. Mr. D. B. accepted the offer, making Stedman, though in debt to Mrs. Godefroy, Joanna and Johnny's new owner. Nevertheless, in addition to the debt accrued to purchase his family, Stedman also had to post bond to the colonial government, a steep fee that discouraged manumission. By late 1776, when Stedman was about to leave Suriname, he had only paid half of the loan back and still had not secured a bond for Joanna and Johnny's freedom. Using his service to the colony to gain sympathy, Stedman convinced Suriname's government to grant Johnny a bond for manumission.

Joanna, however, remained enslaved. Ultimately, unable to pay the rest of the loan to Godefroy or post the required bond, Stedman "sold" Joanna to Godefroy to cover his debt to her. Godefroy promised to provide for Joanna and Johnny, give them a small house to live in, and free Joanna upon her death. While Stedman makes himself out to be the architect of this arrangement in the *Narrative*, the diary suggests it was actually the product of negotiations between Joanna, Seerie, and Godefroy.[31] Whether Stedman ever intended to take Joanna, free or enslaved, to Europe and make her his legal wife—a tragic story central to the *Narrative*, but unmentioned in his diary—is not clear. Likewise, if we can trust the *Narrative*'s description of Joanna's reaction to going to Europe with him, she was apprehensive about leaving her home and the only place she knew. Regardless, the end result was the same. Joanna and Johnny remained in Suriname upon Stedman's departure on April 1, 1777.[32]

---

31. See diary entry for August 25, 1776.

32. For more on Joanna and Johnny, see Natalie Zemon Davis, "Joanna," in *Dictionary of Caribbean and Afro–Latin American Biography*, ed. Franklin W. Knight and Henry Louis Gates, Jr. (New York: Oxford University Press, 2016), 3:416–18.

After Suriname

After departing Suriname in spring 1777, Stedman returned to the Netherlands and to service in the Scots Brigade. Although he dreamed of writing his life story and experiences in Suriname, other events intervened. As the only Scots Brigade officer who went to Suriname and survived, Stedman received a promotion first to the rank of captain and then major, effectively validating his service in Suriname.[33] Word of his time in Suriname spread, which attracted all sorts of opportunities, including an offer to be the governor in Berbice, all of which Stedman declined. It seemed, as his thoughts turned to writing about Suriname, he wished to consign that time of his life to the past, something to be reflected upon, not relived. He not only refused to return to the Guianas, but he also freed his enslaved boy Quaco, now a young man. Yet, without Quaco's consent, Stedman gifted him to the Countess of Rosendaal to serve as a footman. Stedman's belief that he was still entitled to commanding Quaco after manumitting him is illustrative of the deeply racist, paternalistic attitudes he held about Black people and their capacity for full freedom that he developed during his time in Suriname.[34]

As Stedman found a place in the leadership of the Scots Brigade and sought the time and stability to write, three other events further delayed those aspirations. In 1782, Stedman married Adriana Wierts van Coehorn, the descendent of a famed Dutch engineer. Over the next fifteen years, the couple would have five children, George William, Sophia Charlotte, Maria Joanna, Adrian, and John Cambridge. Their children followed in the footsteps of their father and mother. The boys served in the military while the girls married officers.[35]

Meanwhile, shortly after marrying Adriana, larger political events forced Stedman to make a decision that changed the course of his life. During the American War of Independence, the Netherlands intervened on the side of the United States and declared war on Britain, called the Fourth Anglo-Dutch War (1780–1784). The war caused considerable consternation in the Scots Brigade because of its peculiar political status. Although it served the Netherlands, the Scots Brigade was, legally speaking, on loan from Great Britain, and most officers had taken loyalty oaths to Britain's King George III. Thus, the States General forced the members of the Scots Brigade to decide whether to leave the Netherlands and serve Britain or be fully incorporated into the Dutch army.

---

33. James Ferguson, *Papers Illustrating the History of the Scots Brigade in the Service of the United Netherlands, 1572–1782*, vol. II (Edinburgh: Scottish Historical Society, 1899), 442n1.

34. For the offer of the Berbice governorship and gifting Quaco, see Louise Collins, *Soldier in Paradise: The Life of John Stedman, 1744–1797* (New York: Harcourt, Brace, and World, 1966), 217–18.

35. Thompson, *Journal*, viii–ix.

It was not an easy decision. Stedman's brother William chose the Netherlands, while Stedman himself, ever loyal to George III, decided on exile. By 1784, Stedman and his growing family settled in the town of Tiverton in Devon, England.

Finally, Stedman's growing family added another member in 1784, shortly before their exile to England. Johnny, Stedman and Joanna's son from his time in Suriname, arrived to live with his father and stepfamily. Joanna died, allegedly by poison, in November 1782. She was still enslaved. While Joanna and Stedman wrote to each other after his departure, their correspondence ended by 1779, and Stedman did not learn of her death until nearly a year after it happened. Johnny then departed Suriname with 200 pounds sterling his mother had somehow earned and joined his father. Much to Adriana's chagrin, who considered the mixed-race Johnny an embarrassing reminder of her husband's past debauchery, Stedman loved and doted on the boy just as he had in Suriname. From Stedman's view, Johnny was his legitimate eldest son and the equal of his children with Adriana. Nevertheless, perhaps because of how Johnny disturbed the Stedmans' domestic tranquility, Stedman used his connections to find the boy a commission as a first seaman in the British Royal Navy. At the age of seventeen in 1792, however, Johnny drowned in a shipping accident in Jamaica.[36] Johnny's death devastated Stedman. After Johnny's drowning, Stedman wrote to his brother that the boy's death "broak my heart," and he had been "ill" since receiving the news.[37]

After settling in Tiverton, Stedman eased into retirement. Suffering from the aftereffects of the tropical diseases he survived in Suriname, Stedman was in poor health for the rest of his life. Indeed, he seems to have chosen Devon over his family's native Scotland when he went into exile because it was reputedly a good place to recover from tropical disease.[38] Despite the early retirement, he and his family lived in relative comfort between his wife's family money, the sale of his officer's commission for 1,000 pounds sterling before departing the Netherlands, and a pension he negotiated from the British government for his years of military service.[39] He also served as a military recruiter and entertained the local gentry. Mostly, however, Stedman finally found the time to write. By the late 1780s, he had finished a draft of his memoirs from his early life and, as his correspondence with friends shows, the beginnings of the *Narrative*. In 1790, he completed a full draft and spent the next six years working with editors, printers, and engravers, preparing it for publication. It was his

---

36. Davis, "Joanna," 3:417–18.
37. John Gabriel Stedman to Captain William Stedman, August 30, 1792, in *John Gabriel Stedman: A Study of His Life and Times*, by Stanbury Thompson (London: Thompson and Company, 1966), 65.
38. Collins, *Soldier in Paradise*, 219.
39. For the Stedman family finances, see Thomson, *Journal*, 337.

life's work, even if he was not entirely happy with the finished product. John Gabriel Stedman died, allegedly as a consequence of an accident he suffered in 1796, on March 7, 1797, at the age of fifty-two.[40]

John Gabriel Stedman's Suriname Writings

Today, John Gabriel Stedman is known for his writings about Suriname, most significantly the *Narrative*. This book has been in near continuous publication since 1796 and has been translated into more than a dozen languages. Nevertheless, the *Narrative* was the culmination of a nearly quarter-century of reflecting on and writing about his time and experiences in Suriname.

To write the *Narrative*, Stedman relied heavily on a diary he kept during his time in the slave society. This diary, which he referred to as his "journal," recounted his day-to-day experiences, containing his immediate, unfiltered reactions to the situations he found himself in and an openness about his own behavior. It is important to note just how rare it was for people to keep a diary as comprehensive as Stedman's in the eighteenth century, especially white men living in Caribbean slave societies. This makes Stedman's journal a unique artifact. The only comparable figure in this regard is Thomas Thistlewood, an overseer, enslaver, and small plantation owner who lived in Jamaica from 1750 until he died in 1786. An immigrant from Lincolnshire in England, Thistlewood kept a diary from the moment he arrived in Jamaica until just days before his death. Spanning more than 14,000 pages, Thistlewood's diary listed his daily activities and described the people he encountered. Like Stedman, Thistlewood documented his participation in the horrors of slavery, recording the violent, disturbing tortures he meted out to enslaved people and the more than 3,200 acts of rape—written in amateur Latin—he inflicted on enslaved women. Although they are largely chronicles of Stedman's and Thistlewood's monstrous behavior, these diaries are still important sources for scholars looking to study slave societies in the Americas.[41]

Nevertheless, it is important to remember that Stedman's diary is an incomplete, biased record. It is an "ego-document," created by an eighteenth-century man, reflecting his own mindset and worldview. And while Stedman's diary discusses enslaved people, it only captures a glimmer of their lives, refracted through a heavily distorted, racist, and misogynistic lens. In that sense, the lives of enslaved men and women are just as obscured as they are revealed in

---

40. Stedman's age is calculated here using the diary. On April 4, 1776, he noted that it was his birthday, meaning he would have only been fifty-two when he died.

41. For more on Thomas Thistlewood, see Trevor Burnard, *Mastery, Tyranny, and Desire: Thomas Thistlewood and His Slaves in the Anglo-Jamaican World* (Chapel Hill: University of North Carolina Press, 2004).

Stedman's diary, making it imperative not to draw too many generalizations from the document.[42]

Just as Stedman's diary is unique, it also came to serve a larger purpose. Inscribed on the back cover of the first volume of his Suriname diary was a promise to "explain it more at large one day." From the beginning, or at least at the time of completing his first year in Suriname, Stedman designed to write (and perhaps publish) a narrative of his experiences.

Despite his future intentions, Stedman remained unfiltered about his experiences in the diary. Throughout, he revealed much of his character, his behavior as a white man living in a slave society, his thoughts about the world he encountered, and the subjects he took a deep interest in. Some of these subjects, such as his fascination with Suriname's natural history, later appeared in the *Narrative*, but many were obfuscated or removed entirely. The diary reveals Stedman as a man with a propensity for violence who held morally ambiguous attitudes toward slavery and racism. He was a gifted and dutiful, if entitled, military officer who liked to indulge in Suriname's debauched high society.

In the two decades between Stedman's service in Suriname and the publication of the *Narrative*, he reimagined, sometimes dramatically, the meaning and purpose of his time there. Some of this change can be attributed to Stedman's inspiration as a writer. It is important to remember that outside of a few years in Scotland, Stedman received very little formal education in English. Writing, then, did not come easily or naturally to him. To develop his own style, when he sat down to write the story of his time in Suriname, he imitated famous authors of his day. His two favorites were Tobias Smollett, especially Smollett's novel *The Adventures of Roderick Random* (1748), whose eponymous protagonist Stedman believed he took after; and Laurence Sterne, author of the multivolume *The Life and Opinions of Tristram Shandy, Gentleman* (1759–1767). Sterne famously wrote in a stream-of-consciousness style with significant explanatory diversions, which is also a great way to characterize Stedman's *Narrative*. For Stedman, the lengthy asides presented the opportunity to participate in the world of science and write about Suriname's environment, climate, and natural history; discuss plantations, the slave trade, and race; and compose graphic depictions of violence against enslaved people.

A final influence on Stedman was popular nonfiction of the day, such as *The Life and Adventures of Bampfylde Moore Carew* (1745). This book was about a gentry-born man who ran away to live with travelers as a boy and led a life of adventure. Carew's life served as an example of someone subverting class expectations while still living a good life, something Stedman came to revere.

---

42. See Marissa Fuentes, *Dispossessed Lives: Enslaved Women, Violence, and the Archive* (Philadelphia: University of Pennsylvania Press, 2016), for how manuscript records, like Stedman's diary, are created and preserved in ways that make it difficult to discern the lives of enslaved people beyond the violence perpetrated against them.

Indeed, when Stedman died in 1797, it was his final wish to be buried next to Carew, a wish his family sort of fulfilled by burying him in the same cemetery in Bickleigh, just south of Tiverton in Devon.

Using these sources as inspiration for narrative style and his Suriname diary for the details, Stedman began writing in earnest in the late 1780s. Yet, much had changed since his time in Suriname, and Stedman, now a middle-aged family man and respected veteran with a reputation to maintain, sanitized his experience in Suriname. He excised the excessive drinking and, most importantly, his many sexual encounters with Black and mixed-race women. Indeed, he seems to have not only left these experiences out of his draft narrative but sought to excise them from the record altogether. In the second volume of the diary, there are numerous lines scribbled out and, in the ones that can be read, they often deal with sex with Joanna.[43] It is impossible not to wonder if he scribbled these out as he gathered his notes and began to write. As previous editors of Stedman's work have noted, these edits regarding sexuality "had the effect of distorting Stedman's descriptions of an important aspect of contemporary Suriname life."[44]

As he rewrote and distorted some of his experiences, he expanded his thoughts about Suriname's natural history and articulated a reformist vision of slavery and the slave trade, arguing that while slavery could be morally repugnant, it was also a necessary labor system that could be effectively reformed into a more humane institution. These were subjects only briefly discussed in the diary, but obviously, subjects Stedman had thought about considerably in the meantime.

By 1790, Stedman had completed a draft of his narrative. As true in the eighteenth century as it is today, a completed manuscript did not guarantee publication. Especially concerning for Stedman's book was the cost of publication. The manuscript was very long at over 250,000 words, meaning it would span more than one volume. Meanwhile, Stedman intended for the book to include more than one hundred images based on sketches and watercolors he had made in Suriname.[45] These would have to be engraved and, in some more exclusive copies, colored. To offset the expense, Stedman began seeking out subscribers to subsidize the production costs and ensure at least a few copies, especially the expensive, full-color copies, would be sold. Between early 1791 and the publication of the book, Stedman reached out far and wide and ultimately found nearly 200 subscribers, including family; neighbors; fellow soldiers; leading political figures, such as Warren Hastings, a famous governor of British India; and some of the people he met in Suriname, like Thomas Palmer, the New England gentleman turned Suriname planter who Stedman befriended during his time in the colony.

---

43. See diary entries for May 11, May 16, October 16, and October 19, 1776.
44. Price and Price, *Stedman's Surinam*, xxxii.
45. Price and Price, *Stedman's Surinam*, xxxv.

In addition to seeking subscribers, Stedman also found an editor and publisher, Joseph Johnson. Johnson, a political radical, was one of the leading publishers of his day. He had an exceptional reputation, publishing authors such as Mary Wollstonecraft and Thomas Malthus. He also hosted the "Johnson circle" that met for dinners at least once a week where Johnson invited some of the leading minds, especially political reformers, of the time.[46] How Stedman, an unpublished, first-time author came to Johnson's attention is unclear as those pages are missing from his later diary. However, it is possible Stedman cold-called Johnson or even participated in Johnson's circle during a visit to London. Likewise, Stedman may have become known to Johnson, whose radical politics interested him in Stedman's critique of slavery. Regardless, by February 1791, Stedman was regularly sending Johnson material while seeking subscribers.[47]

Equally unknown is Johnson and Stedman's publishing agreement, although it gave Johnson considerable editorial control over the final text of the *Narrative* and how the book would be printed, marketed, and distributed. As the publisher, Johnson intervened in large and small ways. Most significant is that Johnson, without Stedman's knowledge, hired a copyeditor and ghostwriter named William Thompson.[48] It was left to Thompson to edit the text. Not only did Thompson attempt to correct Stedman's unlearned writing style, but he also drastically changed the book. Thompson made "substantial alterations" to "Stedman's views on race, slavery, and social justice, obliterating or warping significant aspects of his Suriname experience and the social commentary he had intended to share with his readers."[49] These changes softened Stedman's antislavery message, completely rewriting or removing accounts of violence and torture. Although Stedman never fully committed to being an abolitionist, Thompson downplayed Stedman's critiques of slavery and positioned him as opposing abolition.[50]

Richard and Sally Price speculate that Thompson, who had pro-slavery sentiments, and Johnson's own political concerns allowed the *Narrative* to be edited in such a way. At the same time he was editing Stedman's work, Thompson was ghostwriting defenses of the slave trade. Johnson, for his part, feared being targeted and possibly imprisoned for his beliefs as the British government cracked down on radicalism in the wake of the French Revolution. Approving Thompson's edits allowed Johnson to appear more moderate.

---

46. For more on Joseph Johnson, see Daisy Hay, *Dinner with Joseph Johnson: Books and Friendship in a Revolutionary Age* (Princeton: Princeton University Press, 2022). More on his relationship with Stedman can be found on pp. 283–86.
47. See, for example, Thompson, *Journal*, 333.
48. For the background on Thompson, see Price and Price, *Stedman's Surinam*, xlv.
49. Price and Price, *Stedman's Surinam*, xlviii.
50. Price and Price, *Stedman's Surinam*, lxi.

When Stedman finally saw the edited and printed text in 1795, he protested vociferously to Johnson, but Johnson seemed much less concerned. Even with Thompson's softening of Stedman's message, Johnson argued the book was still a powerful condemnation of slavery—a conviction vindicated by later reviews and the popularity of the book among antislavery activists.[51]

In addition to Johnson's belief that the book was sufficiently antislavery, larger factors were at play during the *Narrative*'s publication. First and foremost, public opinion on the question of slavery had shifted dramatically as Stedman's book went through the publication process. During the 1780s and early 1790s, public and parliamentary support for reforming slavery, including a possible slave trade ban, grew dramatically. Yet, the wider crackdown on radicalism that started in 1792 during the French Revolution and that had scared Johnson into endorsing Thompson's edits also caused the government to turn against abolition and suppress abolitionist activity. Planters in Britain's West Indian colonies and merchants tied to slavery and the slave trade in Britain played into these fears, arguing any attempt to end slavery or the slave trade would lead to the collapse of the West Indian colonies, the loss of those profits, and the triumph of the French in the Americas. In short, Stedman's *Narrative* was at the mercy of a growing conservative, antiradical sentiment in the British Empire and the 1796 edition reflected that mood.[52]

Moreover, it is essential to remember that although Thompson's changes can account for some of the ambivalent messaging about slavery in the published *Narrative*, Stedman was, ultimately, an ameliorationist. While he was plenty condemnatory of the brutality of slavery, he believed that it could be reformed into a more benevolent labor system. Stedman was not alone in these beliefs. Many pragmatically minded reformers and planters looking to mollify abolitionists subscribed to these ideas. Ameliorationists sought to provide enslaved people with a higher standard of living, which included more food and better housing and clothing, encouraged family formation and Christianization to foster community and order, and created opportunities for redress against abuse. In theory, these measures were supposed to improve the quality of life for enslaved people and end some of the worst exploitation.[53]

In practice, however, ameliorationist policy had the potential to extend slavery by eliminating the most egregious examples of violence and thus satisfying outside observers. Amelioration also proved to be incredibly invasive, mandating enslaved people give up their already-limited free time for religious

---

51. Price and Price, *Stedman's Surinam*, lxi.

52. For more on the backlash against abolitionism in Britain, see David Brion Davis, *The Problem of Slavery in the Age of Revolution, 1770–1823* (Ithaca, NY: Cornell University Press, 1975).

53. More on the ameliorationist movement can be found in J. R. Ward, *British West Indian Slavery, 1750–1834: The Process of Amelioration* (Oxford: Clarendon Press, 1988).

instruction, encouraging and pressuring enslaved women to have as many children as possible to maintain the labor force, and introducing numerous new labor management strategies to maximize the amount of work performed. Likewise, almost every institution created to protect enslaved people from abuse was almost immediately neutralized by the planter class. Certainly, Stedman did not foresee the full consequences of the policies he advocated, but his equivocation on the issue of slavery—present in his diary, first draft, and other Suriname writings—allowed Thompson to edit his words in such a way.[54]

Between mid-1795 and February 1796, Stedman battled with Johnson over the fate of his book, refusing edits and insisting changes and additions be made to the text. In a January 1796 letter to his sister-in-law, Stedman complained his book "was printed full of lies and nonsense, without [his] knowledge." When receiving the first print run of the text, Stedman claimed to have "burnt 2000 vol[umes] and made them print it again." He asserted that despite the "villainy and folly" of his editors, he "overcome them all" and looked forward to the printed edition that would be released the following month.[55] Nevertheless, the substantial differences between the 1790 draft and published *Narrative* suggest that Stedman did not, in fact, overcome his editors, and their version of the text won out in the end.

In some ways, the numerous illustrations Stedman wished to include were just as important as the text itself. Since his youth, Stedman had been an avid artist and especially loved watercolors. While in Suriname, he sketched and painted the people, plants, animals, and scenes he encountered. And, from the moment he started drafting his narrative, he believed illustrations would appear in the final published version. Unlike the text, Stedman had a much more active hand in recruiting engravers and guiding their work. He initially requested that 106 images be included, and while Johnson was onboard, the final version contained 80 illustrations. Stedman worked with a number of engravers for the *Narrative*, including famed artist, poet, and printmaker William Blake (1757–1827). Blake engraved 16 of the 80 total plates. These included many of those containing human subjects, including the portrait of the Ranger and the various scenes of torture inflicted on enslaved people. As he helped Stedman transform his sketches into engravings, Stedman and Blake became friends, and working on the images for the *Narrative* probably informed Blake's abolitionism.[56]

---

54. For more nuanced interpretations of amelioration, see Justin Roberts, *Slavery and the Enlightenment in the British Atlantic, 1750–1807* (New York: Cambridge University Press, 2013); and Sasha Turner, *Contested Bodies: Pregnancy, Childrearing, and Slavery in Jamaica* (Philadelphia: University of Pennsylvania Press, 2017).

55. Thompson, *Stedman*, 75.

56. For more on the engravings, Blake's work in the *Narrative*, and his and Stedman's relationship, see Geoffrey Keynes, *Blake Studies: Essays on His Life and Work* (Oxford: Oxford University Press, 1971), 98–103.

Stedman did not live long enough to see his *Narrative*'s lasting impact. Johnson's predictions about its potential for success and powerful message were right. The book was an overnight sensation and enjoyed a wide readership. Especially compelling were the engravings contained in the book, which became some of the most iconic images of plantation slavery. Shortly after his death, Stedman's *Narrative* spread across Europe and the Atlantic, translated into multiple languages. Each new edition allowed readers to reinterpret Stedman's experiences, and abolitionists extracted—literally in some cases—parts of the book to make moral, political, and economic arguments against slavery.

In short, Stedman's *Narrative* took on a life of its own, far removed from the author's original intentions. Subsequent generations ignored his diary as they reread and used Stedman's *Narrative* for their own purposes. Stedman himself, however, started this process by reinterpreting the material in his diary to write a compelling and poignant book about his time in Suriname. He left behind a very specific and nostalgic version of his experiences far removed from the version of events recorded in his diary. Reading the diary alongside the *Narrative*, then, ultimately allows readers to unpack the ambivalent legacy of John Gabriel Stedman and examine the way he selectively (mis)remembered and rewrote key moments of his time in Suriname.

Reading This Edition

Central to reading John Gabriel Stedman is understanding who he was. This edition foregrounds Stedman's identity in his writings while modernizing, standardizing, and clarifying the text for readers. The text consists of three parts: Stedman's diary from his time in Suriname, edited chapters from Stedman's 1796 *Narrative*, and an appendix placing selections from the diary beside the excerpts from the *Narrative*.

This edition contains the first modernized, yet faithful, transcription of Stedman's diary from his time in Suriname. It is based on the manuscript housed at the University of Minnesota's James Ford Bell Library. While it is not the first time the diary appears in print, it is the first to contain all of Stedman's unfiltered observations and take into account his way of writing and recording what he encountered. In 1962, British antiquarian Stanbury Thompson published the *Journal of John Gabriel Stedman*. It contains a transcription of Stedman's entire diary and an account of his life. Yet, Thompson's edition is heavily sanitized, removing reference to Stedman's sex life and violent acts, and is based on Thompson's guesswork when he transcribed Stedman's unclear handwriting and grammar. In this volume, however, readers will encounter Stedman unredacted and a much more honest transcription.

When reading Stedman's diary, the author's biography matters. John Gabriel Stedman was half-Dutch and half-Scottish. While a boy, he lived with an uncle in Scotland, where he received a rudimentary education in English. He spent much of his young adulthood, however, in the Netherlands, where he would have read and spoken Dutch. And yet, as the publication of his *Narrative* shows, he generally wrote in English. While he may have written in English for privacy as much as anything else, it was not formal, proper English but rather reflective of Stedman's background. The diary is full of words and phrases from Scots, a dialect of English spoken in Scotland. Yet, he also occasionally used Dutch words and referenced Dutch popular culture.

This passage, from October 24, 1775, illustrates Stedman's use of language:

> I get two letters, one from my mother and one from Alexander Cunningham. Fowler gets a letter from his Jo in verse, from Vader Cats.

xxxvii

Although it reads strangely at first, the second sentence from the passage demonstrates Stedman's blend of Scots and Dutch. "Jo" is a colloquial Scots term for lover or beau. Sergeant Fowler, a fellow Scot who served under Stedman and whose first name the reader never learns, received a letter from his love. It was not just any letter, however. It was in verse, or a poem, and Fowler's lady used "Vader Cats" as a template for composing the poem. "Vader Cats" is a reference to Jacob Cats (1577–1660), a popular Dutch poet and moralist during the seventeenth century. His poems and stories became (and still are) popular for the moral instruction of children in the Netherlands, thus the affectionate "Vader," Dutch for "father." In short, when writing this one sentence in his diary, Stedman blended Scots with a deep familiarity of Dutch culture.

Throughout the transcription of the diary, Scots words and phrases have been highlighted. The same is true for any Dutch words or references. To maintain the text's original intent and give the reader a sense of how Stedman wrote and, by extension, thought, they have not been "translated" to modern English. Doing so would remove a cornerstone of Stedman's identity and style. Instead, any words or phrases unclear to modern English readers will be clarified in the footnotes.

Moreover, the diary is full of abbreviations and shorthand. Often, Stedman did this to save space in the narrow margins. Other times, however, he shortened or, perhaps better worded, redacted more offensive entries, such as writing "fuck" as "f——k" or "rogered" as "r——g——r." Yet, his abbreviations and redactions are random and highly idiosyncratic. For example, often in the diary and despite its length, Stedman fully wrote out the placename "'s-Lands Welvaren," which was the outpost called "Devil's Harwar" in the *Narrative*. He likewise used "me" interchangeably for "my" and "mine." This edition spells out Stedman's redactions and abbreviations, adds articles at the beginning of sentences, and modernizes the possessives he used to avoid confusion and make the diary as readable as possible.

In addition to the diary, this edition contains eight chapters from the 1796 *Narrative*. As described in the Introduction, the *Narrative* is exceptionally long, containing more than 250,000 words, and was originally published in two volumes. Much of the *Narrative*'s heft comes from Stedman's long, discursive descriptions of everything he encountered in Suriname, from the colony's flora and fauna to its plantation economy. It also contains a considerable amount of moralizing on slavery and commentary about race. Moreover, Stedman's writing style can be confusing. He often wrote overly long and complicated sentences in the passive voice and started them with verbs like "being," making it difficult to identify the object of his discussions.

This edition takes a middle-road approach to modernizing and transcribing Stedman. Much like his use of Scots colloquialisms in his diary, Stedman's unusual sentence structure is a key part of his identity as a writer. For that reason, the passive voice remains. Nevertheless, some of the phrasings within the sentences have been clarified to make it easier for modern readers. Likewise, to cut down on the length of Stedman's chapters, most of his digressions describing the plants and animals of Suriname have been heavily edited or cut altogether. The chapters, then, largely relate to the themes identified as significant by historians and literary scholars who have studied Stedman: race, gender, and sexual relations in a slave regime; plantation production; maroon life and ways of living; and Stedman's humanitarian critiques of slavery and violence more broadly. Wherever the editor cut material in the text, it will either contain "..." for shorter edits of words and phrases or a short, italicized summary for longer selections. Finally, the spelling of all proper nouns, including names of people and places, has been standardized across the diary and *Narrative* to avoid confusion.

This edition also contains an appendix, which juxtaposes passages from Stedman's diary with the 1796 *Narrative*, illustrating how Stedman changed the text and often the meaning of his experiences in the two decades between his Suriname expedition and the publication of his book. Readers will be able to examine these differences in depth, and if necessary, the full context of the diary entry and/or passage is provided. The excerpts provided are transcribed and modernized in the exact same way as the main text of the book.

Finally, it is important to note that the diary and *Narrative* reflect the harsh realities of Stedman's career as a soldier and life in an eighteenth-century slave society. Stedman's writings contain descriptions of extreme violence, sexual exploitation, misogyny, anti-Semitism, racism, and generally demeaning language. As a product of Stedman's moment in time, these features of the texts, although abhorrent to modern readers, open a world very different from our own and create opportunities to reflect on the human experience, past and present.

The Suriname Diary of John Gabriel Stedman

Editor's note: John Stedman's diary, which he referred to as his "journal," was the primary source he used to write the Narrative. *In it, he recounted his day-to-day experiences in Suriname. It contains his immediate, unfiltered reactions to the situations he found himself in, and he is open about his own behavior. Today, there are two existing volumes of the diary. The first, called* Volume I *in this edition, covers Stedman's departure from the Netherlands in November 1772 until April 1774. To save space,* Volume I *of this edition begins with Stedman's arrival in Suriname in February 1773. The second volume,* Volume II *here, starts in October 1775 and ends in December 1776. What happened to the journal containing Stedman's entries from May 1774 through September 1775 is unclear. However, in the* Narrative, *Stedman noted dropping the volume in the water, and while he was able to recover it, it may have more rapidly deteriorated than the other two journals. Likewise, it is unclear if Stedman kept a journal at all for the period from January 1777 until his departure on April 1, 1777. For a fuller discussion of the diary, see the* Introduction.

Note on citations: Unless otherwise noted, all definitions and etymologies come from the Oxford English Dictionary (OED). *Scots terms and definitions come from either the* OED *or* Dictionaries of the Scots Language (https://dsl.ac.uk/), *while Dutch etymologies can be found at* Etymologiebank.nl, *a website created and hosted by the Instituut voor de Nederlandse Taal (Institute for the Dutch Language).*

Volume I: February 1773–April 1774

Throughout Volume I, *if Stedman wanted to add additional information to a day's entry, he would start the note with "NB" at the end of an entry. Moreover, Stedman made a number of editing marks, such as stars, asterisks, carets, and crosses, that noted his desire to amend or add material to that day's entry. The corresponding information can be found at the beginning of the journal with the appropriate notation. Much of that material has been crossed out, although it is unclear if Stedman did that during his time in Suriname or when he wrote the* Narrative. *For this volume, every time Stedman desired material to be added, the material will be included at the end of the intended entry date and denoted by starting a new paragraph with an asterisk at the beginning. Likewise, if it was intended as a new entry, it will begin with an asterisk before the date itself.*

1773

February

February 2: We sailed up the River Suriname and heave anchor at 1pm before Fort New Amsterdam.…The fort and other ships salute us, which we return. We all dress in our uniforms and kept a guard of one officer and seven file[1] on the quarterdeck. Captain Becquer is dispatched in the sloop to Paramaribo to acquaint the governor of our arrival. Several colonial officers come to pay us a visit.

February 3: Several more gentlemen come to see us in tent boats rowed by negroes, all naked. We get several refreshments sent to us, such as oranges, salads, etc.

February 4: Our soldiers are sent ashore to take a walk in Fort New Amsterdam and refresh themselves. Colonel Fourgeoud goes to Paramaribo incognito.

February 5: Write to mama and Colonel Gordon.

February 6: Receive a kind invitation from Mr. Lolkens to accept of his house in Paramaribo.[2]

February 7: Walk alone in Fort Amsterdam where I see nothing except undesirable misery. I pay a visit to the commandant.

---

1. I.e., "rank and file" soldiers or privates.
2. Lolkens invited Stedman to lodge at his home.

February 8: We lift anchor at 3pm after saluting Fort New Amsterdam and they us. We sail up the river with beating drums and flying colors and heave anchor about 4pm before Paramaribo, after being saluted by the fort citadel Zeelandia with 11 guns and we thanked them with nine....

February 9: Our troops were disembarked at Paramaribo. A few soldiers faint. The whole corps of officers dine at the governor's table. I get fuddled[3] at a tavern. Go to sleep at Mr. Lolkens's, who was in the country. I fuck one of his negro maids.

February 10: Am spotted like a leper by the mosquitos. Go aboard and fetch my baggage ashore. Dine at Mr. Kennedy's, who gives me the use of a fine negro boy[4] to attend me while here. I sleep at Mr. Lolkens's.

February 11: Settle in my own house which was shown to me by the quartermaster. This made me very content, since I had little satisfaction on the voyage, always having our coarsest provisions for dinner. For supper, I ate damned ill-prepared black biscuit and cheese—and the same for breakfast. Amusements we had none of any kind. The time was passed in sleeping and talking nonsense. No wit was taken notice of and a fart was seemed more diverting. Liveliness and agility were looked on as very ill manners and the height of indecency. In short, in order not to have my eyes hurt by the most sour discontented countenances and my ear injured by the sound of the worst scraped fiddle—besides the unwelcome smell which often met my nose—I was decent enough to pass most of my time in the mast high above my shipmates reading in the round tops[5] or hauling a rope for exercise. After passing into the tropics, every morning I washed in salt water, while *Monsieur*[6] powdered his hair.... The only accident that befell me was, letting my bunch of keys drop in the sea from on top of the yardarm and falling on my bum on the quarterdeck, which broke my snuffbox.

Now hearing the negroes are at peace and most disturbances over, I don't want for time. Hearing of nothing except bread and cheese for officers and nothing for the men since we came, I don't want for appetite, so this day I dined at Mr. Demelly's and sup with my neighbor, the watchmaker.

* NB It has been discovered that we used the same tub used to bring soup to the table and excrement[7] overboard. When at sea a few days after our arrival, the magistrates told the colonel that the colony had no use for the troops.

---

3. I.e., drunk.

4. This is the boy Quaco who accompanied Stedman during his entire sojourn in Suriname and returned home with him.

5. The crow's nest of the ship.

6. Most likely, Colonel Fourgeoud.

7. In the diary, Stedman wrote "E——ts," suggesting "excrements."

February 12: Dine at Mr. Demelly's. After dinner, I take the ladies to the parade which mounts at 4:30pm. I sup with several gentlemen.[8]

February 13: Dine at home on cheese and bread. A guest is glad to take share.[9] I sup at Mr. Beugel's. The company takes a midnight walk after drinking wine and water, singing old songs, sweating to death, and talking nonsense.

February 14: Dine at Mr. Demelly's where I breakfast daily until I get my own things prepared.

February 15: Dine at Mr. Texier the Commandant's where I sup likewise.

February 16: Dine at headquarters for reasons of state after being asked by three gentlemen.

February 17: Dine at headquarters. Sup at Mrs. MacNeil's. I meet with much civility. The gentlemen send me rum, lime juice, oranges, sugar, etc. and the ladies lend me all the furniture I want.

February 18: Dine at Mr. Lolkens's. Sup at Mr. Van der Oevers. I write to mama, Gordon, Vonck, Stuart, Reygersman, Lagh, Dundas, and Rosetta.

February 19: Dine at Mr. Kennedy's, who offers me the use of a riding horse when I please.

February 20: Dine at Mr. Kennedy's.

February 21: Dine at the major's with Captain Rughcop.

February 22: Dine at Mr. Gordon's. Drink to friendship with [illegible].[10] A negro woman offers me the use of her daughter while here for a certain sum. We don't agree about the price.

February 23: I dine at Mr. Lolkens's. He introduces me to Mr. Huijsman who pays not the least attention. I sup at Mr. Kennedy's. We have a dance after supper. An old widow with a good fortune is in love with me. Am advised to marry her to which I can't agree.

February 24: I dine at Mr. Kennedy's. A poor negro girl breaks five pewter plates, which I see, and so by paying the whole save her from a horrid whipping.

February 25: Dine at the mess house and sup in my room with two mulatto girls[11] on bread, cheese, and a bottle of claret.

---

8. In the eighteenth century, "dinner" referred to what we would call lunch and was often the largest meal of the day, while "supper" was the evening meal.
9. Stedman never identified this guest.
10. In the diary, Stedman wrote "k———n," and it is unclear if that is the name of a person, a type of drink, or a curse word.
11. It is possible that one of these two girls was Joanna.

February 26: Dine at Mr. Rynsdorp's with all our officers. Sup onboard the *Boreas*. Dance there until 7:00 in the morning and then had breakfast.

February 27: Ate breakfast and then took a ride with six chaises full of ladies and gentlemen. Dine at the mess house.

February 28: Dine at Mr. Kennedy's. I get what they call *rootvont*.[12]

March

March 1: Dine at Mr. Lolkens's. Sup at Mr. Beeltsuijders's. Leave the company not feeling well. Receive a cordial and two fine oranges from a mulatto girl.[13]

March 2: Asked to dine at Mr. Kennedy's and to sup and dance at Mr. Stolker's. Refuse both and stay in.

March 3: Am not well.

March 4: Draw twelve ounces of blood.[14] I am asked to sup and dance at Demelly's. Can't go. The *Boreas*, Captain Van de Velde, sails down the river for Holland after the common salutations. NB On board was Mrs. D. B——e——, a curious pasquil.[15]

March 5: Go for the air to Sporksgift, a coffee plantation in Matapacca Creek belonging to Mr. (Captain) MacNeil. I take powders and recover. Mr. MacNeil turns off his manager[16] for breaking trust and killing four negroes. He gives a feast to all the rest.

March 9: I return to Paramaribo. NB During my absence, three negroes were hanged on the boat and two whipped below the gallows. On the 8th of March, it was the Prince of Orange's birthday, so Colonel Fourgeoud gave a genteel supper and ball to the ladies and gentlemen. The *la salle de danse*[17] was the officer's guardroom. The price for two fiddlers was 120 Dutch florins.[18]

---

12. This was what Stedman called "prickly heat" in the *Narrative*.
13. In the *Narrative*, Stedman later acknowledged it was Joanna who sent him the oranges.
14. Bleeding, the act of being cut and having blood drained, was a common medical treatment in the eighteenth century. It was used for all types of ailments.
15. What Stedman meant by "curious pasquil" is not clear. Nevertheless, "pasquil" was another word for a satire or a lampoon. Perhaps Stedman considered Mrs. D. B——e—— funny or some sort of vexing problem.
16. I.e., MacNeil fired his overseer. See Chapter V of the *Narrative* for details of this story.
17. I.e., a dance hall.
18. Stedman used the word "hollands" to describe the currency, indicating they paid with money from the Dutch Republic and not the local Suriname currency.

March 11: Dine at Mr. Lolkens's. I deliver Mr. Van der Meij his letter, which he gave a sooty[19] reception. Lolkens got his letter long before. Both were from my friend Mr. Reygersman.[20]

March 12: Dine at Kennedy's. Three girls pass the night in my room.[21]

March 14: Dine with young Rynsdorp.

March 15: Dine at Demelly's.

March 16: Dine at Kennedy's. That night fell down with my hammock.[22]

March 17: Dine at Demelly's.

March 18: Dine at Kennedy's.

March 19: Colonel Fourgeoud goes up the Commewijne River to see the colony. The fort and three ships salute him.

March 21. Dine at Lolkens's.

March 22: Dine at Lolkens's.

March 25: Dine at Kennedy's. Their[23] boy is three years old.

March 26: Dine at Kennedy's. B———e comes to me and stays the whole night.[24]

March 28: I went down the Suriname River with young Mr. Rynsdorp to these plantations:

> Elizabeth's Hope—coffee
> Rynsfort—coffee
> Limeshope—coffee
> Groningen—coffee
> Schoonoort—sugar

April

April 6: Returned to Paramaribo with Colonel Fourgeoud and company.

April 7: Dine at Kennedy's. A discovery concerning B———e.

---

19. I.e., foul or dismal.
20. These "letters" were most likely letters of introduction that spoke to Stedman's character and helped him build social connections once he arrived in Suriname.
21. Stedman's use of the term "girls" here was not only derogative but also literal. One of them was probably Joanna, who would have been fifteen at the time and thus not legally an adult or "woman," but rather a "girl" in the eyes of the law.
22. Stedman slept in a hammock, and it probably somehow dropped from being suspended.
23. The original diary says "the," but Stedman was discussing Kennedy's son.
24. It is unclear who Mrs. D. B———e——— was, but she occasionally appeared in Stedman's diary. Most likely, she was one of the "three girls" who stayed with Stedman on March 12, and he may have courted her.

April 8: Dine at Kennedy's. I have a remarkable discourse with B——e.[25]

April 10: Dine at Kennedy's. Succor to Joanna.[26]

April 11: Dine at Demelly's. Joanna, her mother, and Q——'s[27] mother come to close a bargain with me. We put it off for reasons I gave them. The *Westellingwerf*, Captain Crass, arrived in the river after a 37-day journey from Plymouth to Suriname.

April 12: Dine and sup at Lolkens's.

April 13: B——e and Joanna both breakfast with me. I call myself.[28] Muster was before Fort Zeelandia. B——e sleeps with me.

April 14: Dine at Gordon's. I am introduced in the Society.[29]

April 15: Sup at Lolkens's and came home drunk. His son goes to Holland. X[30]

April 16: Dine at Lantman's. He, Mr. Rughcop, and I visited Captain Crass onboard his ship.

April 18: Dine at Mrs. Demelly's.

April 20: Colonel Fourgeoud heads up the Suriname River.

April 23: Joanna comes to stay with me. I give her presents worth about 10 pounds sterling and am perfectly happy.

April 25: A sailor onboard Captain Crass's ship lubs[31] himself in delirium. Dine at Demelly's.

---

25. While Stedman could be recounting his conversation with B——e, it may also be sexual innuendo.
26. I.e., Stedman provided some sort of aid and comfort to her. This is the likeliest interpretation of the original: "secrer to J——n" given what comes next in the diary; that is, he started to woo her and provide financial support.
27. This seems to be the third girl Stedman was courting.
28. Stedman used an archaic Scots form of the word "call" here. Given the context of the entry, it either means he chastised himself for his behavior—we today would say "call out"—or he prepared himself for the muster by dressing in his uniform.
29. Stedman probably referred to meeting with leading officials of the Society of Suriname, the private company that governed the colony.
30. Stedman marked this entry with a large, bold "X," suggesting it was meant to trigger his memory.
31. This verb is a corruption of the Dutch word "lubben," meaning castrate. In the 1790 draft of the *Narrative*, Stedman recounted the story of the sailor who castrated himself while suffering from a high fever. See John Gabriel Stedman, *The Narrative of a Five Years Expedition against the Revolted Negroes of Surinam: Transcribed for the First Time from the Original 1790 Manuscript*, ed. Richard Price and Sally Price (Johns Hopkins University Press, 1988), 97. Hereafter cited as "FD" to indicate it as the first draft version of the *Narrative*.

April 27: Captain Barens of the frigate *Vigilance* dies. First mate Cornelius Zeebrandt is now captain.

April 28: Captain Barens is buried. Joanna slept at Mrs. Demelly's. I redress Bob Campbell's dispute.[32]

* We hear that the free negroes have destroyed a village and killed half of Baron's gang and took three more prisoner.[33]

May

May 1: Colonel Fourgeoud returns.

May 4: 300 free negroes received.[34] Dine at Mr. Lolkens's.

May 5: Dine at Mr. Kennedy's. Captain Crass heads down the river, sailing for Demerara.

May 7: Dine at Mr. Demelly's.

May 8: Dine at Mr. Gordon's. Give my wedding.[35]

May 10: Free negroes have a ball. I arrest a soldier for picking a Jew's pocket. He was whipped and sent away.

May 11: Dine at Mr. Kennedy's.

May 12: Mr. Kennedy escapes breaking his neck when his horse fell. I get a fever. It lasts two days. I keep to the house until the 17th.[36]

May 21: Lieutenant Colonel Lantman dies.

May 22: He is buried. Seven negroes are executed, six are hanged, and one is *rabraakt*,[37] and a white man is whipped.

May 23: Major Westerloo is made lieutenant colonel.

> Captain Becquer—major
> Captain-Commander Rughcop—a company commander
> Lieutenant Van Coeverden—captain-commander

---

32. This was Lieutenant Robert Campbell, who served under Stedman.
33. This passage refers to the Rangers, who destroyed a maroon village and successfully attacked Baron, one of Boni's chief lieutenants, and his men.
34. These are the Rangers, who Stedman saw muster for the first time on this day.
35. Stedman proposed to Joanna, offering to free her, educate her, and make her his "Suriname wife."
36. In the diary, Stedman did not provide a date, instead leaving it blank. In the draft of his *Narrative*, he noted it was May 17. See FD, 100.
37. This is the Dutch term for being broken on the rack.

Sous-Lieutenant Du Peron—lieutenant
Ensign[38] Ower—sous-lieutenant
and Sergeant Nys—ensign

May 24: Having got a supply of provisions from Holland, we think to sail half June[39] and began to ballast the ships. I am very sorry to leave Joanna.

May 25: A plantation being run down[40] and its director murdered by the negroes,[41] we are to stay here by the request of the governor and magistrates.

May 28: I dine at Mr. Kennedy's. Sous-Lieutenant Van Zende gets his demission[42] by asking for it after being long under arrest for some quarrel.

May 29: Dine at Mr. Kennedy's. The transport ships are discharged.

May 30: Dine onboard the American bark[43] with Captain Minott.

June

June 2: Dine at Mr. Lolkens's.

June 3: Dine at Mr. Kennedy's.

June 5: Onboard the frigate *Johannes and Elizabeth*, Captain Coke.

June 6: Dine at Mr. Lolkens's. Ensign Dederlin is made 2nd lieutenant. 2nd adjutant and ensign titular Mewis is made effective ensign. Sergeant Luck is made ensign titular and 2nd adjutant.

June 7: Dine at Mr. Kennedy's. Since no more disturbances were heard of, we are desired to go away because we are very expensive to the colony. We soon resolve to leave.

June 8: Dine at Mr. Demelly's.

June 9: Colonel Lantman's goods are rouped.[44] I dine with Joanna. I resolve to lie with her no more for certain good reasons.[45] I gave her a gold medal to remember me by. My father gave my mother the medal the night I was born.

June 11: The ships are reengaged and ordered to prepare to leave. I dine at Mr. Kennedy's.

---

38. Stedman used the Dutch term for an ensign, "vaendrig," in the diary.
39. I.e., in the middle of June.
40. Attacked.
41. Stedman often referred to the maroons generically as "negroes" in the diary.
42. Resignation.
43. A type of sailing ship with three or more masts and square rigging. Also spelled "barque."
44. An archaic term for a public auction.
45. Perhaps Stedman hoped to avoid a pregnancy right before his departure.

June 12: Sup at Mr. Kennedy's with two gentlemen from Tobago,[46] Mr. Kerry and Mr. Campbell.

June 13: Dine at Mr. Kennedy's.

June 15: Dine at ditto. Get news of Lieutenant Lepper and several men being shot by the negroes.

June 16: Some pasquils[47] are found against the governor and council. One thousand ducats offered to discover the author.

June 17: Dine at Kennedy's.

June 18: We are once more begged to stay, still, since the last bad news.[48] We once more agree to remain and, so again, discharge the ships. Mr. James Campbell invites me to take a jaunt to the island of Tobago, which I decline, expecting soon to be sent on sharp[49] commands.

June 21: Surgeon Renard dies and is buried the same day. Two captains, myself, and ten subalterns[50] are warned to prepare for command. Until now, the only duty was everyday one captain for picket,[51] one subaltern for guard duty, and three subalterns onboard the transports until the victuals were all on shore in the magazine.

* Mr. Van de Velde escapes being hanged in the bushes when his horse jumped through a hedge while racing with me.[52]

June 23: Dine at Mr. Demelly's.

June 24: Dine at Mr. Kennedy's. I receive a complement of coffee, sugar, lime juice, porter,[53] cider, Madeira,[54] claret, and rum from his lady.

---

46. An island in the Caribbean to the northwest of Suriname. The British acquired Tobago in 1763 and actively developed the island into a major plantation colony. As Stedman noted in the *Narrative*, he received an invitation to visit the island from Kerry and Campbell. They most likely were looking to recruit Stedman to settle in the colony.
47. I.e., satires. It is unclear if these were printed or orally transmitted.
48. I.e., the June 15 attack on Lieutenant Lepper.
49. When related to military affairs, "sharp" means fierce or vigorous. In essence, Stedman turned down the opportunity to travel to Tobago because he believed he would see combat.
50. In military terms, a subaltern is any junior officer ranking below a captain.
51. The picket was a group of soldiers always at the ready in case the enemy attacked. In this case, a captain always had to be in charge of the picket.
52. For some unknown reason, in the draft of the *Narrative*, Stedman recounted the story of Van de Velde's accident in October 1773. See FD, 176. Nevertheless, he does not note riding a horse in the diary entry for October 16, 1773, below.
53. A dark beer with a high alcohol content. It is unclear where it would have come from in Suriname, but it may have been imported from North America.
54. A type of fortified wine from the Portuguese island of Madeira.

* Master Lolkens gives me six bottles of muscatel wine, two bacons, hams, 12 spermaceti candles, one stoop-bottle[55] of sugar candies, and Mr. Gordon gave me four salted tongues and some muscat.

June 25: I put the liquor in bottle cases for the expedition: two stoop-bottles of claret, one stoop-bottle with porter, and one stoop-bottle with cider, but the latter spring to pieces to my sad vexation.[56]

June 26: At home with my girl. Some English gentlemen pass the evening with me over a chirping glass.[57]

June 27: Worthy Colonel Gersdorph dies. I dine at Master Gordon's.

June 28: The colonel is buried. I have the honor to carry one corner of the cloth.[58] I dine at home with Joanna.

June 29: A remarkable discourse with a freemason. I go to see Mr. Roux and his fine cabinet of Indian curiosities. The soldiers for command are ordered to be ready to go at a call.

> Major Becquer is made 2nd lieutenant colonel
> Captain Rughcop—major
> Captain-Commander Tulling—a company commander
> Lieutenant Van Halm—captain-commander
> 2nd Lieutenant Stromer—lieutenant
> Ensign Meyer—2nd lieutenant
> and Sergeant Matthew—ensign

* It is remarkable that Captain Tulling, who is now in charge of the company but was before a sea officer, got his first lodgings in the house of a lady that he had taken up in a boat at sea after she and several others had floated in her boat about 16 days in the greatest distress. NB at Paramaribo they met by chance, the one not knowing the other was in the place. A singular affair happened recently. All the sudden, a young fellow wanted to enlist as a soldier in the Society troops, but came to make his bargain at quite an unreasonable hour. The officer bid him to come at another time or go to the devil. The young man answered, "very well" and drowned himself directly. I have seen a boy of ten years old give a stroke to the face of an old negro woman for touching his hair when powdered and a Dutch sailor almost knock[ed] down a negro for not pulling off his hat at passing. A Jew knocked a woman in a swoon with his

---

55. Stedman used the Dutch word "stoop" to describe these. They were most likely tall, narrow cylindrical bottles with short necks that would be stopped with a cork topper.
56. Natural carbonation may have caused the bottle to explode.
57. An eighteenth-century phrase that meant to be cheerfully drunk.
58. I.e., the funeral pall.

cane for not walking fast enough after being short fettered.[59] A Jewess, out of jealousy, murdered a young mulatto girl in a horrid manner by putting a hot iron in her private parts. For that, she was sent to the savannah.[60]

June 30: Dine at Mr. Lolkens's. I beat a smous.[61] Captain Medlaer, 2nd Lieutenant Campbell, 2nd Lieutenant Meyer, one sergeant, two corporals, and 28 men leave to command Jew's Savannah. The captain on picket duty in Paramaribo is removed and a subaltern put in his place.

July

July 1: Dine at Mr. Kennedy's. Captain Tulling, Lieutenant Randwijk, 2nd Lieutenant Swildens, Ensign Meavis, two sergeants, three corporals, and 32 men leave to command the Commewijne River. I read in the Dutch papers that I have got lieutenant's pay in the Honorable Major-General Stuart's Regiment.[62]

July 2: I see the torpedo fish, have some Dutch gentlemen over for a hearty glass, and get orders to command the Cottica River. I give over command of my company. Dine at home. At six that evening, embark on two punts.[63] Myself, 2nd Lieutenant Hamer, Ensign MacDonald, one sergeant, two corporals, 18 men, 10 negroes, and a white pilot are onboard the *Prince William VI*. Lieutenant Stromer, 2nd Lieutenant Ower, one sergeant, one corporal, 14 men, 10 negroes, and a pilot are onboard the *Seven Provinces* bound for Patamacca Creek. In each frigate are provisions for one month besides two *double-haake*,[64] two blunderbusses, spades, axes, a saw, and a quantity of gunpowder. I take leave of poor Joanna and leave her in a flood of tears. She takes the care of all the baggage.

July 3: In the morning, about 4am, the ships lift anchor and set out on a cruise. Both are under my command. That evening heave anchor before Fort New Amsterdam, since we were windbound.[65] A small boat insults our fleet. I give chase with our armed sloop with a sergeant and two men. The rogue escapes us by the help of a dark night.

---

59. I.e., restrained.
60. I.e., Jew's Savannah, a Jewish settlement about fifty miles upriver from Paramaribo.
61. "Smous" was an eighteenth-century pejorative term for a Jewish person. In FD, Stedman recounted the story of him assaulting a Jewish man after that man attacked one of Stedman's soldiers for urinating on his fence.
62. Another name for the Scots Brigade.
63. A small, shallow, flat-bottomed boat. Probably similar to the barges that Stedman later described in the *Narrative*.
64. A type of small cannon.
65. The wind prevented them from sailing any farther.

July 4: I visit Mr. Kleijnhans at his plantation, Elizabeth's Hope. He treats me civilly and gives a quantity of refreshments for the crew. We set sail and anchor that night at Matapacca Creek.

July 5: The crew cook and walk[66] on plantation L'Adventure. We load the muskets and hoist a pennant. Anchor before the Perica River.

July 6: Crew cook and walk at De Alia. I teach Mr. Hamer subordination.[67] We load the pistols. Anchor before Limenbourg.

July 7: Crew cook and walk at Bokkenstein. Fire called out aboard without reason.[68] The fleet anchors at Coopman's Creek.

July 8: I beat the pilot of *Seven Provinces* frigate and almost fall overboard. We load the *double-haake* and blunderbusses before noon and anchor before the post 's-Lands Welvaren.[69] I go to shore with my officers to speak to the commandant. I deliver three sick men to go in his hospital, a horrid sight of poor scarecrows.[70] At dusk, lift anchor and go higher up the river and drop anchor again before the quitted[71] post Barbacoeba.

July 9: Heave anchor before Coermoetibo Creek off the River Cottica.

July 10: Send away the report of my arrival and a letter for the lovely Joanna. I dispatch the *Seven Provinces* frigate to Patamacca and send a sick negro to the post 's-Lands Welvaren.

* A soldier scalds himself with a keg of hot groats.[72]

July 11: Go ashore in Coermoetibo and build a hut to cook under. When finished, it dropped to pieces. We again begin to build it up and call the place "New Scotland." It was the only place fit to set a fort on shore within the hearing of a cannon shot. At night, we anchor in the mouth of the creek again, which we call "Devil's Corner."

July 12: Finish the hut and cook under it until…

July 14: Sail to Barbacoeba. Get a report from Fourgeoud's post at Patamacca via the *Seven Provinces* frigate.

---

66. Probably refers to a midday break when the soldiers would have disembarked, cooked for the rest of the day and the next morning, and exercised before rowing on.
67. I.e., he disciplined him using violence, most likely a slap or whipping.
68. A minor fire broke out near the stove.
69. The place Stedman and his men will nickname "Devil's Harwar."
70. I.e., men on the verge of death.
71. Abandoned.
72. I.e., a hot cereal made of boiled whole grains.

July 15: Build a hut at Barbacoeba and sail for 's-Lands Welvaren for repair. I got ashore and speak to the captain.

July 16: Return on board. Discord between my officers. Write to Fourgeoud, visit my sick soldiers, and get the vessel repaired. A carpenter escapes drowning. The captain gives me some fruits.

July 17: Sail for Devil's Corner after losing an anchor among the roots. The men cook at Barbacoeba. Get a letter from Fourgeoud. Anchor at Devil's Corner.

July 18: Make patrol to Perica Creek.

July 19: Since New Scotland is dangerous to cook at because it is on the rebel side of Coermoetibo Creek and where a strong command was lately murdered, we set the hut on fire and boil onboard. We are now opposed by all the elements. No ground to cook safely, almost choked by the smoke of the cook's fire, the air poisoned by mosquitoes, and all set adrift by the heavy rains which fell regularly every day.

NB The small rainy time begins about January 1 and lasts until the end of February. The small dry time from then until the last of April. Then begins the great rainy time until about the last of August. Finally, again begins the great dry-time until about the New Year.

Yet the poor fellows[73] still like it better than at the fort where, after being well used at first, must put up now with salted pork, groats, and peas in moderation. There is no butter, cheese, tobacco, or drams and only receive two pounds of bread for one man and one bottle of oil for 10 men per week. Here,[74] at least, they get their belly full at present.

July 20: Sail down river and anchor at Cassipora Creek. I often think about the fort where I had my wife, riding horse, two servants white and Black, free bed and board, wine in my cellar, and money in my pocket.

July 21: Anchor at Barbacoeba. I send out a patrol. Two men recovered and returned. I write to Joanna, Demelly, Heneman, Kleijnhans, Lolkens, and Kennedy.

July 22: Send a sergeant and one man to the hospital. Anchor at Devil's Harwar. Get a letter from Joanna.

July 23: Fire blunderbusses and great guns.

July 24: Anchor at Perica Creek.

---

73. The soldiers.
74. I.e., on the boat.

July 25: Pay a visit in a yawl[75] to the *Seven Provinces* frigate. Hear story of a witch.[76]

July 26: A false alarm on the river. Go to help the *Seven Provinces* frigate. The witch offers me a cat.

July 27: Anchor at Devil's Harwar.

July 28: Send two men to the hospital. A recovered negro returns. One man dies at the post. I hear Captain Medlaer sent the hands of two rebel negroes, killed by free negroes in Jew's Savannah on the Suriname River, to the fort. Poor Lieutenant Stromer comes down sick. I send Lieutenant Hamer to command his vessel[77] and, with him, the recovered negro.[78] Also, a woman and child, who escaped from the bush negroes,[79] came down to us. They had been stolen about a month before. By her account, the rebels crossed the Cottica River above plantation La Rochelle. Get report that 2nd Lieutenant Cottenburgh, one corporal, 10 men, and a craft with provisions are at 's-Lands Welvaren. Also received a letter from Fourgeoud. Sail down at once and anchor at Cassipora Creek in a damned condition. The boat was crowded with all sorts of people—and I had almost forgot a Jew. The sick groan, the negroes beg, the Jew prays, the soldiers swear, the child cries, the mother sings, the fire smokes, the rain beats, and the whole stink confounded.[80]

July 29: Anchor at 's-Lands Welvaren. There, we deliver Lieutenant Stromer and one sick man. Place 2nd Lieutenant Cottenburgh's command and the victuals. Get a sick man from *Seven Provinces* against orders and a foolish letter. I at once answer it.

July 30: I send an officer down to buy dram[81] for the soldiers. They cook on shore. I finish storing the provisions that came with 2nd Lieutenant Cottenburgh.

July 31: One man goes to the hospital and one man comes out. I get [a] letter from *Seven Provinces* with something more to purport. I answer it directly. We cook ashore. I take in some provender[82] and send report to Fourgeoud.

---

75. A small rowboat.

76. In the *Narrative* and first draft, Stedman recounted the story of an elderly enslaved woman who hailed him from the shore. She lived alone after being deemed useless and banished by her owner, who was Jewish. After the encounter, the Black men in Stedman's party swore the woman was a witch. See FD, 131–32.

77. The *Seven Provinces* or *Cereberus*.

78. Throughout the diary, Stedman described people of African descent using "negro" and its Dutch cognate "neger" interchangeably. This edition standardizes the terminology, using the English word.

79. An old term, now out of use, for the maroons.

80. An older definition of the word "confounded" means "to mix up."

81. I.e., a provision of liquor, most likely rum.

82. I.e., food or provisions.

August

August 1: I leave the civilian captain and sail to Cassipora Creek. I hear more troops are sent out.

August 2: Sail to Devil's Corner. Meet craft from the *Seven Provinces* going to fetch provender. Ensign MacDonald returns with the drams. I shoot an ape[83] and eat him with a piece of kapok tree,[84] longing for a fresh dinner.

* A damned insolent discourse I overhear from Mr. L———r.[85] Jump in at the window and hold my fist below his nose, which makes him good at once.

August 3: Get report of poor Lieutenant Stromer's death. Send up to fetch his things.

August 4: Sail to 's-Lands Welvaren. Meet the sergeant with the provender. The officers and men go ashore, and I bury the deceased officer[86] at the post. After which, I give a glass to all the gentlemen of us and the Society.

August 5: Send the goods of the deceased to Paramaribo along with a report to Fourgeoud and a letter for Lieutenant Colonel Westerloo. I also wrote a letter for Joanna and sent her a calabash and two plaits of my own hair. Get some fish from Patamacca Creek. I give it to the captain of the post and have a good meal of salt provisions. Men bait[87] ashore.

August 6: My sergeant returns recovered. Take on bread and sail to Barbacoeba. The men cook ashore at Barbacoeba.

August 7: Sail to Devil's Corner. The men boil[88] in the woods.

August 8: Send out a patrol to Patamacca Creek. The men boil in the woods. At 8pm, we hear a drum that we suppose is the bush negroes.

August 9: MacDonald falls sick. Two Society officers pass headed for Patamacca. Get letters from Fourgeoud, Campbell, Demelly, and Lolkens, who sends me hams, tea, sugar, wine, porter, etc., which I part too generously. I send down for provisions and a man sick to 's-Lands Welvaren.

---

83. Stedman did not shoot an ape, which is not native to South America, but one of the monkeys he described in the *Narrative*.
84. It is unclear what Stedman meant by "eat him with a piece of kapok tree." Kapok, or the silk cotton tree, is native to northern South America, and Stedman would have certainly encountered it in the jungle. It is not clear if he cooked the monkey over kapok wood, used a kapok skewer to cook the meat, or actually ate a piece of kapok along with his dinner.
85. Unclear who "Mr. L———r" was.
86. Lieutenant Stromer.
87. I.e., rest and relax.
88. I.e., cook their food.

August 10: Got the provisions. Men boil in the wood. I shoot two apes.

August 11: Send out a patrol to 's-Lands Welvaren and two sick men. The men cook in the wood. MacDonald is hard sick but won't be transported. This morning we again heard the drum.

August 12: Men boil in the wood. I shoot two large apes. Two Society officers come from Patamacca. Give me a letter from the *Seven Provinces*. We are driven from our anchor by a remarkably strong wind.[89]

August 13: Men boil in the wood. MacDonald is a little better.

August 14: Six scarecrows stop tide.[90] Make a patrol downriver.

August 15: Nine more scarecrows stop tide. Get letters from Fourgeoud, Westerloo, Heneman, and Joanna, who sends me wine, sugar, lemons, biscuit, paper, etc. Second Lieutenant Ower comes down sick. Give him letter I got for him. Get a letter from *Seven Provinces*. Send Ower to the post with a letter for the captain, send down to 's-Lands Welvaren for provisions, and give another letter for Captain Orzinga. This day got 200 florins from Fourgeoud for the men.

August 16: Got provender from 's-Lands Welvaren. Send 2nd Lieutenant Ower, who is worse, to Paramaribo and send a letter to Fourgeoud. I pay five florins for the wrights[91] who repaired my ship and made poor Stromer's coffin. My Black boy is hard sick.

August 17: Get letter from 2nd Lieutenant Cottenburgh at 's-Lands Welvaren. The men boil in the wood.

August 18: Send down patrol with money for the sick and to the *Seven Provinces* a letter with money and provender. My men cook in the wood. Get report that 2nd Lieutenant Cottenburgh has fallen sick.

August 19: Send MacDonald in his place[92] and my sergeant sick to hospital. At night, get letter from the *Seven Provinces* and report from MacDonald that Cottenburgh is very bad. That moment, I sent a letter to Fourgeoud and orders to take Mr. Cottenburgh to Paramaribo. The men boiled in the wood. This day, for the first time onboard, I get the ague.[93]

August 20: I am a deal better. Get letter that *Seven Provinces* has retired to Post La Rochelle with only six men in all. Men cook ashore.

---

89. In original: "remar. st. wind."
90. I.e., the sick men Stedman referred to as "scarecrows" died. Stedman used an older form of the word "tide," meaning a point of time in a person's life.
91. I.e., carpenters.
92. I.e., to replace 2nd Lieutenant Cottenburgh at 's-Lands Welvaren.
93. I.e., a high fever.

August 21: Send two men to assist them[94] and a letter to the lieutenant to return to his post. The men cook in the bush. Have the whole day a violent fever. Am now in a bad condition. Only 15 people remain of my 42 able men. Hard sick myself and there are neither medicines nor the least refreshments for me to be had within the hearing of a cannon shot.

August 22: The fever continues.

August 23: Am still very sick. Send two sick men to the hospital. Eight more scarecrows stop tide at 's-Lands Welvaren.

August 24: Lay in a violent fever.

August 25: Still no alteration. Get account that 2nd Lieutenant Ower died on his way to Paramaribo. Get letter from Fourgeoud and 50 florins for the sick and orders to take possession of 's-Lands Welvaren and arrest a thief. I also received letters from *Seven Provinces*, Lieutenant Colonel Westerloo, MacDonald, Captain Orzinga, Lolkens, and Joanna. One man returns recovered. Three Society soldiers pass for Patamacca. I order *Seven Provinces* to come down.

August 26: Am without fever but weak. We sail for 's-Lands Welvaren. I shoot a snake 18 feet long. Meet provisions headed for Patamacca.

August 27: *Seven Provinces* frigate comes down likewise. I take possession of the post, hospital, etc. at 's-Lands Welvaren and hoist the Prince's pennant.[95] Since I only had 20 of 54 men, I take 21 from the Society's captain. This makes just 41. I flog three negroes and beat the pilot.[96]

August 28: Society troops set off for Patamacca. Get letter from Dr. Kissam. Several men fall sick.

August 29: Two soldiers die in hospital. Send report to Fourgeoud and letter to Westerloo. At 11pm get account that three plantations, Peru, Zuyingheyd, and L'Espérance, are destroyed by bush negroes, all the white people are murdered, and that the rebels must pass close by Post 's-Lands Welvaren. I make all the men take arms. All considered, there are not above 12 able men to defend the post, which used to keep 300. The men in the hospital broke out and arose to certain death in a view to avoid it, several of the men dropping down and never rising. Only two small chest of powder was all the ammunition. The soldiers

---

94. The *Seven Provinces*.

95. The flag of the Dutch Republic. Before, soldiers from the Society of Suriname controlled 's-Lands Welvaren and would have hoisted their flag.

96. In the draft, Stedman revealed that the pilot was the thief mentioned on August 25. See FD, 152.

I got from the good captain[97] were sought out scrim,[98] all having rotten limbs, ruptures, agues, open wounds, etc. I myself was very weak. I send a report to Patamacca.

August 30: The men are still under arms. Send a report to Fourgeoud. Provisions passed to Patamacca.

August 31: The men are again on watch the whole night. A man dies.

September

September 1: I now make the negroes do the soldiers' duty since I did not have soldiers sufficient. Two waiters[99] desert the hospital after robbing it. At last, I get one corporal and 10 men from Patamacca.

September 2: I have now altogether 19 privates after making the two surgeons give me a written declaration that all the rest are unfit from any service. A Society officer comes down from Patamacca to me. I send my craft down to fetch dram for my men.

September 3: Get letter from Fourgeoud and word from Joanna. Kennedy sends down 12 bottles of Madeira. Gordon sends me a barrel of biscuits. My sergeant Cabanus is made ensign. I send him, Ensign MacDonald, and one sick Society soldier to fort Paramaribo with the money, goods, arms, etc. of the deceased men along with a prisoner for stealing. Get a letter direct from plantation Alida and report to Fourgeoud asking from him more men, more powder, better provisions for the officers, and medicines for the sick—all of which I wanted. I write to Joanna. I get one more man from Patamacca. I hear 2nd Lieutenant Cottenburgh is dead. Three of my five officers are now dead.

September 4: Another man dies. Get 18 jugs of dram.

September 5: One more dies. A large craft from Paramaribo arrives with provisions, one subaltern, one surgeon, three sergeants, two corporals, one drummer, and 29 men. I receive an order to seek the track of the rebels. Send to the fort a sick Society corporal and a report for Fourgeoud.

---

97. Stedman is referring to the Society soldiers in this sentence.
98. I.e., Stedman had to resort to these men as reinforcements. Stedman used an archaic meaning of the word "sought," meaning to resort to or have recourse to. "Scrim" is a Scots word for a piece of fabric used to reinforce something, such as plaster, bookbinding, etc. In this specific context, Stedman's tone suggests he had been forced to resort to using ill and nearly dead Society soldiers.
99. Stedman was probably referring to the enslaved people that served as nurses and servants in the post's hospital.

September 6: Stow the victuals in the magazine, clean the arms of the sick, and consult about patrol.

September 7: I set out at 6am with one subaltern, two sergeants, two corporals, 40 men, a guide, and eight negroes to seek the track of the rebels. After crossing the cordon,[100] I discover it near halfway between 's-Lands Welvaren and Soribo.[101] We arrived there at 8pm but had to leave 10 men behind in the jungle. We were all miserably fatigued after half swimming through morass; climbing over fallen trees, roots, etc. and creeping on our bellies under them; and marching through the most scorching heat while the sun shone and Hell's darkness after it set at 6pm. Most of us were scratched, stung, and some even blinded by insects. Cotty were we in the *macas*[102] notwithstanding four negroes with cutlasses continually cutting up a track.

September 8: We rest at Soribo. Send company of Society troops to fetch back my invalids.[103] They bring seven back and the other three returned to 's-Lands Welvaren. I get some provisions and a letter from Lieutenant Colonel Becquer. I write a report to Fourgeoud that I discovered the track of the rebels, but too late owing to my being too weak in men, powder, etc. when it was time to find it.

September 9: Leaving four men sick at Soribo, the rest of us are refreshed and march off at 4am and come to 's-Lands Welvaren at 4pm. I am in rags without a stocking or a shoe and striped red and blue up to the haunches.[104] My messmates in Paramaribo have not only taken away my house by the chief's[105] wise order, but have also sealed up my goods to throw them untouched on a *koopdag*[106] in case I should die.[107] For that reason, I could not get a stick of my own since I went up on this cruise and now all is worn and torn. I find Lieutenant Colonel Westerloo has come to 's-Lands Welvaren with Quartermaster Coene. I make the colonel a report of my discovery and give him command of the post, hospital, magazine, etc. I go in the river to wash, since I was covered in dirt,

---

100. The defensive perimeter around 's-Lands Welvaren.
101. Soribo was a military post on Perica Creek maintained by the Society of Suriname and staffed with their soldiers.
102. I.e., they were entangled in the briars. "Cotty" is an antiquated term meaning entangled, while *maca* is a term used for thorns or briars across the Caribbean.
103. The ten men Stedman left behind.
104. I.e., bruised up to the thighs.
105. Colonel Fourgeoud.
106. In the diary, Stedman spelled it "coopdagh." A *koopdag* is a sale of goods ordered by judicial authorities to settle debts or after someone's death. It is similar to a sheriff's sale or estate auction in the English-speaking world.
107. The actual word Stedman use here is illegible, but the context implies in case of his death, so this edition uses "die."

blood, etc. That evening I am indisposed. NB I was rather weak when I went to the bush.

September 10: A craft comes from the fort with two subalterns named Portuguese and Matthew, a quantity of provisions, and soldiers for 's-Lands Welvaren. Joanna sends me a letter with 15 stoop-bottles of rum, biscuit, sugar, bacon, ham, etc. I was far from well this day. By the surgeon's advice and 's-Lands Welvaren now having troops in abundance and thus nothing to dread, I ask leave to go to Paramaribo[108] to get recovered. The time for that, however, was when I was bedfast.[109] As for now, I could not yet be missed. I grow desperate, swear revenge against Fourgeoud, knock down my sergeant,[110] stroll unarmed through the woods, come home again, and get mortally drunk.

September 11: Have the whole day a fever. Get my hair cropped.

September 12: By a letter, Fourgeoud seems to call some of my actions into question. With justice, Lieutenant Colonel Westerloo supports me notwithstanding the most horrid invectives I throw at the former in public and sink in the lowest of spirits. I am now reckoned wrong in the head and, after a private consultation, get leave to go to Paramaribo. News comes that the negroes burnt Mr. Nyboor's plantation in Patamacca and murdered him.

I said I got leave and so, about noon, I walk to the waterside supported by a negro. None of the other officers have time to conduct me there—some are corking the gin bottle, others beating out their pipes, and the whole just going to give their hands and jawbones a different occupation. I sleep in the boat and make the negroes pull for Paramaribo. I do not have the benefit of my own servant or one white attendant. But how could they afford to lose one man since they did not have above 100 and the bush negroes are not more than three or four days journey from them?

September 13: I deliver two letters from Colonel Westerloo to plantation Vreendenburgh, one for Captain Stoelman and the other to go to Fourgeoud.

September 14: About 2am, I find myself before Mr. La Marre's door. Send in the boy to ask for a lantern, but La Marre himself comes out and offers me, his brother-in-law (he having my girl's sister),[111] the best room in his house and all necessary attendance with the greatest hospitality. I accept the offer. Joanna is sent for and I am not unhappy. I write to Westerloo and send for a physician.

---

108. Often when Stedman referred to Paramaribo, he called it "fort." This edition uses the town's name to avoid any confusion.
109. I.e., bedridden. Somehow, Fourgeoud knew Stedman was going to request a leave and preemptively denied it in his orders to Westerloo.
110. This is the sergeant who allegedly assaulted Joanna, as detailed in the *Narrative*.
111. In the draft of the *Narrative*, Stedman calls Joanna's sister La Marre's "wife." See FD, 161.

September 15: I get my things and get out clean linens, etc.

September 18: In a letter from Mrs. Stedman,[112] get account that my good friend Mr. Vonck died December 25, 1772.

September 20: I have got the ringworm, but soon get better by an excellent recipe.

September 26: Have blood drawn twice.

September 28: Get letter from plantation Rosetta and from Van de Velde.

October

October 2: I am ordered to take the care of the colors and the regimental chest.[113] For that reason, I was preferred to the rank of commandant of our troops at Paramaribo. I get a sentry placed before my door. Mr. Brandt, the old commandant, leaves the fort.

October 3: Mr. Texier, the Society commander, comes home sick.

October 4: I begin to show my power by discharging the damned sour gripe gut[114] claret, which had been brought for the sick officers and men. Instead, I bought good wine. I suppose I should have bought something dearer out of the money that was kept in the regimental chest. I was also sorry that I could not transmogrify[115] all the salt beef and pork, groats, hard peas, etc., which was ordered for the sick officers as well as the men, into a good wholesome diet.[116]

October 6: The fever left me, but I was still unable to walk because of two sores on my thigh. I go out in Kennedy's chaise, visit the governor, and dine at Demelly's.

October 8: Crawl out and see the selling of my dear Joanna and the whole plantation.

October 10: Receive a letter from Westerloo and two from Fourgeoud. I write to Dr. Campbell, James Campbell of Tobago, Mrs. Vonck, and my brother. I dine on board the *Harmony*, Captain Tom Timmons.

---

112. Stedman's mother.
113. The "colors" were the regiment's flag, and the "chest" was a physical chest that held the regiment's money for purchasing supplies and provisions.
114. Similar to the term "rotgut" used to describe poor-quality liquor today.
115. I.e., transform.
116. Here, Stedman lamented not being able to exchange the preserved foods for fresh provisions but was under orders to continue giving them to the sick.

October 11: I dispatch Fourgeoud's letters and my own. I hear Fourgeoud, with all the troops, has gone into the bush and that, in place of Stromer, he has advanced Robert Campbell to 1st lieutenant, Rulagh to 2nd lieutenant, and Sergeant Coene to ensign and quartermaster. In place of Cottenburgh, Mewis is now 2nd lieutenant and Sergeant Cabanus is his ensign. And, in the place of Ower, Noot to 2nd lieutenant and Sergeant Ghim to quartermaster.

October 12: Write to Fourgeoud and Brandt. Give Geelguin one letter from Holland and Fourgeoud two. Send Lieutenant Randwijk and two quacks with medicines to the Commewijne River and medicines to 's-Lands Welvaren. La Marre goes on command with 25 free mulattos.

October 13: Send Fourgeoud a packet and three letters from Holland.

October 14: Dine with Mrs. Godefroy and sup at my girl's.

October 15: Visit company and dine at the governor's. Get packet from Holland for regiment and letter from La Marre.

October 16: Buy two more anchors[117] of wine for the regiment. Get letter from Tulling. A dispute with a sailor concerning my girl. Fun on our officer's mount.[118]

October 17: From a negro's back, get letter from Portuguese and write to 's-Lands Welvaren. Matthew comes home sick. Send off Fourgeoud's packet and oil for Tulling. I dine onboard the *Peggy*, Captain Lewis.

October 18: Dine at Mr. Day's. Westerloo comes sick from Patamacca. I fetch him home in a coach and get physicians. I send two men's chests to 's-Lands Welvaren.

October 19: Dine at Texier's. Get Dr. Kissam to Westerloo, in addition to Van Dam,[119] and stop the passage by a sentry. I send medicines to the Commewijne River.

October 20: Randwijk returns home sick. I make a maid drunk.

October 21: Breakfast with my girl. Dine onboard the *Olive Branch*, Captain Bogard.

October 22: Dine at Kennedy's. Mr. Coene and Hamer come here sick.

October 23: Breakfast with Joanna. Write to Stanhouse and La Marre. Receive a small chest of Fourgeoud's from Kennedy's.

---

117. A type of wine barrel.
118. In the first draft of the *Narrative*, Stedman recalled a race with Van de Velde on October 17, 1773, but, in the diary, noted that the race was on June 23, 1773. Here, he may have been out for a joyride after being ill. See FD, 176.
119. Seems to have been a doctor that was already attending Westerloo.

October 24: Being now recovered, I resolve to go into the bush with Fourgeoud. Give over command to 2nd Lieutenant Meijer and ask for a boat. Refused as 15 florins a day was too little for them. Damn them for their economy.

October 25: Get the offer from a Dutch sloop. Refuse it with disdain. Get drunk and play damn…[120]

October 26: Get three dozen wine from Kennedy and six bottles from Lolkens. Take leave from my girl and leave the fort with assistance from a boat with men supplied by four different English captains. They hoist their pennants and acknowledge me in the boat, where we drink a glass at parting. I salute them by discharging one gun and pistol, which they answer by three cheers. I sup at Fort New Amsterdam. Row the whole night and breakfast at plantation Sporksgift.

October 27: Row to plantation Charlettenburgh. Give a letter from Kennedy. Write Joanna and Kissam. Discharge the English boat after giving them 10 florins and compliments to their captains and having treated them with wine and roasted duck all the way from the fort.

October 28: Set off in tent punt.[121] Come to plantation Mondesire.

October 29: At plantation Lepair and see the three broke plantations.[122]

October 30: After dining at plantation Lebanon, go to Post 's-Lands Welvaren.

October 31: To Coermoetibo Creek.

November

November 1: Sea cow.[123] I arrive at Wana Creek where I find a punt full of provisions. Sent back a party with letters for Joanna, Kissam, Reeder, and Hertsbergh. Also sent six turkeys for Joanna.

November 2: Eat shield hog.[124]

November 3: Rughcop comes to Wana Creek with his command.

---

120. The rest of the line is illegible. It is unclear what Stedman meant here, although, in the *Narrative*, he recounted a night of drunken behavior that involved a fight between soldiers and sailors.
121. I.e., a small boat with a tent covering most of the deck.
122. I.e., the three plantations that Stedman noted had been attacked and sacked on August 29.
123. In the draft of the *Narrative*, Stedman described how the Rangers showed him a manatee or sea cow swimming in the river. See FD, 184.
124. Stedman's term for an armadillo.

November 4: Fourgeoud comes also with his men and he receives me coldly. On their way here, they discovered three empty villages. While there, they buried seven heads of soldiers put on pins[125] by the negroes and one old woman they took prisoner. He also stopped a mutiny among his men over bread three days before.

November 5: Bob Campbell acquaints me that the previous evening, Fourgeoud had given the damnedest description in place of introducing me to a number of Society officers with whom I was unacquainted, which hurt me. I am sent to join Mr. Rughcop. I am little thought of by my messmates, all Germans.[126] I must have patience.

NB Damned short allowance and clean water is allowed.[127]

November 8: I go on patrol with 20 men and 20 from the regiment come home.[128] A Society captain affronts me with his tale. I challenge him on any weapons. He chooses cutlasses. We go out and fight a duel at once. I sent him to the camp with a cursed slash in the right shoulder, two inches from his throat.

November 10: Poor Bob Campbell goes sick to 's-Lands Welvaren. I send my foul linens to Joanna with a letter. Also write to Kissam. Fourgeoud uses me cruelly by God.

November 13: We march down Coermoetibo Creek. Camp at night in a heavy rain with no huts.

November 14: March on a bad road. Only receive a half ration of rusk biscuit[129] in 24 hours and nothing else but water.

November 15: March on bad roads in heavy rains.

November 16: Come to a plantation that I used to call New Scotland, but properly named Jerusalem. We were wet and half starved. Receive a letter and some biscuit, half of which was stolen, from Joanna. I sleep on the ground, no hut.

---

125. These were the heads of Lieutenant Lepper and his men, whose story Stedman told in the *Narrative*.

126. Messmates were the people that soldiers and sailors dined with and were important social connections in military and maritime settings. The fact that Stedman's messmates at Wana Creek were German is not surprising, given the large number of Germans that served in the Dutch army, especially foreign expeditionary forces, in the seventeenth and eighteenth centuries.

127. The fact that the men were allowed clean water suggests a shortage of liquor.

128. I.e., all the men survived the patrol and returned to camp.

129. A hard, twice-baked wheat flour biscuit consumed by soldiers and sailors.

November 17: I force the *bassia*[130] to make a hut at once. Am very sick. Offered the opportunity to go down[131] by Fourgeoud, which I reject disdainfully.

November 18: Am well again. Get account that poor Campbell died on the 17th. Am sadly low-spirited. I attack Fourgeoud and ask for reasonable satisfaction concerning his damned tongue. He denies the whole in a dirty way and accuses other people. Mr. Rughcop is now the 11th officer sent home sick from the command. We are almost starved. I eat broiled fish without bread or salt.

November 19: Buy Dutch trousers because Fourgeoud did not approve of my English ones.

November 20: A captain with 20 men and 20 more from the regiment is sent down to Boekoe. I discourse with Fourgeoud regarding Scotsmen, for whom I ask for double punishment when they deserve it.

November 21: Get account that Rughcop is dead. Fourgeoud with a command marches to Boekoe. I ask to go without success. I am given command of 400 people, Black and white, at Jerusalem, but 200 are sick. Send down 60 free negroes and 30 sick soldiers to 's-Lands Welvaren. Write to Joanna and Kissam and to Patamacca and 's-Lands Welvaren for provisions.

November 22: Some negroes are arrested for stealing some pork, which I decide strongly.[132] Get letter from Zeebagh which tells me that my letters, etc. are neglected. I write at once to Portuguese.

November 23: He sends me back my letter to Joanna of the 10th and the foul linens I had sent her. I send them down once more and write again to Portuguese.

November 24: Captain Zeebagh and Lieutenant De Graaff come from 's-Lands Welvaren, recovered. I get some rum from 's-Lands Welvaren. Zeebagh picks a quarrel with me about the command. I at once challenge him at sword and pistol which he most gallantly refuses and begs my pardon in the most condescending manner.[133]

---

130. The enslaved driver on the plantation. He was in charge of keeping all the other enslaved people working and on task.
131. I.e., down the river to either 's-Lands Welvaren or Paramaribo.
132. I.e., forcefully. In the draft of the *Narrative*, Stedman recounted this episode. The regular soldiers were quite upset with the Blacks for stealing pork and demanded vengeance. Instead, Stedman divided the pork between the offenders, the soldiers, and the executioner responsible for detaining the thieves. See FD, 204–5.
133. Stedman used "condescending" in the eighteenth-century sense, meaning to back down or submit in a conciliatory manner.

November 26: Was bled in the toe last night by a bat.[134] Walrave and Stoelman come to Jerusalem and give me a letter, some biscuit, cheese, and tea from my friend Kissam. Fourgeoud and his command returns to Jerusalem after capturing two unarmed negroes, who he brought with him. One was not hurt, but the other had his leg and thigh shot to smash[135] and was tied to a long pole like a hog in the most inhuman manner. He died of his wounds that day.

November 27: Fourgeoud told me that Mr. Stoelman had made free[136] behind my back, I ask that he may call himself to account. But it was not him. Fourgeoud owns he was mistaken and begs me not to speak of it. Fourgeoud discharges all the free negroes and sends them off.

November 29: Captain de Borgnes becomes major, Lieutenant Portuguese becomes captain commandant, and 2nd Lieutenant Swildens becomes 1st lieutenant.

November 30: March back to Wana Creek. Keep St. Andrew's Day[137] with Sergeant Fowler and Thompson.

December

December 1: March again. Dispute between Mr. Richards and me concerning my hut. Put him out.

December 2: Have a singular dream concerning my brother Willy.[138] I discourse with Fourgeoud's *valet de chambre*, whom I shall henceforth call Sancho, but not on account of his master.[139] He tells me what he had advised Fourgeoud to write to His Highness and what he had wrote to worthy Colonel Gersdorph's mistress, in Holland, about what officers were to be looked over and what officers were to be advanced.

December 3: We march in bad weather to Wana Creek again. I am warned for the second time by Fourgeoud not to whistle or speak above my breath. A hangman is to be sent from Holland to hang, burn, etc. all who disobey his

---

134. In the middle of the night, a bat bit Stedman's foot.
135. I.e., broken to pieces.
136. I.e., slandered Stedman's reputation.
137. St. Andrew's Day is the feast day for St. Andrew, Jesus's apostle and the patron saint of Scotland. St. Andrew's Day falls on November 30 and is Scotland's national day. As a Scot, Stedman would have celebrated with other Scots in his command.
138. Stedman's brother William George Stedman (1748–1807), was also in the Scots Brigade but did not deploy to Suriname.
139. After Sancho Panza, the peasant who served as Don Quixote's squire in Miguel Cervantes's classic tale. Stedman made it clear with the clause following Sancho that he did not think Fourgeoud was an ignorant fool like Don Quixote.

commands in the least. I challenge Mr. Richards. He begs pardon in tears. I give him a dram and send him about his business.

December 4: I treat them all with good rum punch—the last I had.

December 7: Get intelligence that the bush negroes passed close by the camp and over Coermoetibo Creek.

December 8: We march after them or, rather, from them, but I am not heard when I voice my opinion. We cannot find one after marching until dark without bread or water. I get in a hot quarrel with Master Keller, whom, after a fruitless challenge, I curse as a dirty scoundrel and all the rest that were his mates.

December 9: We march again to Wana Creek. The colonel goes to reconnoiter the other side of Coermoetibo Creek. The last negro we caught is set at liberty.

December 10: March after them again, the same way we marched on the 8th. Find an old negro camp. Can get no water to drink.

December 11: March. Find an old banana ground.[140] No water still.

December 12: March again. Still no water. The men faint. I lick the drops from fallen leaves, creeping on all fours like Nebuchadnezzar.[141] We turn back for drink. Gausarie[142] is sent to spy. We sleep in an old negro camp. A sad work about a dub.[143] Am refused my own dram by Fourgeoud. Instead of giving my own, I steal double from him.[144] The "old shaver"[145] swears to shoot the first that speaks, having just heard my voice begging from his negro cook.

December 13: We come to Wana Creek. Fourgeoud gives a single glass of claret to his own officers. I get none. Receive a letter from Joanna and Joanna's brother. A small patrol sent out.

* I was refused a dram from the "old shaver" and steal a bottle.

---

140. I.e., old plantain walks cultivated by the maroons.
141. This is a reference to chapter four of the Book of Daniel in the Old Testament. In it, the prophet Daniel tells the Babylonian king Nebuchadnezzar II that he will be driven mad and live and behave like an animal for seven years. This would include walking on all fours until God would restore him. It was meant as a parable that all earthly beings, no matter how powerful, had to bow to the power of the Hebrew God.
142. A free Black man who had been a rebel leader during the 1763 Berbice Rebellion before changing sides and helping the Dutch quash the rebellion. He then fell under the protection of Colonel Fourgeoud, who brought him to Suriname for this expedition. See Marjoleine Kars, *Blood on the River: A Chronicle of Mutiny and Freedom on the Wild Coast* (New York: New Press, 2020).
143. I.e., a muddy, stagnant pool of water. Stedman used the Scots term "dub" to describe an attempt to dig a pit to find water near the old maroon encampment.
144. In the diary, Stedman wrote "steal double," but in the draft of the *Narrative*, he makes it clear that he stole it from Fourgeoud.
145. Stedman's nickname for Fourgeoud.

December 14: Gausarie returns, fruitless. Gets little thanks.

December 15: Two captains, two subalterns, and about 50 men are sent to Marowijne[146] to look for the command from November 20.

December 16: Fourgeoud orders a snake to be shot after refusing to kill game. A soldiers' resolution.[147]

December 17: Have a swollen foot, a cold, a looseness,[148] and hunger. Joanna sends me, in this distress, a ham, two stoop of rum, a sugar loaf, biscuit, eggs, etc. I give the "old fouter"[149] the ham. Write to Joanna and send her all my linens, being allowed but one carrier. Every evening get a sentry to stop my mouth.[150]

December 18: I pass my time making baskets for the girl I love.

December 22: I write to Klaasje[151] Brindel. I now walk barefoot, all my shoes, stockings, etc. being torn.

* December 27: A Society soldier has been condemned to be shot after planning, with six others, to abandon their post out of hunger. He is pardoned on the spot and loses his senses.[152]

December 28: Get account that Fredericy has arrived at the Commewijne River. Get letter from Kissam and also from Coeverden, who sends me 10 bottles of claret. Give five to the "old rogue,"[153] and so think it is best to butter an old foe by necessity.

December 29: A command consisting of the major, myself, one subaltern, and 40 men is sent out again. We sail a punt to plantation Bergshoven.

December 30: We disembark and march. We forget powder and lose the way. I beg that I may be followed and it is granted. I march north and find a savannah. I discover the path where the command that marched the 15th had passed.

---

146. The river that makes up the border between Suriname and French Guiana.
147. It is unclear what Stedman meant with this line, although a considerable amount of suffering occurred in the encampment.
148. I.e., diarrhea.
149. I.e., Fourgeoud. A "fouter" is a Scots term of derision, meaning an objectionable or worthless person.
150. It seems Fourgeoud sent a sentry to quiet Stedman down or to stop him from complaining.
151. Shorted form of the name "Nicholas" in Dutch.
152. The practice of court-martialing a soldier who deserted, sentencing him to death, and then pardoning him was relatively common and a way for officers to assert their authority while avoiding making the soldier a martyr.
153. Fourgeoud.

December 31: We follow it. March in water above the middle[154] the whole day. Must go back and camp near Coermoetibo Creek. The major uses me with disdain. I curse him and challenge him. He refused. I go off mad and run myself in swoon on a tree.[155] He offers his condescension and I pity him. We make it up.

1774

January

January 1: We return to Wana Creek.

January 3: Write of Bob's death to Dr. Campbell. I write to Joanna. Two captains, three subalterns, and 60 men are sent out to cruise on the way to Patamacca. Fredericy and Mewis return with a bush negro.

January 4: We march for Patamacca Creek over high, strong mountains.

January 5: March in heavy rains. The "old rogue" [illegible].[156] I hear Bob Campbell wrote two singular letters before his death. A carrier deserts.[157] We come to Boni's[158] country where a previous command had found rice and buried heads.[159]

January 6: The command rests and only I must march in water up to the middle the whole day with one officer and 10 men to discover a creek. I swim it alone and make a report thereof. Ask for a bit of my own ham and glass of my own wine, which could scarcely be granted.

January 7: We march. Camp over Patamacca Creek. Fourgeoud calls General Stuart *crasseaux*.[160] I deny it and leave the company. Am obliged to ask for shot from Sancho the Knight who refused to give me more than four.

January 8: We march to plantation La Rochelle in Patamacca and arrived in rags, most of us without shoes. My feet had suffered too much. We found there a number of wretches just ready to undergo the cursed misery that was

---

154. I.e., the waist.
155. Stedman fell headfirst into a tree as he stormed off after his fight with the major.
156. The word may be "murmurs." In the draft of the *Narrative*, Stedman described Fourgeoud as enraged about the weather and marching conditions.
157. One of the enslaved men the soldiers employed as a porter fled.
158. The leader of the maroons.
159. The original diary just stated, "had found rice and buried heads," which is clearly a reference to the command Stedman described on November 4, 1773.
160. I.e., a French term of derision meaning filthy or wretched.

ever felt by a heap of withered pale-faced mortals, except ourselves.[161] The bush affords not the least satisfaction, but exposes man to being troubled with [many illnesses][162] and many insects[163] in addition to tigers, snakes, etc. In the creeks and rivers, there are caiman and piranhas or "prick biters."[164] Besides all these, there is the inconvenience of trees, shrubs,[165] sharp stones, deep swamps, savannahs, warm days, cold nights, heavy rains, short allowances,[166] etc. I represent[167] Fourgeoud that the men are mostly barefoot and long for some refreshments. He curses the shoemakers and praises Hannibal's frugality, to whom he compares with Laurant.[168] In the space of three months, he had nothing but stinking Irish beef and creek water, by God, for officers and men alike. I jaw[169] with Captain Larcher who told me he never shifted[170] shirt or stocking until they rotted from him, slept in boots, and never combed his hair or washed. I left him. I spoke to a director[171] who told me he had seen the Devil. I left him and went alone to pare my nails. I had win some [illegible] but got none.[172]

NB The old negro woman, marching between the creek and the post, paid homage to her deceased husband's bones, who had been murdered on her account and was buried below a tree in the wood.

January 11: The command sent out. A third comes in but saw nothing.

January 12: A negro and his wife come to us of themselves.[173]

---

161. When Stedman and the rest of his party arrived at La Rochelle, there was another group readying to head into the jungle, thus "ready to undergo the cursed misery."
162. Here Stedman listed twelve different ailments, most of them in Dutch, which are near impossible to identify today.
163. Stedman listed eight types of insects.
164. Stedman used the local term *peree* for piranha. For the slang term, Stedman wrote "p——k biters."
165. Stedman listed the species of trees and shrubs.
166. I.e., low ceilings.
167. I.e., tell.
168. This is a reference to the legendary Carthaginian general Hannibal (247–181 CE), who was frugal and able to cross the Alps and attack Rome with limited supplies. Laurant was Fourgeoud's quartermaster, the person in charge of logistics, and not up to the task. Thus the unfavorable comparison to Hannibal.
169. I.e., chat or gossip.
170. I.e., changed.
171. I.e., plantation overseer.
172. "Win" is a Scots term for drying food. The food Stedman dried is unclear, and he only wrote an "f."
173. These were two maroons who willingly surrendered to Fourgeoud.

January 13: I and other officers are sent to Paramaribo to repair.[174] Thank God. Away in a tent boat. Welcome at 's-Lands Welvaren where I meet letters from Joanna, Lolkens, La Marre, who also sent me 20 bottles of claret, 4 stop of rum, tea, biscuits, lemons, etc. From Lolkens, I received one barrel of butter and two sugar loaves. I send dear Fourgeoud the butter and 10 bottles as presents—the rest we drink going down the river.

January 14: Sup at plantation Mondesire and away down we went.

January 15: Stop at Fort New Amsterdam. The major is wearing long ruffles taken from a drum major. Arrive in Paramaribo. Go to La Marre's to lodge, barefooted and in rags. Send for my girl, my dear girl, who had heard that I was dead and to whom I gave a hearty welcome.

* Buy a new hat and gold lace for Quaco since he had attended me faithfully during the three months in the woods.

January 16: I wait and dine at Mr. Kennedy's. Come home lame, since I was no longer used to shoes.[175] Joanna is good for nothing. Was sod cripple last night.[176]

January 17: She makes me an odd discovery, which makes me think.[177]

* Am almost taken[178] stealing Fourgeoud's eggs to make hot posset.

January 18: I hire her from her master for 10 bits[179] a week and her to sewing for myself.

January 23: Send for Master Kennedy's chaise and dine with him.

January 26: Go onboard the *Zeelust* to take leave of Colonel Westerloo. He goes to Holland to recover from a lameness. Lieutenant Randwijk also gets

---

174. I.e., recuperate.

175. Stedman wore shoes to Kennedy's after having not worn them in so long, causing his feet to swell and making him unable to walk.

176. It is unclear exactly what Stedman meant by "sod cripple," but given the context, he most likely was impotent after drinking too much at Kennedy's. In the draft, Stedman noted Kennedy got him drunk with whisky. And Joanna was perhaps "good for nothing" because she could not help him get an erection. See FD, 232.

177. Here, Stedman most likely learned of the practice of hiring an enslaved woman as a concubine. In the draft, his entry for January 16 is a long description of Paramaribo and the behavior of the people who lived there. In one part, he described hiring concubines, suggesting Joanna informed him of the practice. If he could not purchase her outright, he could at least hire her, which is exactly what happened in the next diary entry. See FD, 239–40.

178. I.e., caught.

179. A bit was a small denomination coin worth about sixpence or half a shilling.

leave to recover. I write to mama, Reygersman, Bob Cunningham, and Jan Van de Velde.

January 28: Dine at Mr. Gordon's.

January 29: A fight at La Marre's, which I separate and horse whip the mob.

January 30: Get a strike from a horse.[180] Give Joanna a silver purse, which I got from Rosetta, and bought her a new blanket. Offer several things to sell, having received no pay or ransom. I hear Lieutenant Randwijk's voyage is stopped for certain alleged reasons and until further orders can be given. All the officers go to Patamacca to be sent on duty. I can't yet follow because my feet have not yet recovered.

January 31: Dine at master Lolkens's. Pay near 100 florins for new bush equipage. Received three bottles of rum from Fredericy. Since December 1st of last year, we receive our full pay, commissions, maintenance, etc.

February

February 1: Each officer in Paramaribo is now allowed, in place of victuals, at the rate of, for each ransom,[181] 100 florins a year.

February 2: This day, it is a year since we arrived in Suriname. This day I hear Lieutenant Colonel Becquer is dead and makes the company vacant for me. I get fuddled, drinking to good success and my mother's health, which is this day past the grand climacteric.[182]

February 3: Ride with Heneman in the morning and dine at Mr. Demelly's. Write a letter to Fourgeoud.

February 4: Dine at Mr. Gordon's.

February 6: Pay a visit to the governor and commandant. Dine at Mr. Kennedy's.

February 7: Dine at Kennedy's. Sup with my girl, Heneman, and sister.[183]

February 8: Received Fowler's letter. Mentions the lumber and spin house.[184]

---

180. Most likely got hit by a horse while walking in Paramaribo.
181. When Stedman used the word "ransom," he was referring to the officers' commissions, which bound them to remain in the military.
182. I.e., his mother turned sixty-three years old. This is a reference to astrological "climacteric," or important, birthdays.
183. I.e., Joanna's sister, who was La Marre's, now Stedman's landlord, concubine.
184. A "spin house" was a term for a women's prison where the prisoners would often spend their time spinning thread.

February 9: Give two gold rings to Heneman and Medlaer. Am disturbed at midnight by La Marre's[185] bastards below and a German beating his wife above.

February 10: Dine at Lolkens's. Get the news that I have the company. Major de Borgnes becomes lieutenant colonel; Captain Medlaer, major; Lieutenant Perret Gentilly, captain commandant; and Heneman, lieutenant.

In place of officers Major Rughcop and Lieutenant Campbell were advanced Captain de Borgnes to major, Captain Commandant Brandt to company, and the two 2nd lieutenants, Geelguin and Swildens, lieutenants.

Came home fuddled at night after buying a Turkish blade to carry into the bush—or rather to a post. I have been ordered to take the command of L'Espérance[186] and the Commewijne River.

* Here Fourgeoud stops advancement and treats his field officers as corporals and worse.

February 11: Dine at Demelly's.

February 12: Dine at Mrs. Gordon's. Give Fourgeoud a chest of candles that I had received from La Marre at Patamacca, a mistake not yet given.

* The rats eat my commission because I left it, by accident, on a table the whole night.

February 13: Dine at Mr. Kennedy's.

February 14: Dine at Mr. Smith's. My friend Lolkens sends me cheese, butter, and sausages to take to my post. I hear Fourgeoud is in the bush and going to march to Boucou and Marowijne.

February 15: Dine at Kennedy's.

February 16: Mrs. Godefroy sends me three sugar loaves, tea, and coffee. I hear the company was engaged in battle. Captain Fredericy and two men wounded.

February 17: Dine at Mr. Smith's and set off for plantation L'Espérance after getting: from Lolkens, six bottles of arrack;[187] from La Marre, 12 bottles of claret; from Gordon, two tongues;[188] and Mr. Goetzee, some lemons. I had a wonderful visit from Mr. Laghman, an officer. Sleep at plantation Sporksgift.

---

185. Stedman just wrote "L——s" here, but given he was living in La Marre's house at the time, it was most likely his children making the noise.

186. Also called "The Hope."

187. A liquor distilled from the sap of coconut palms or sugarcane along with rice or another grain. Arrack is popular in South and Southeast Asia, but it is unclear if Lolkens obtained it from the Netherlands's extensive Asian trade or if it was made locally in Suriname.

188. I.e., salted beef tongues.

February 18: Dine at plantation Jalosee. Sleep at plantation Arentrust.

February 19: Arrive at L'Espérance.

* It is remarkable that Accara[189] discovered one of the Society negroes to be his brother. In Paramaribo, he found his wife and child.

February 20: Van Halm heads to plantation Klarenbeek.

February 21: Get letter from Van Halm. Write to Joanna, Medlaer, La Marre, and Lolkens. Get provisions for the post from Paramaribo.

February 22: Go to Klarenbeek.

February 23: Write to Kennedy and Gordon. Get dram. Visit plantation Hazard.

February 24: Visit new ground.[190]

February 25: Place Lieutenant D. Moulin under arrest for 24 hours.[191] Visits from Klarenbeek. I go and see the sugar mill work.

February 26: The officers, Du Peron and Hamer, come here. Letters from my mother and Medlaer. Walk new ground.

February 27: Letters from Joanna, Lolkens, and Gordon. Joanna sends soft soap[192] in a *pagaal*.[193] Go to Fauconberg and Klarenbeek.

February 28: Go to Fauconberg. Letter from Fourgeoud with paroles.[194] Letter from Perret. Get ananas[195] and cassava from Cojo.[196]

---

189. Stedman spelled the name "Ackeraw." Accara had been a leader of the slave rebellion in Berbice a decade earlier. He turned on his enslaved comrades, however, and joined with the Dutch, who rewarded him for his service. That was especially true of Fourgeoud, who became something of a patron to Accara. In Suriname, Accara was in charge of all the enslaved porters aiding the expedition against Boni. See Kars, *Blood on the River*.
190. Most likely referred to land recently cleared for cultivation.
191. Stedman never stated why Moulin was placed under arrest.
192. One of two types of soap manufactured in the eighteenth century. Soft soap was semi-liquid, cheaper, and usually shipped in barrels, while hard soap would be aged longer than soft soap, which allowed it to harden and be shaped into bars. Stedman spelled "soft" as "sauf" in the diary.
193. I.e., a creole word, from the Carib *pagala*, for a type of woven, waterproof basket with a lid. Stedman's use of *pagaal* here is important. It is one of the few times in the diary where he used words from Suriname's creole language. The term has changed over time, and today, in modern Sranan Tongo, the word is *pagara*.
194. An older definition of "parole" means a password or watchword military officers would use to communicate with each other in coded language.
195. I.e., pineapple.
196. Cojo was a free Black and Joanna's uncle.

March

March 1: Guests from Klarenbeek. I do write to Joanna, Fourgeoud, Medlaer, Kissam, Lolkens, Perret, and de Borgnes. Change Hamer out for Geelguin. Send my lists to the major and a boat for my sweet Joanna to Paramaribo.

March 2: Letter from Van Halm. I go to see the sugarcane plant. Discover two casks of spoiled risp[197] on the magazine.

March 3: Letter from de Borgnes and Perret, who sent two melons. Send to plantation Cupy a letter from Perret, Lieutenant D. Moulin, a corporal, some rations, and clothes.

March 4: De Graaff Rineval gives me some *rolpens*,[198] herring, etc.

March 5: Mr. Rulagh and one sergeant go sick to Klarenbeek from Wana. I receive letters from Mr. Brindel, La Marre, Lolkens, Kissam, Gordon, and Medlaer, who sends pepper and fish for the post. In the magazine, three kegs of greens spoil. I receive from Paramaribo, 50 bottles of wine, a chest of candles, some fishhooks. Mrs. Godefroy sends potatoes. Joanna sends sweetmeats as she passes by and whom I conduct to her plantation.[199] I stay with her all night. A society soldier passes from plantation Rietwijk.

March 6: De Borgnes inspects the buildings and sends negroes to repair them. Get letter from Van Halm. Write letter to Medlaer.

March 7: Get letter from Van Halm. Mr. Cabanus comes with a director, plaintiff, and free negro delinquent.[200] I give the last a cursed trimming[201] and chase them both away. Send Mr. Geelguin sick to Klarenbeek along with two sick soldiers and two ditto who were well. Two directors dine here along with Mr. Cabanus. Sleep at Fauconberg.

March 8: Give six shillings and some meat to Joanna's grandfather, who is old and blind. Drink to the prince's and Willy's health. Tom the cook comes from Klarenbeek.

March 9: Halm and Francen dine here. Sleep at girl's plantation.

---

197. Most likely, Stedman's phonetic spelling of "rasp," a Scots term for raspberries, but in this context, probably applied to some sort of dried berries or other fruit that spoiled.
198. A Dutch dish of minced beef in tripe.
199. Joanna grew up at plantation Fauconberg, thus making it "her plantation."
200. The "plaintiff" had a complaint against the Ranger ("free negro") who caused some offense. It is unclear if the plaintiff was free or enslaved, but the presence of a "director" or overseer suggests the latter.
201. I.e., a beating.

March 10: Charles MacDonald arrives from Paramaribo with letters for Fourgeoud and the officers. I receive letters from Medlaer, Mistress Vonck, and Volkman. Sleep at the girl's.

March 11: Send the packet for Colonel Fourgeoud to plantation Rietwijk.

March 12: Am craved[202] for oars lost by the former commanders. Get letter from Perret and some watermelons. I write to Perret. Sleep with girl.

March 13: Got some fish from Mr. Francen. Send the cook to Paramaribo and write to Medlaer, Lolkens, and Mr. Brindel. Get a letter from Van Halm. D'Onis and a little Frenchman dine here. Quarrel with three Frenchmen. Send small basket[203] to Mrs. Godefroy and one to Kennedy.

March 14: Send to Mr. D'Onis for dram. Go to sleep at Joanna's. We quarrel.

March 15: Agree again. Get letter from Larcher, who sent two men. One was wounded. Send him and one more sick to Klarenbeek. I hear a man was shot and another lost, while one of the captured[204] negroes deserted.

* This poor man[205] had been forced to stay behind by necessity and desperately wounded by the negroes, who had disarmed him. He was almost condemned by Fourgeoud when he appeared the next day.

March 16: Change three post negroes. Four freemen pass by here. Go to sleep with Joanna.

March 17: Get timber from Mr. Francen. Letters from Francen and Perret. Mr. D'Onis sends deer meat, etc. I write to Perret and send him some provisions. I sleep at Fauconberg.

March 18: A letter from Van Halm.

March 19: Five more negroes come to the post. Get a letter from Mr. Palmer and answer it directly. My house being finished, I give a merry night to the negroes who made it and go to lay with Joanna.

March 20: Send off three old negroes. Go to dine with Mr. Lolkens at plantation Fauconberg where I also sleep.

March 21: After dining once more at Fauconberg and walking to the brick manufactory called Appe-Cappe,[206] with a droll Dutch ship captain, I return to my post where I part with Lolkens after receiving from him Mr. Passalage's

---

202. A Scots term for when someone demands payment.
203. Most likely a *pagara*, which Stedman learned to make while out in the field.
204. "Taken" in the original diary.
205. The soldier "lost" in the March 15, 1774 entry.
206. This brickyard belonged to the governor of Suriname, Jan Nepveu.

address.[207] I receive letters from Medlaer, Stuart, Kissam, Gordon, Kennedy, and Brindel in addition to three officers' commissions and 100 florins for the posts. Medlaer sends a man; Mr. Kennedy sends me a banknote; Mrs. Gordon, three bottles of English muscat, a cask of Boston biscuit, and a small keg of oysters; Mrs. Godefroy, some fine biscuits and two sugar loaves; Lucretia,[208] some cakes. Besides all this, I have commissioned and receive one barrel of flour, one barrel of mackerel, one keg of sausages, one jug of vinegar, and one ditto of sweet oil.

March 22: Write to Colonel Fourgeoud and send him 33 hammocks. Write also to Lolkens and Passalage. I bring my provisions to my house and put it in proper order. Go to Fauconberg and bring back Joanna. Get a letter from Hamer.

March 23: Write to Medlaer, Dr. Ludwig, and Mr. Francen.

March 24: Receive letters from Lolkens, Francen, Hamer, Halm, Perret. Send Quaco down to plantation Vriedyk with Mr. Kennedy's banknote.

March 25: Give three bottles of claret to the sick and distribute the received 100 florins among the men—40 florins to the men in the hospital, 40 to the men at Klarenbeek, and 20 to those at Cupy. I hear one Mr. Hamell is captain-commandant. Mr. Rulagh and Mr. Du Molin dine here. Get a letter from Mr. Polser in answer to Mr. Kennedy's banknote, who sends back to me with Quaco, a fine hog, two fine sheep, fat and good, and a basket of garden greens. I give post Klarenbeek one bottle of vinegar and 10 candles and the same to post Cupy. Joanna and I drink to Kennedy's health.

March 26: Turn my sheep and hogs loose and resolve to dine at home with Joanna.

March 27: Joanna and I go to Fauconberg and come home at night. I give presents of mackerel to the officers, directors, negroes, etc. I give the last of the bananas to Joanna.

March 28: I have a fever. Still go and swim with Joanna. A punt with provisions comes. Get letter from Medlaer.

March 29: Mr. Cabanus dines here. I get a letter from Fourgeoud. Send two negroes to Klarenbeek. A damned rascal spoils my bread.[209]

---

207. Passalage was the man managing the estate and holding the debts of Joanna's deceased owner. Any reference to him during this time was Stedman negotiating with him to purchase Joanna.

208. Joanna's aunt.

209. It is unclear what this last sentence referenced. It is not included in the *Narrative* or draft. Perhaps it was some insect or animal that destroyed or ate Stedman's bread, or he possibly used "bread" in the sense of a meal that a soldier or enslaved person ruined somehow.

March 30: A strong fever. Mr. Ebber gives me three bottles of Rhenish wine. Get letter from Perret. Send provisions to Perret.

March 31: Get letter from Dr. Knllaert. Receive one officer and eight men from Klarenbeek and take three men from plantation Callis. Send two sick men to Klarenbeek. Nine negroes and a tent corial.[210] Four free negroes pass from Rietwijk.

April

April 1: Send a command of one officer, 20 men, a punt with provisions, two crafts, and a canoe to plantation Tempatee. Write letter to Fourgeoud and send him a packet of letters. Had got a letter from Fourgeoud this morning, also a letter from Mr. Hamer.

April 2: Send away my monthly lists. Write to Medlaer, Gordon, Brindel, and Kennedy. Give half ration to negroes and make them repair the magazine. Get half a *pingo*[211] and a letter from plantation Killenstein Nova. A party arrives and I get a letter from Hamer.

April 3: Another party comes. Four free negroes repass. I buy two hens to keep alive. Get a letter from Perret and write a letter to him. Two negroes are whipped, with mitigation, for being two infamous thieves, etc.

April 4: Am this day 30 years old. Joanna gives me a cock and two hens and I make a henhouse. Yesterday, it was four freemen passed, but today it was only three.

April 5: I perceive smoke in the bush opposite my house. Suspicious, I went out on patrol with one corporal and six men, but to no purpose. Get a letter from Mr. Hamer. Mr. Francen comes to us from Klarenbeek.

April 6: Nothing extra.

April 7: Sergeant Hartman dies. I decide a quarrel between officers. Write to Rosenback and Killenstein Nova and give them mackerel. The first comes to ask what was in his letter as he could not read. They both send me greens. I buy two hens.

April 8: Bury Sergeant Hartman. About seven in the morning, hear seven great guns at distance. Relieve three men from Callis. Review the whole post. Send an officer and 11 men to Perica Creek and keep the rest on piquet.[212]

---

210. A type of dugout canoe used in the Guianas.
211. A type of wild boar in Suriname.
212. I.e., on active duty.

In the afternoon, I get a letter from Pape. I also take the sergeant from Callis and alter the night post. Sergeant Fowler comes from Paramaribo, brings some provisions for the post, a cook for me, some clean linens, pepper, and letters from [illegible] Gordon, my brother, Kissam, Brindel, and Medlaer. Discover a soldier wounded in the head after getting in a duel.

April 9: Send the cook to Fourgeoud and write him a letter. A Society Command comes here from Rietwijk with my own command. They bring account that plantation Kortenduur was attacked yesterday. I send the sergeant and three men back to Callis. A damned dog has complained about me. Letter from Mr. Kennedy. I buy two hens from the sergeant.

April 10: Command back to Rietwijk to push it.[213] I write to Kennedy. My hens begin to lay.

April 11: A surgeon's command arrives from Wana Creek along with September, a captured bush negro. I send eight men to Klarenbeek and three to Callis. They report the former news of a Society soldier being killed is false, but rather that the "old shaver"[214] was vexed that the wounded man of ours had not been killed. And that when he forbade seeking the lost man and firing on the rebels, instead ordering to take them with hands, those very rebel negroes laughed at him.

April 12: I get lemons from Golbagh. I shoot a *sabaco*,[215] a snipe, and two *kemphaantjes*.[216] Mr. Hoed sends fish and greens. I receive letters from Perret and Hamer. Write Perret and send provisions. I replace my night post. Two freemen pass. Mr. Huysman and Mr. Matouring come to stay on this plantation.

April 13: Send provisions and arms to Hamer. Two officers and a command come from Wana Creek with a prisoner, a surgeon, and a madman. The whole post is flooded. I send one officer and a command to Klarenbeek and some men to Cupy. A Society sergeant brings goods for Colonel Fourgeoud.

April 14: I send him away. A punt comes from Tempatee loaded with about 150 men, Black and white, along with Major Abercrombie, Meyland, De Graaff, and Cabanus. I break my sword on the strongman.[217] Send negroes to Pathuysen and militia to Perica Creek. Send Cabanus and some men to Klarenbeek.

---

213. Stedman used "push" in the military sense. He wanted the soldiers to push back against the perceived maroon offensive.
214. Fourgeoud.
215. A type of heron, which Stedman spelled *sabacoo* in the draft. FD, 264.
216. It is unclear, but probably some sort of wild bird.
217. This word is nearly illegible in the diary. Based on the draft narrative, however, Stedman described how all these poorly disciplined soldiers arriving at the post caused pandemonium, and he had to restore order. He referenced breaking his sword while subduing one of the "ringleaders" in an attempt to restore peace. FD, 262.

Letter from Fourgeoud. I write to D'Onis. He writes me back and sends his boat with eight oars. I send it to Fourgeoud and write him. We unload the two punts. Three sick Society soldiers stay here. I give Huijsman mackerel, and he uses us all damned impertinently.

April 15: Send two punts and three craft to Fourgeoud and write him a letter. I curse Huijsman and scold Matouring, who both leave the plantation. I hear the officer that brought over about 300 men, which, except a few, he murdered on the passage and made his subaltern throw himself out the cabin window, is likely to win his process.[218] Lieutenant Randwijk is set off for Holland.

April 16: Lady Sheffer dines with me. Get a letter from Perret. Several sheep on the plantation poisoned either by *duncane*[219] or cassava water.[220] Discover symptoms in Joanna.[221]

April 17: A boy and girl cruelly used by Huijsman, a negro infant lately drowned for crying by Mrs. Stolker's[222] own hands, and a negro forced to jump in boiling sugar by a director's cruelty and who later died. A negro was lately whipped to death on this plantation. On the 14th instant,[223] a Dutch sailor drowned before the post. I beat a negro for deserting. I mess with the officers and send Joanna to her plantation.

* For killing this negro,[224] Mr. Ebber pays about 1200 florins as punishment by which I lost a wager of four ducats to Lieutenant Randwijk.

April 18: Mr. Cachelieu and Deloge come to see me. The last hears my mind.[225] I buy six hens. Heneman gives me one more. Director gives me roast pork.

April 19: Remark on German cruelty and French indecency. Get a letter from Van Halm. Write to Tulling and J…no no, I mean Van Halm and Fourgeoud.[226]

---

218. It is unclear what episode Stedman referred to in this passage. He does not reference it in the first draft or *Narrative*. It may have just been another rumor he heard while out in the field.
219. A type of poisonous shrub in Suriname.
220. For cassava to be edible, the roots have to be soaked to wash away the poisonous cyanide present in the plant. Since the cyanide leeches into the water, the water is also poisonous.
221. This may be the moment when Stedman learned Joanna was pregnant.
222. Stedman abbreviated her name in the diary but spelled it out in both the draft and *Narrative*. FD, 340.
223. I.e., this month or April 1774.
224. In the April 17, 1774 entry, Stedman noted the "negro…lately whipped to death." It was Ebber who murdered the man.
225. Stedman most likely complained of the cruelties he witnessed the previous day, especially the behavior of the overseer.
226. Stedman did not cross out "Tulling and J" and instead corrected himself mid-sentence.

April 20: Fourgeoud at Rosenback, where I go to see him with Heneman and Colonel de Borgnes, who had come to me first. Send provisions to Rosenback and Klarenbeek. From Medlaer, I received a letter, provisions, and two men and, from Perret, a letter and four sick men. At Rosenback, I saw the troops landed and get back my sergeant. News of the campaign: a negro woman lost, a negro's arm broke, and a poor man died by neglect alone.

April 21: Brandt and Coeverden come to see us. Send victuals and clothes to Rosenback and some mackerel to Fourgeoud. A corporal and nine men come back. Three Society soldiers go away. Boats and passengers come up and down. I send to ask for Joanna.

April 22: Golbagh sends some greens. Mewis, Swildens, and Meyer come. Send general list to Fourgeoud. Quarrel with Du Peron and leave the mess.

April 23: [Illegible] comes here. All the plantation negroes are whipped for sleeping too long. I get drunk and send to Joanna.

April 24: Provisions to Fourgeoud. Two freemen pass.

April 25: Coeverden and Brandt come to see us. Letter and two sick men from Cupy. Write there and send provisions. Send five sick men to Klarenbeek. Get leather capes and give them out. Send beer to Fourgeoud. Get letter from de Borgnes. I carry oil, meat, etc. to Joanna. It was at a desperate risk as I had to pass Rosenback against orders, forge a pass, and cheat Fourgeoud in person. The boat was disguised, and it was rather late in the evening when it occurred.

April 26: Outsleep my time, the sun is up, and I must pass while all are stirring. I resolve, jump ashore, and cut home through the woods. The boat is taken, sent to me arrested, whom I examine and acquit. And so, I came off with flying colors, having made the sergeant drunk with new rum and fresh with a dunk in the water. The negroes I well rewarded. Send Heneman to Fourgeoud who orders shortness of allowance and wants an officer and daily report.

April 27: I send him paper and provisions. Get greens from Cachelieu and letter from Perret.

April 28: Send Du Peron to Fourgeoud and some beer. Cabanus comes to see us. Francen goes to a plantation to recover his health. Colonel Fourgeoud and Van Guerick come here. The former gives a paper with orders, full of the most damned nonsensical stuff that ever was read, such as, ordering to ask if any bush negroes are at their plantation then to chase them away, but not to follow unless I am sure of them for which I shall always be accountable. Or, if I attack without success, I must be punished and, if I don't attack at all, I will also be punished. God damn him, amen.

April 29: Send Mr. Du Peron and get some of those orders altered. Fourgeoud goes to Paramaribo with several officers. I take command of the whole battalion dispersed in this fine river. NB When Fourgeoud was here yesterday, I let him see my house and told him of my girl in such a way that, by God, he was obligated to approve both—and behaved civilly.

I give out some orders and send for my girl who is not well. Station[227] is still. I receive two letters from Swildens and one from Cupy. I write and send away by opportunity.

I hope now to live quietly for some time in my own house, with Joanna and my boy Quaco on a pleasant spot with two sheep, 20 hens, and a fat hog for company. I have about 200 florins worth of my own provisions, getting from the magazine only salt beef, groats, risp biscuit, and new rum, half bottle per week. And that is all upon honor and so wishing for better I conclude this volume.

Written on the inside of the back cover of this volume of Stedman's diary is the following inscription:

This small journal contains the space of one year, six months, and one day and is written with the greatest attention and founded on facts alone. By Captain John G[abriel] S[tedman], who shall explain it more at large one day if Providence spares him in life.

---

227. It appears as an abbreviation—"Sta"—and given the context of the diary, all being peaceful and quiet, it makes the most sense.

Volume II: October 1775–December 1776

Stedman wrote Volume II *of the diary on large sheets of loose-leaf paper that he then folded. Some pages read vertically, while others are horizontal. The first page of this diary is missing about an eighth of a page, and the October 20 entry begins abruptly.*

1775

October

October 20: …one of which discovers four large fields west of plantation Cofaay, planted with cassava, rice cacao, pistachios or pine nuts, etc.

October 21: We march to them with the 1st Division and destroy them all, first with the sword and then with fire. After that, we return to Cofaay and camp in the east part of it since our camp was in flames.[1] NB The poor bush negro was left in the fields half-dead, half-alive when we left in the morning. So ended the life of this most miserable wretch.[2] The rice and other foods at Cofaay, which was cut down this morning, is now also set fire and reduced to ashes.

October 22: We march east. Have again the 1st Division pass the fire bush at Meyland's camp and sleep where the bush negroes were heard shouting and dancing[3] about the first time.

October 23: March to Cassipora Creek. I have the vanguard and we camp where we camped on September 13.

October 24: March. I have the rearguard. Come to plantation Jerusalem. I get two letters, one from my mother and one from Alexander Cunningham. Fowler gets a letter from his Jo[4] in verse, from Vader Cats.[5] Tulling had come to

---

1. Somehow—and Stedman was unclear—the soldiers' camp caught fire while they were out burning the maroons' fields.
2. Stedman and his men captured a rebel a few days before this who was severely emaciated and near death. He stayed behind in the camp when the soldiers went to destroy the fields and perished when the camp burned. See FD, 449.
3. Stedman used the word "baniarding" in the original, a word that, based on context clues, suggests dancing.
4. "Jo" is a Scots slang term for sweetheart.
5. Refers to Jacob Cats (1577–1660), a popular poet and moralist during the seventeenth century. His poems and stories became (and still are) popular for the moral instruction of children in the Netherlands, thus the affectionate "Vader" or father.

Jerusalem, but is sent back again. He was dispensed from further duty until further orders for having overstayed his furlough and also having married without giving proper notice to Colonel Fourgeoud. The major and all the captains give a request for him to the colonel, but it was to no purpose. Captains Meyland and Perret and Mr. Larias go down. Perret was drunk and threw all his money among the negroes. Fourgeoud had a hot fever, ordered a man arrested for hosting the party, and commanded a deadly silence.

October 25: The poor devil[6] got a damned gantelope[7] with the slings.

October 26: Mr. Kier goes down sick. I write to Dr. Kissam and send for rum. Also write Kempen for goods.

October 27: Get letter from Tulling to send down his wine and his chests. Am not well and take physick.[8]

October 28: Captains Meyland, Perret, and Larias come back and bring news that Mr. Muselin is dead, so God help the putor.[9]

October 29: Write mama and Alex Cunningham.

October 30: Captain Van de Sande goes down sick.

October 31: Died Sergeant Vader Kaay, a relation to Colonel Seyburg. I felt mesel.[10] S——y, H——l, M——l, and myself tipple.[11]

November

November 1: Five and twenty negroes deserted from the command. I receive a letter from Jamie Gordon and one from Mr. James Campbell at Tobago. Also one from Kissam.

November 2: A man was beat for asking for shoes.

November 3: Colonel Seyburg goes out with a command and 10- or 12-days allowance. Mr. Theirs of the Society and Mr. Mathieu go down sick. I write two letters, one to Mrs. Godefroy and one to Mr. De Graaff.

November 4: Account comes that about 50 armed negroes had been swimming across the Cottica River above Barbacoeba.

---

6. I.e., the man arrested for hosting the party the previous day.
7. I.e., the gauntlet. In this case, the soldiers used leather slings to beat the offender.
8. I.e., medicine, possibly a laxative.
9. I.e., the stench or foul odor.
10. I.e., loathsome, repulsive, or wretched.
11. I.e., drink. It is unclear who the other men were.

November 6: Receive three salt herring and some potatoes from Mrs. Tulling. The news comes from Holland that the troops are to return and that the officers, Neys and Geelguin, were in the proposed only, the first six weeks and the second two months. My things come from plantation Mocha. The director, Mr. Kempen, gives me bananas, *bakovens*,[12] ananas, etc.

November 7: Two Society officers, Hertell and Segelar, come here. Account that poor Ensign Chevaille is dead. I receive a letter from Mr. De Graaff that my girl and my boy are not well and I have a damned hole in my ankle, which makes me melancholy.[13]

November 8: Another Society officer, a Mr. Siegvelder, arrives. I am bit by a bat.

November 9: Am bit again and, most confoundedly, almost faint.

November 10: Word comes that the 25 runaway carry-men[14] were taken by the Rangers.

November 11: Mr. Mathieu and two directors come to Jerusalem.

November 12: Colonel Seyburg returns with his command. No news. I receive a letter from Mr. Geelguin. The officers—Captains Orzinga and Fredericy and Subalterns Vischer and Soomer—arrive in a tent boat. I write a letter to Captain Tulling. Meyland and the two directors go down.

November 13: The officers Pasterille and Walters go to Paramaribo.

November 14: Our whole corps and the Society soldiers go to bid farewell to Fourgeoud.

November 15: Colonel Fourgeoud leaves the command and goes to Paramaribo with Captain Van Guerick. Takes Monsieur Mathieu with about 13 men as an escort. NB This gentleman did his utmost to make Captain Perret and I fight a duel, as we had an insignificant quarrel the night before. For which, Captain Perret had asked pardon and was sorry, so we got good friends again. This hurt the villain [Mathieu] so much that not being the master of his tongue, I gave him the challenge to fight me for Perret, which he most swiftly did refuse and

---

12. I.e., bananas. An older spelling of *bacove*, the word used for bananas in Suriname. There, the Dutch usually used for banana, *banaan*, refers to green plantains. See the Instituut voor de Nederlandse Taal's word bank (https://anw.ivdnt.org/) for more.

13. The "hole" was from a wound Stedman received in an earlier engagement with the maroons.

14. I.e., the porters who ran away on November 1, 1775.

set off. Tulling, having left some wine and four *kelders*.¹⁵ I give the wine to Colonel Seyburg and send Tulling the *kelders*. The carry-men are sent off and new ones come in their place, of which I have the inspection.¹⁶ Mr. Mewis goes down. Mr. De Graaff is put in arrest about Gibhart¹⁷ by Colonel Seyburg, who is now commandant. Colonel Seyburg has a hot fever and raves much.

November 16: Receive a letter from mama dated February 19. I write a letter to Dr. Kissam. Mr. De Graaff released. Mr. Meyer goes down sick to Paramaribo.

November 17: Mr. Noot goes down sick. Fredericy gives me a silver compass.

November 19: Captain Meyland returns to Jerusalem. I am [illegible] sick.

November 20: Major Medlaer goes out with a command of 150 arms.

November 23: Colonel Seyburg presents me with six bottles of wine.

November 24: A patrol of five men come from Patamacca.

November 25: I bore a hole in Quaco's right ear. I write a letter to Mr. Kempen at Mocha.

November 26: Mr. Florette came from Patamacca.

November 27: Monsieur Laurant got a hell of a flogging for sleeping. This day, my little boy turns one year old. I treat the captains and drink to his health. We sing and play and the negroes dance to the banjo.¹⁸

November 28: I write a letter to Mr. Kempen and desire my things may be sent to Paramaribo.

November 30: This being St. Andrew's Day, I treat the captains and the private men of Stuart's Regiment. Receive letters from Madam Tulling and Dr. Kissam. Receive a jug of rum from Paramaribo. Give a stoop to Fourgeoud and one to Captain Fredericy. Tulling under arrest and imprisoned at Fort Zeelandia.

---

15. *Kelder*, the word for "cellar" or "basement" in Dutch, was also used in the eighteenth century—especially in Suriname—to describe a chest divided into compartments and often used to transport the square bottles Stedman described elsewhere in the diary and *Narrative*.

16. By "the inspection," Stedman probably meant supervision or management.

17. Judas Gibhart worked for Colonel Seyburg, largely as his assistant and spy. De Graaff's arrest was related to intelligence Gibhart provided Seyburg.

18. In the original diary, Stedman wrote "dance banjar." "Banjar" was the common spelling of "banjo" in the eighteenth century and was an instrument created by enslaved people drawing upon their West African heritage. Stedman was one of the first Europeans to describe the instrument and acquire one for European exhibition. The banjoes he encountered would have been made using gourds.

December

December 1: Monsieur Florette sets out for Patamacca. This day, the command that set out on November 20 was expected home, but did not appear. Their allowance for 12 days is now finished and we expect something extra happened. And, to add to this, on the 27th last, two shots were heard from this post and, on the 25th, a gang of bush negroes passed close by post 's-Lands Welvaren on this side of the river. Judas Gibhart's man, who was to run the slings, was pardoned at the entering.

December 2: I send Quaco to Paramaribo with a letter to Mr. De Graaff dated Jack's[19] birthday and with a miniature of the house we lived in on L'Espérance, made by myself as a compliment. I send a curious basket of my own making to Mistress Godefroy and some things to Joanna. An express goes to Paramaribo to inform command that Major Medlaer has not returned yet.

December 3: The command comes at last. They caught a pregnant woman and her little boy. The woman said the country we took was named Gado-Saby, the most recent called Busy-Cray, and that Captain Arico still had another village named Fishee Hollo. Corporal Schoelar and Philip Van der Bos, a soldier, were poisoned eating bitter cassava found in a little ground in which the above negroes were found.[20] I make [illegible][21] kneel and cry for taking away my negro. A dead sea cow comes down the river. It had the marks of two shots and by all appearances killed by the bush negroes when we heard the firing on 27th last. Mr. Cabanus, who took the above-mentioned woman, and two men carry her and the boy to Paramaribo. I write a letter to La Marre. Give Hamell the prodigal[22] in six pieces as a compliment.

December 4: The surgeon asked two subalterns if I was really sick and if he could swear it. He answered I was not fit for duty.

December 5: The sergeant sent to me to ask if I was not fit for duty. I answered I am not. The adjutant Judas[23] was then sent to me. The same answer. When, at last, two captains and the other surgeon came to me a final time, but still to no purpose. Captain Perret got the same messages, gave himself as recovered, and was called a malingerer, a man of bad conduct for his pains, and threatened

---

19. Stedman and Joanna's son.
20. Before cassava can be consumed by humans, its roots must be washed. Otherwise, it is poisonous. Both of these men died. See FD, 452.
21. The name Stedman wrote here is near illegible. It is possibly "Horary" or "Horace."
22. I.e., a wayward person who has come back.
23. Judas Gibhart, Seyburg's assistant. Since Stedman disliked Gibhart and found him duplicitous, the use of his first name and omission of his last name may be more than coincidental here.

to be sent into the woods even if has to be carried in a wheelbarrow by Colonel Seyburg. I am forbidden from appearing anymore until I give myself as recovered.

December 6: News comes that Fredericy of the Society and Lieutenant Bush of our troops, were both made captain-commandants in Fourgeoud's regiment. The Stenhouse who was [illegible]'s mistress,[24] came here with Mr. Schadts, who left his wife in Holland. A little before that arrived one Pater, an ensign in the Society troops, who left his wife for whoring and spent about three or four hundred guilders.

December 7: I give myself recovered, but am not actually so.

December 8: Get letter from Colonel de Borgnes that he is going to be married to widow[25] Crawford. Mr. Hertell goes down with the sick Society soldiers.

December 9: Some good men return in their place from 's-Lands Welvaren. The negroes of the command are dancing.[26]

December 10: A command negro dies.

December 11: Two command negroes arrive. A punt with provender comes. A sergeant and two men from Patamacca to ask about a man lost in the woods. A little below Coermoetibo, as we went ashore to shoot *pingoes*, we hear the rebels struck plantation Killenstein Nova on the 5th, burning the house and the two white men in it. Only the director was burnt with the footboy. 33 women taken away, several of whom were killed. A young mulatto boy got a leg chopped off by the villains. Wants confirmation. I receive my things from Mr. Kempen at Mocha. Quaco returns from Paramaribo with candles and sugar from Joanna, who was very sick and the boy also. Both are better, but the bitch from Virginia was killed.[27] Get letters from Kissam, Brindel, Halfhide, and Mr. and Mrs. Tulling and lemons and oranges from Mrs. Godefroy. Captain Orzinga of the Society goes to Paramaribo with a swelled hand. I answered Hertell and Colonel de Borgnes's letter, wishing him joy.

December 12: Give all the lemons and oranges to the sick. Sergeant Van de Kaay's goods were rouped.[28]

---

24. This is a Dutch woman, and Stedman referenced her in more entries below. She spent a bit of time with the soldiers. It is unclear whose mistress she was before her arrival, as the name is illegible.
25. The word is illegible, but de Borgnes did marry a widow with the last name Crawford.
26. In the original diary, Stedman wrote, "dance baniard."
27. In July 1775, Stedman received a female English pointer, a type of hunting dog, from Virginia as a gift from Charles MacDonald. FD, 376.
28. I.e., auctioned after his death.

December 13: Mr. Hertell arrives. Vinsack and 80 freemen entered the woods from Hagenbosch. A *coriaal*[29] with Indians passes going to Marowijne.

December 15: A shot fell.[30] Soomer to Patamacca for men.

December 16: Sick negroes go down. Cabanus and Meijer come from Paramaribo. Get letters from James Douglas. I hear from Fowler that Willie and Hultman were purloined on 27th August in Zutphen.[31]

December 17: Sick soldiers go down. Write to Fredericy and Hamer. Medlaer goes down to recover from nothing. Perret and Fredericks go down the river. At last my foot is healed to my great joy.

December 18: Mr. Soomer comes back with six men.

December 19: A punt with provender arrives from 's-Lands Welvaren. I hear that a damned puppy brother was broke infamously for using his old weapons but pardoned by the prince.[32]

December 20: Two Society soldiers under arrest for boxing each other.

December 21: Put my boy and my things on the punt. The two bullies were put on sentry. I give a declaration to Colonel Seyburg about Claas Creek. Perret and Captain Fredericy return. The man inquired about on the 11th was found in Perica.

December 22: The whole post breaks up and we march for Wana Creek. Two punts with provender and the sick go there also. Society sick go down. Gibhart and Pape go down sick. I have the vanguard. We meet *pingoes* and kill some. An old negro man lets the bread fall in the water for which he got his head broke and was left behind.[33] A Society soldier was also left behind. We camp in an old camp made by Colonel de Borgnes.

NB At Jerusalem, the crickets were as numerous as grains of sand, destroyed everything.

December 23: Have the rearguard. Pass Cayman's Creek. I swear a dear oath to leave this regiment.

---

29. A type of canoe used by the Amerindians of the Guianas.
30. I.e., one of the Rangers.
31. This line referred to Stedman's brother William, who married Charlotta Hultman in September 1775. "Purloined" means "to be stolen," and it seems Stedman made a joke here about the nature of marriage.
32. "Puppy" in this context meant an "affected or conceited" fool, while "brother" referred to a fellow soldier. In this instance, a foolish soldier Stedman knew used old weapons, was punished for it, but then received a pardon from the Prince of Orange.
33. In the original, Stedman used the archaic "missed" for "left behind."

December 24: Have the rearguard. Sad rain and deep swamp. We pass over Java Creek and make camp.

December 25: Have the vanguard. Rain and swamp. All wet. We make camp an hour below Wana Creek at the Coermoetibo River where Fourgeoud ordered all the cocks to be killed. The two craft were there before us. One of their negroes drowned.

December 26: I am sent to reconnoiter Wana Creek with 60 men. No news, much water. Give Seyburg a written report. The captains dine with him. Sick men go down. Negroes come.

December 27: Captain Meyland and 60 men are sent to plantation Bergshoven.

December 28: He comes back. Much water. No news. The negro that was lost on the 22nd returns with his head in a sad condition.

December 29: I write Mr. Gordon and Mr. Halfhide.

December 30: A boat comes with dram. The drowned negro found below Java Creek. I get several packages containing coffee, pepper, sausage, small beef, cheese, *tayers*,[34] sour water, fish, mutton, etc.

December 31: Mr. Hertell, Larias, and Pater go down sick. Captain Perret also goes down sick. Mr. De Graaff goes to 's-Lands Welvaren on business. A punt with sick soldiers and sick negroes goes down also. New negroes come. Boat from Magenberg says that new men were at Appe-Cappe and Vreendenburgh and that Post Oranjebo was received by us. Also heard that Mr. Gibhart is dead along with three men sent from Jerusalem. Some women taken from Killenstein Nova escaped from the bush negroes and came to Jew's Savannah and said that only about five more were still alive.* Late in the evening Captain Fredericy arrived with ensigns Matthew, Swildens, and Coene. One man lost. Twenty-two others found at 's-Lands Welvaren. Colonel de Borgnes married to Madame Crawford on 24th past. Two bush negroes found and taken alive at Cassawinica Creek, while another found dead in Perica Creek.

*Since proven not true. Most living still.

---

34. A type of sweet potato.

1776

January

January 1: Compliment the colonel and others with my head powdered.[35] Hamell, Cranbe, Cabanus, and myself set off. We sleep in Coermoetibo Creek. Breakfast at 's-Lands Welvaren.

January 2: Command marches in quest of Fissy-Hollo. De Graaff goes to Wana Creek and Hertell down with us. We dine at Mocha with Becquer. Mr. Moryn passes. Stop at plantation Beekslied.

January 3: Dine at the new fort with Van de Sande. We reach Paramaribo in the evening. I take Hamell with me to De Graaff's house. I find Joanna with a large hole in her right breast and the poor boy very sick. Tulling is released from arrest.

January 4: Wait on Fourgeoud and dine with him. Our departure confirmed.

January 5: Dine with the governor. Receive a letter from General Stuart. Write to De Graaff, Fredericy, and Fowler. Give a neat copy of Paramaribo[36] to Mrs. Godefroy. Sup with de Borgnes.

January 6: Letter from Brindel. Send him a flute. Dine with Tulling. He and de Borgnes go to Wana Creek.

January 7: Dine with Demelly.

January 8: Dine with Godefroy. Letter from De Graaff.

January 9: Dine at MacNeil's. Luik made adjutant. I roger[37] Joanna.

January 10: I dine at home. Sup with Black Miss mulatto Sampson.[38] News comes that Dederlin is pardoned.[39] Received three months provisions.

January 11: I dine with Mr. Palmer. Write to De Graaff. An officer and 20 men head to Jew's Savannah.

---

35. I.e., he powdered his hair, which men did for formal occasions in the eighteenth century.
36. I.e., a painting of the town.
37. I.e., had sexual intercourse. In the original diary, Stedman wrote "R——," but wrote "R——r" in subsequent entries. See January 15, 1776, below. "Roger" was a common slang expression for sex in the eighteenth century.
38. This oddly phrased line referred to Zubly Sampson, who had been married to a white man and was recently widowed. Stedman spent the day with her. See FD, 465.
39. Dederlin was one of Fourgeoud's lieutenants and had been placed under arrest for cowardice in June 1775.

January 12: They return. No news from De Graaff only that I turn out Hamell, who goes to new fort with Medlaer. Travails[40] after buying a hat for Johnny. I write letters to Mrs. Vonck and Heneman. I dine with Captain MacNeil.

January 13: The command comes from Jew's Savannah with no news. Colonel Seyburg, Bolls, and Vischer arrive. Receive a letter from Fowler and a declaration from the surgeons. I box the barber and dine with Captain MacNeil.

January 14: Dine there again. A great dance[41] at Fort Zeelandia.

January 15: I swim with Donald MacNeil[42] behind Fort Zeelandia. Buy him a bow and arrows. Dine with MacNeil. I roger Joanna.

January 16: Get a hell of a fever and stay home.

January 18: I slip out to see a curious mulatto ball.[43]

January 20: Am better. Visit Stuijvasand's[44] cabinet of paintings. Persuade Cachelieu that D'Onis was in Mandrine's complot[45] in the cause of Lieutenant Perrinett.[46] I dine at Godefroy's.

January 21: Dine with Mr. Bolls. Win a jug of rum from Mr. Palmer.

January 22: Dine at Godefroy's. I go to see the foolish club of [illegible][47] at Mr. Larias's. De Graaff comes.

January 23: Dine with Mr. Texier. Write James Campbell on the island of Tobago.

January 24: I take physick. De Graaff to plantation.

January 25: Draw nine ounces of blood from my foot.

January 26: Mr. Neyseus, a surgeon from Holland, arrives. Coeverden's two children also arrive.

---

40. This word is largely illegible, and there is no indication of what happened in either the draft or *Narrative*. Perhaps this was the cause of the fight with Joanna.
41. Stedman wrote "baniard in Zeelandia" in the original.
42. This is most likely Captain MacNeil's son.
43. This was a gathering and party for free people of color. See RD, 465.
44. The name is mostly illegible. A more idiomatic translation for English speakers may be "Stuyvesant."
45. I.e., conspiracy.
46. It is unclear what Stedman referred to here. A "Perrinett" has never been introduced before this moment unless Stedman meant the "Perret" who other soldiers attempted to get to duel Stedman in December 1775.
47. It is unclear what Stedman wrote here, although he did underline it. There were a number of social clubs, often hosted in private residences, for free white men in Paramaribo at this time.

January 27: Two commissioners appointed to give their men refreshments[48] and two to time ships.

January 28: I go out. Dine at MacNeil's. Walk to Beekuysen. A negro woman killed by a Frenchman.

January 29: De Graaff comes from the plantation. MacNeil's family goes to Sporksgift. I dine with the "old shaver," who assures me the pictures I gave him were now being engraved in Holland.[49] His own picture is only now going there to be engraved, at the request of the Haren van Amsterdam,[50] since it had been detained for so long by Mr. Muselin's death. Received from Mr. Luik, the adjutant, 500 guilders, 47 stuivers, and 10 pennies, thus having paid off debts that were worth 600 guilders, 70 stuivers, and 10 pennies. I send Van der Meer 10 guilders. Mrs. Godefroy complements me with paints. The foot where I was bled last inflames, which occasioned a strong fever as the orifice had been struck too deep.

January 30: Get room from De Graaff in the yard. Nine guilders from Vischer.

January 31: A visit from Medlaer and Bolls.

February

February 1: De Graaff away.

February 2: A poor negro woman in the *diaconia*[51] gets 400 lashes without crying. Some sick men arrive.

February 3: I draw Mr. Corral. He gives me some paints.

February 4: Mitie dies at De Graaff's house. Supposedly poisoned.

February 5: Give two dragoons to Mr. Gordon. *Diaconia* indecent.[52]

February 6: Write a satire against the bitch.[53] De Graaff comes.

---

48. "Afreshnics" in the original. Most likely an archaic use of the term.
49. Stedman made sketches and watercolors of many of the things he encountered in Suriname. Here, he seemed to have given some to Fourgeoud to be engraved in the Netherlands.
50. The city of Amsterdam was one of the main investors in the Society of Suriname, which administered the colony. The reference to "Haren" here refers to the committee in Amsterdam in charge of overseeing the colony's affairs.
51. A term used for an almshouse administered by the Dutch Reformed Church, the official state church of the Dutch Republic, and by extension, Suriname. "Diacony" in the original journal.
52. In the draft, Stedman documented the terrible conditions of the poorhouse and how abusive the woman who ran it was. See FD, 472.
53. I.e., the woman who managed the *diaconia*.

February 7: Hesseling returns from Holland. Vischer lights[54] Larias.

February 8: Fight Pater. Hamell, Luik, Cabanus, and Rulagh to Maagdenburg. De Graaff away.

February 9: Vischer dines with me.

February 11: I dine with the governor.

February 12: De Graaff comes.

February 13: De Graaff demits Joanna.[55] I dine at Godefroy's.

February 14: La Marre dead. He made above 20 children. Dine with Godefroy and pay, in retail, 500 guilders (Holland money) for Joanna.

February 15: La Marre buried. I write to Fauconberg for my check. My chest was seized at La Marre's.[56] Francen, Noot, and Hesseling come. Fourgeoud gets a letter from Holland.

February 16: I write De Graaff about Joanna. Sells me a [illegible] for 20 guilders.

February 17: Chatteauview and Mewis. My chest released.

February 18: Dine at Godefroy's. Soldiers go to Maagdenburg.

February 19: Dine with Tulling. Seyburg comes from plantation Alkmaar.

February 20: Visit Fourgeoud and hear that the letter from the 15th instant brought news for us to stay six months longer. He also tells me that the Scots Brigade goes to England and that a recorder is here making a paragraph to gazetteer.[57] I dine with Mrs. Godefroy.

February 21: Go with Rynsdorp to visit his plantation Schadelyk. Fall through a cotton hammock. Meet a man here who lost his sight in one night from the bats.

February 22: I go to Alkmaar and draw that plantation.

February 25: Mr. MacNeil's family comes here.

---

54. I.e., cheers up.
55. De Graaff had been the person in charge of Joanna after her enslaver fled, and she was sold to cover her mistress's debts. It seems De Graaff agreed to sell her, most likely to Elizabeth Godefroy, on this day.
56. La Marre had "married" Joanna's sister, so Stedman stored things at his home, including this chest. Officials in the colony most likely impounded it while they assessed La Marre's property.
57. It is unclear what the latter line, "a recorder is here making a paragraph to gazetteer," meant, although a "gazetteer" was a term used to refer to newspaper accounts produced supporting the government. It was most likely a government official (the "recorder") writing in support of the soldiers' mission to place in newspapers in Holland (the "gazetteer").

February 26: Society soldier shot for mutiny in Paramaribo.[58]

February 27: Receive a letter from Mrs. Godefroy and go to Paramaribo.

February 28: Wait on Fourgeoud. Get reprieve. De Borgnes and others come to town. Letter from Fowler. Dine at MacNeil's. A small French ship fired at. Estates Wayampibo and Vossenburg complain. Roger Joanna.

February 29:[59] Get 10 bottles of gin from Mrs. Godefroy. I dine with Mr. Gordon.

March

March 1: The major and several officers set off. A ship catches fire.

March 2: Receive a ham from Hulser.

March 3: Receive tea and sugar from Godefroy.

March 4: 7000 guilders stolen from Blike.[60] Only on this day did the major et. al. depart.

March 5: Dine with MacNeil. Receive coffee from Godefroy and ring from Fredericy. Came home fuddled. Mrs. Nag——l is a hot bitch.[61]

March 6: Graman Quassi has gone to Holland to complain. He carries letters of recommendation from Fourgeoud.

March 7: De Graaff away.

March 8: Prince's birthday. Dine with the governor and Fourgeoud. Compliment Mrs. Godefroy with a painting of Alkmaar. Joanna gets chintz.[62] Rynsdorp treats the soldiers.

March 9: Two negroes hanged. Dine at Godefroy's. Get soap, wine, tobacco, rum, and biscuits.

---

58. In the original journal, Stedman only stated the soldier was shot, but in the draft, noted it was for mutiny. That has been added for clarity in the entry. See FD, 480.
59. 1776 was a leap year.
60. Stedman does not clarify what "Blike" was, but it was most likely the plantation Bliekveld, also known as Blikkreek. It was on the upper reaches of the Commewijne River and vulnerable to maroon attack.
61. Stedman never revealed the full name of this woman, but she was married and asked Stedman to sleep with her. It was most likely Nagel's wife. See FD, 483, and *Narrative*, 2:211. The term "hot bitch" is quite vulgar but also descriptive, meaning, in modern English, "a bitch in heat" or a female dog ready to breed.
62. I.e., a multicolored cotton fabric that was popular for dressmaking in the eighteenth century.

March 10: Tulling and Van Halm come. Dine with Godefroy. Get tamarind and soap from Nagel, jalap and tamarind from Wolfe, tamarind and sausages from Rynsdorp.

March 11: A negro's foot cut off. Mr. De Graaff comes to town. Dine with Godefroy and present her with her own picture.

March 12: Dine at Godefroy's.

March 13: Dine with ditto. Receive candles from MacNeil. My hens come. I complement Joanna with a fat hog and her mother with a young turkey.

March 14: De Graaff gave farewell to Mrs. L——a——t.

March 15: I kill the hog myself. Send a piece to Godefroy and one to De Graaff. Joanna prepares me a pot with suet[63] and one with sausages. Mrs. Beugel lets me have three bottles of orange *stroop*[64] and 20 spermaceti candles.

March 17: Dine at Colonel Texier's. Before dinner, I discover two beautiful girls washing naked in the alley of the governor's garden. I hear the post 's-Lands Welvaren has been abandoned and that the freemen are encamped at Wana Creek.

March 18: Bowman's bark[65] sails with Lieutenant Hertell to Marowijne. Mr. De Graaff goes to his plantation. I send my things to L'Espérance.

March 19: Dine at Mrs. Godefroy's. Go onboard the freighter *Der Goede Vrienden*, commanded by Captain Nyholt, with the governor. Write my cousin Reygersman and send him butterflies.

March 20: Dine at Mrs. Godefroy's. The newly-raised negroes and mulattos bring up, from Wana Creek, a woman, two children, and the hands and ears of several shot bush negroes.

March 21: I dine with Mrs. Godefroy.

March 22: I am asked to go to the Dutch play by Mrs. Kleijnhans. I sleight her. I dine with Tulling, then go visit the negro that had his leg cut, and lose a silver knee buckle. Captains Fredericy and Van Guerick along with John Fowler set out to meet the Owca and Saamaka.[66]

---

63. I.e., lard.
64. Dutch for syrup.
65. Unclear who or what "B/bowman" refers to, but it may be a reference to Amerindian allies sailing with Hertell.
66. Owca and Saamaka were maroon groups whose legal existence and independence had been recognized by the Dutch after previous maroon wars. At this stage in the war with Boni, the Dutch feared an alliance between them and other maroon groups and sought their own alliance to inflict further damage on Boni.

March 23: Dine with Mrs. Godefroy. Go and see Mr. Schouten's excellent collection of drawings and stamps.

March 24: Dine at Mr. Demelly's.

March 25: Dine at Lieutenant Colonel de Borgnes's. Jack goes out in clothes for the first time. Van Zandt dead on the Guinea coast. Mr. De Graaff comes. Make Fourgeoud buy a spinet[67] for Miss MacNeil.

March 26: I write to Mrs. Volkman. Visit the governor and ask him for 200 acres of land, which is taken into consideration. Mr. d'Halbergh was bit by an iguana as he was about to celebrate his 25th wedding anniversary in two days' time.[68] He asked his officers to stay until then, but Fourgeoud refused. We were ordered to go off the next day, which I longed for much. I have been troubled at Paramaribo by the air infected with heat and struck by *wassee-wassee*,[69] ringworm, *rootvont*, lice, a sore hand, a sore foot, and a sore nose constantly and all at the same time. During this time, that good woman Mrs. Godefroy sent me my victuals regularly and the best attendance. Before my arrival, Joanna and the boy had also been very bad. They both had sore eyes which blinded them for three weeks and almost forever. The boy had the strongest convulsions and the mother lay in hot fevers, both in danger of life and, added to this, a most painful sore in her right breast and left thigh. She and Jack are now pretty well and she makes good progress in reading, writing, and catechizing, which she has now been off and on for about three months.

March 27: The boat that was supposed to carry us is nowhere to be found, but we were able to get off in a tent boat with Mr. Van Dale and Mr. Emnick. We were kindly entertained at Elizabeth's Hope and had breakfast with Mrs. Kleijnhans. From there, Mrs. Dutrie accompanied us in a sailboat to plantation Alkmaar where we get a boat and six oarsmen, arriving at Sporksgift in the evening.

March 28: Remain at Mrs. MacNeil's and deliver the spinet that Fourgeoud bought for Miss Marijke. I am entertained along with the other officers. The boat that we had missed at Paramaribo arrives here and I give the steersman[70] a beating.

March 29: I am sick, having slept above green coffee the whole night,[71] but we set off and arrive at plantation Goldmine. We are well entertained by

---

67. I.e., a type of small harpsichord popular in the eighteenth century.
68. What Stedman originally wrote in the diary regarding this event is nearly illegible, but he mentioned it in the first draft. See FD, 488.
69. I.e., a type of wasp.
70. "Sturman" in original.
71. Stedman must have slept in a coffee-curing building where he would have breathed its perspiration all night.

Mr. Schadts and Miss Steenhouse alias Madame Peek Van Zeelen, who is a real beauty and vastly entertaining. She plays on all sorts of instruments, sings to a degree of sweetness, and draws prettily in addition to riding well on horseback, fencing, dancing, and is a remarkably good shot. I was only her master at the noble art of swimming, which I was to have taught[72] her if I had stayed awhile longer.

March 30: I make it to L'Espérance which was commanded by Mr. Rulagh, as Captain Portuguese had left sick two days before. We go over and sleep on the new ground with Mr. Blenderman, who entertains us very civilly.

March 31: Captain Hamell comes from Klarenbeek to see me. We leave Blenderman. I got to post L'Espérance and Hamell to Klarenbeek. I write a letter to Colonel Fourgeoud and send the lists.

April

April 1: I put my things in order, send for my hens, and begin to build a neat new summer house.

April 2: I write to Mr. Halfhide and the director of Nuten-Schadelyk. I send a corporal and a sergeant to Paramaribo on orders from Mr. Medlaer.

April 3: I send for dram.

April 4: Send four sick men to Maagdenburg. Mr. Hamer passes on his way to Paramaribo and Monsieur Matthew comes here under my command. I continue to mess with Mr. Cabanus, being resolved not to eat at one table with the one just mentioned.[73] This being my birthday,[74] I give them both a dinner, a glass of punch, and claret. Having wrote to the major via Klarenbeek, I receive a letter from Captain Hamell. I send the boat from here to the burgher officer[75] because it was leaky and ask for another. Receive letter from Fourgeoud and one from Captain Van Halm that his brother, an ensign, who was ready to go with him to Holland, died suddenly.

April 5: Send Van Halm's mourning letters to Maagdenburg and a patrol to Appe-Cappe. Get a boat from Mr. Timme, but send it back for being too small.

---

72. "Learned" in original.
73. I.e., Matthew.
74. "Anniversary" in original. Stedman turned thirty-two years old on this date.
75. Unclear who the "burgher officer" was, but most likely the Mr. Timme referenced later.

April 6: I escape being drowned by Mr. Cabanus.[76] I catch four negroes running away from command and deliver them to Mr. Timme. I receive greens from director Van Dyk and dine with Mr. Blenderman.

April 7: I go and dine at Klarenbeek and receive a letter from the major at Maagdenburg.

April 8: Mr. Timme sends a boat with six oars. I receive provender from Maagdenburg with a letter from Sergeant Hartman. Two men, Timmis and Spinklus, are under arrest for being impervious ligs.[77]

April 9: Before the sortie, I let them both receive 40 *coup de bâton*[78] and keep the last in irons until 8pm. Having found my eggs broken and stolen, I made a discovery—the hens eat them in the nest. Receive letters from Fourgeoud, Texier, Sergeant Muller, and Captain Portuguese, who goes to Holland. Mr. Noot, who passes for Maagdenburg, dines with me. I get greens from different plantations. Sergeant Counter is sent back with news that Mr. Gekel disappeared with an English bark. I send a hog, goat, and letter to Maagdenburg, that passed here.

April 10: Send patrol and Mr. Cabanus to Klarenbeek.

April 11: Send down a sick negro to Mr. Timme. Mr. Francen comes for a visit.

April 12: Write Mr. Texier, Van Halm, and Portuguese. Mr. Matthew on patrol near Rietwijk. Captain Bolt, who had passed for Appe-Cappe the day before, dines with me today.

April 13: Society soldiers assemble here. I ask Hamell, Bolt, Heneman, Timme, and Matthew and give them an excellent dinner. Send compliments to Joanna and Jack with Willie, Hamell's man. I challenge Cabanus for not being civil. He asks pardon and promises to mend. I roger his girl.

April 14: I shoot a caiman.[79] More men and negroes assemble at this post. Captain Bolls and Matthew go to Lamarouge. Hamell and I dine with Timme. A letter from Fourgeoud, in crossing, is lost in the river. The accident makes me mad—I do not know what to do. I resolve to break up the major and Van Dale's letters and examine the carrier in the presence of several officers. This sheds[80] a little light on how to act tomorrow. Hamell, Heneman, and Andrew Bolt, not my officers, sleep at this post. Hamell leaves it about 12:00. Jew Olivier also sleeps here.

---

76. This passage is awkwardly worded, and it is unclear if Cabanus attempted to drown Stedman or saved him from drowning. Stedman does not mention this episode elsewhere. Given Stedman's animus toward Cabanus below, he may have attempted the former.
77. I.e., liars.
78. I.e., blows with a cane or other type of stick.
79. A reptile native to Central and South America that is related to alligators but smaller.
80. "Gives" in original.

April 15: I order 13 men of each post to Oranjebo and from there to Maagdenburg. I write to the major, Van Dale, and Captain Hamell. Also send up three sick men and ask for provender from Maagdenburg. The Society command with the two captains, Heneman and Bolt, set out for Perica Creek. I send a letter to Luik and beg a copy of Fourgeoud's letter if it is possible to help me out of doubting that I had not done what I was supposed to do. Mr. Stedfelt, the apothecary, passes for Paramaribo.

April 16: The grenadier cook escapes a drubbing. Mr. Cabanus patrol to Klarenbeek. Account that Hamell is sick. He writes me a letter.

April 17: I make ready for command.

April 18: Colonel de Borgnes, Tulling, Sergeant Smith pass for Maagdenburg. I also send Mr. Matthew there and conduct him to Klarenbeek, where I pay a visit to de Borgnes. De Borgnes and 100 men are to set out Wana Creek and Marowijne on April 23. I find Hamell recovered. De Borgnes leaves Klarenbeek to proceed and gives orders for Captain Hamell to follow. We both convoy him to Crawassibo and then returned to Klarenbeek where I slept that night. The negro Gausarie sets out for Maagdenburg also. I get a negro in place of the sick one sent off.

April 19: I return to L'Espérance.

April 20: Receive letter from Halfhide that Joanna and Jack are well and a letter from Mr. Luik with a copy of Fourgeoud's that was lost in the river. It corresponded directly with the way I had acted. Mr. Hamer passes from Paramaribo for Maagdenburg, where I also send two sick soldiers. I send a barrel of moldy bread to Mr. Blenderman.

April 21: Mr. Swildens passes, sick, from Maagdenburg to Paramaribo. Receive a letter from Master Rulagh, who now commands Klarenbeek, with an account that Captain Hamell set out for Maagdenburg the day before. I write Mr. De Graaff to bring Joanna and Jack. I dine with Mr. Gourlay at plantation Bergshoven. Get provisions from Maagdenburg.

April 22: Mr. Cabanus dines at Tomasberg.

April 23: I take a general review of all my men who protect the plantation. There are 28.

April 24: I send a patrol to plantation Egmont. Mr. Francen delivers one from Maagdenburg. Receive 40 shifts[81] for the men. Get in a compliment from Mr. Timme, a pantaloon.[82]

---

81. I.e., a type of undergarment.
82. A type of trousers.

April 25: Get from the Jew Olivier, a young ram as a present. I give Mr. Francen 20 shifts for the post Klarenbeek. A boat crosses from Maagdenburg and goes down to Paramaribo.

April 26: I send a compliment of an excellent fat ram for breeding to Mr. Gourlay, who sends me two pretty young ewes in return. I send home Captain MacNeil's books and write him a letter. I also write to Mrs. Rynsdorp and Mr. Gourlay. Give the drummer Claas a *straff guard*[83] for sleeping. I see a moderate-sized snake killed, but it had swallowed a frog of monstrous thickness, which I cut out of his belly quite alive and only covered with a bluish slime. I get an answer from Gourlay.

April 27: Discover a man named Claas [illegible][84] to have a sort of fallen sickness and find a nest with 12 hen's eggs.

April 28: I go pay a visit to Master Thomas Palmer at his plantation Fairfield, but breakfast with Mr. Gourlay first. I buy a guinea's[85] worth of ducks. I send a pot of salt meat and pork to Joanna and beg Mr. Gourlay to bring them to L'Espérance. Sergeant Counter goes to see Mr. Merlon. I shoot an iguana, but lose it. Hear of the rebels being beat by Mr. Vinsack and the rangers.

April 29: Stay still, with Mr. Palmer.

April 30: He gives me a chest of clean corn.[86] I return to L'Espérance and call at Cachelieu while passing.

May

May 1: I send down the monthly list. Captain Bolt's command passes. Cabanus goes to Abecable.

May 2: ———

May 3: Mr. Cabanus comes back and with him is Mr. Francen, who dines with us and returns. I receive a letter from Fourgeoud with the confirmation that

---

83. *Straff* is the Dutch word for punishment, but it is unclear what Stedman meant by "straff guard." Possibly, there was a special type of punishment for guards found sleeping on duty.
84. In the original, Stedman crossed a few words out and scribbled an illegible line above it.
85. A gold coin minted in Great Britain containing a quarter ounce of gold. It was originally meant to be worth one-pound sterling, but as the price of gold increased throughout the eighteenth century, so did the guinea's value.
86. I.e., maize that had been shucked.

11 rebels were taken by Vinsack and orders to acquaint the negroes of Goet-Accord and Crawassibo to be in readiness for defense.

May 4: At 4am, I go to the above-mentioned plantations and speak with the people. The first made for little difficulty, for wanting the five best negroes who were on command. Crawassibo had only four arms in very bad order for use. I write Fourgeoud and acquaint him of the situation. I warn post Klarenbeek to be in readiness. At Fauconberg, my sheep have made two lambs and I now have 10 total from the two that Walter Kennedy gave me in 1774. They are designated for my little boy and his mother, who I daily expect at L'Espérance, where I have built a nice house for their reception. It is made in imitation of Boni's, in his country of Busy-Cray. I send a letter to the honorable Thomas Palmer.

May 5: I dine with Mr. Blenderman. Visit *mijn heer*[87] Otto Cling at Tomasberg and also Mr. Timme whom I complement with three black loaves.[88] I receive a letter from Monsieur Rivieres at Goet-Accord that three negroes are returned, which he begs to keep and a letter from De Graaff that he will be coming.

May 6: My kitchen is blown down in a storm. Two free negroes headed to Perica pass here. I review the whole post and order 25 men to be in readiness at a call and also select a craft to be adrift in readiness with three oarsmen in it. Exchange some old groat barrels for two jugs of dram from Mr. Blenderman. Send off an old boat. Mr. Francen passes here for bread.

May 7: Mr. De Graaff, Captain Van der Pott, and two others come to L'Espérance and dine with me. They bring Joanna and Jack to come and see me. Quaco breaks all my pewter and china. I treat all the men and all the negroes.[89]

May 8: The same over in the morning. Mr. Cabanus goes and dines at Knoppemombo. I send for provisions to Maagdenburg. Write the major, send him greens, and send two sick men. I receive a new boat for the one sent off.

May 9: Mr. Gourlay came to pay me a visit and brought me some trifles he bought for me. He and I go dine with Mr. De Graaff at Knoppemombo. Joanna and Jack were with me there. Came home late. Gourlay sleeps with us at L'Espérance.

May 10: He goes back to Bergshoven. Mr. Braham comes to pay me a visit. I give him a dinner and receive him damned coolly for his "civility"[90] at the

---

87. An affectionate Dutch honorific meaning "my gentleman."
88. Probably loaves of black bread.
89. This entry ends with a line mentioning Joanna, but it has largely been crossed out and is illegible. Based on subsequent entries, such as May 11, 1776, it probably referenced sexual activity. Why these latter entries concerning sex are crossed out when earlier ones are not is unclear.
90. Stedman meant this to be sarcastic. The editor added the quotation marks to denote that fact.

[illegible] when I was sick, notwithstanding his cabots[91] and fresh butter. De Graaff sends me oranges and lemons. Some Society soldiers from Cupy arrive here.

May 11: They leave for Perica. I roger Joanna.[92]

May 12: A visit from Mr. Rulagh. He brings two men. Joanna, myself, and Jack go to Fauconberg to see Mr. De Graaff. Joanna dressed in her worsted suit, a proof of her sense and modesty. Jack receives in homage from all the negroes, eggs and fowls. At this plantation and Rosenback, the negroes complain of having to work hard.

May 13: I form a regular list for the mess, in which I have received Mr. Cabanus. I send a letter and land tortoise to Mistress Lolkens with Captain Zeeman's sloop. Mr. Cabanus goes on the rammle.[93] I am almost mad because a negro killed the wrong duck and lamed another. Get some corn and a letter from Thomas Palmer. I answer it at once and invite him to come. A letter from Fourgeoud with an order to ask for men. I at once wrote to Major Medlaer because I only had 13 men fit for service.

May 14: Mr. De Graaff passes for the Cottica River. Mr. Fleming, his director, sends me greens, flours, and sugars. Sergeant Counter comes with provender from Maagdenburg, but forgot groats. He brings some plasters, but the medicines were refused—I suppose because we do not have a surgeon on the river. I receive a letter from Major Medlaer and one from Johann Coene, a soldier, for dram.

May 15: Mr. Blenderman comes here and tells that two days before, his negroes caught two of his runaways and killed one from plantation Hazard. For that one, he sent the hand to Paramaribo. Mercier, who is the director of Hazard, sends me greens and a watermelon. He is a peaceable man, but his master was a rascal who forced the negroes to fly into the woods by killing them daily with his whip. I had forgot another such fellow, a director, when I was last in town, he had killed a house girl. As he was going to return to his plantation from Paramaribo, he cut his own throat out of remorse, as he was stepping into the boat. I also forgot that the day before the lost rebels were taken, they killed one named Valentine from Fauconberg, who was suspected of intending to poison the rest. It is remarkable that those savages have been defeated twice now just the day after doing their cruel execution.

---

91. Most likely refers to a type of salt fish.
92. Stedman attempted to scribble this line out, but it is legible beneath.
93. "On the rammle" was a Scots slang term meaning to engage in noisy or boisterous behavior, especially under the influence of alcohol.

May 16: Mr. Rulagh and Mr. Noot come here. The last brings one sergeant, four corporals, and only 25 men from Maagdenburg for the whole river. Fourgeoud also sends me a surgeon, named Romelyn. Having reviewed the whole, I send the sergeant, one corporal, and 10 men to Klarenbeek, write a most satirical letter to Medlaer, and send him a basket of lemons and oranges. Mr. Timme and the above officers drink a glass of punch with me. Roger Joanna.[94]

May 17: Mr. Cabanus comes home sick with fever. Mr. Merlon from Killenstein Nova dines here.

May 18: I discharge all the arms. There are 28 arms for the picquet ready at a call. Give general orders for the guard in writing. Received a damned ceremonial letter from Mr. William Stedman and wife and another from Mrs. Van Calker. Some letters pass for up the river. Account that Mr. Marsellis and Mr. Kennedy are dead in Europe and Mr. Huysman, the owner of this plantation, at Paramaribo. I receive a scrape from Mr. D'Onis.

May 19: Mr. Francen passed down and up. I order a waiter for Mr. Cabanus. He's very sick.

May 20: Am awaked at midnight by Mr. Rulagh's negroes. He sent me an excellent *heijmar*[95] and promises himself to come and eat it.

May 21: He does not come, but sends Mr. Francen in his place. I receive provender from Maagdenburg and letters from the major and Bolt with the news that we set sail in July or August—which I won't believe until I'm out of Braam's Point.[96] I also learned that the king had asked the Brigade to come over and afterwards thanked them, but to no use.[97] I write a letter to them both and acquaint the major that Mr. Cabanus is bad past recovery. I sent a patrol today to Rietwijk. No news, although the officer has gone to Soribo.

May 22: ———

May 23: About Hersfelt and a plantation. Trebulon comes down Bottle Creek and after him, Colonel Seyburg in an open corral and in the company with a damned drunken rascal, the director from Rietwijk. He got drunk in a moment, broke glasses and pipes, begged tobacco, beef, and bread, debauched one of the negroes, and was damned impertinent. The colonel dined with me and set sail for Maagdenburg. Get fish from Knoppemombo. Mr. Braham dismissed from

---

94. Once again, this last line has been scribbled out.
95. It is unclear what type of food this is, but it was possibly a type of fish. While the first draft does not detail the events of May 18, 1776, Stedman does discuss fishing in that part of the draft. See FD, 495–96.
96. Braam's Point is the piece of land where the Suriname River meets the Atlantic Ocean.
97. King George III of Great Britain invited the Scots Brigade to fight against the rebels in the future United States, but the leadership refused.

Wayampibo. Two sergeants and four men come from Paramaribo. I receive a letter from Mrs. Rynsdorp.

May 24: Write to Major Medlaer and send one sergeant and one man to Klarenbeek.

May 25: I shoot Accara's hog[98] and begin a garden. I write to Appe-Cappe and beg Mr. Thys to send me the Society surgeon to consult with the one I have here, which was done accordingly. Both agree that poor Cabanus stands a bad chance of not recovering from his illness. Mr. Schadts, Mrs. Stenhouse, and her brother pass here for Black Creek. They finish 20 eggs and half a ham of bacon. They give a jug of dram to the soldiers, who give Mrs. Stenhouse three cheers.

May 26: Mr. Timme gives me a deer's foot. I send a patrol to Klarenbeek. Get a piece of an old Dutch jack[99] for a flag from the director of Appe-Cappe. I ask Dr. Romelyn how poor Cabanus fares and he told me with a self-sufficient grin that Cabanus would step off with the ebb. And so we stand a chance to set out, all of us, one after another—not a rank is now in the colony above me but were in America before he is not stepped off yet.[100] I send up and down for a bottle of old Rhenish. At last get two from Mr. Rotarious.

May 27: Joanna makes Cabanus a ladle.[101] He is not worse. Colonel Seyburg passes from Maagdenburg and steps ashore for a moment. He drinks two glasses of claret and carries off the bottle and glass only after his man takes a draught at boat side. Seyburg approved much of all the regulations and the remarkable change he found upon this post crew—where I found everything dirty and wild and not like a place that was inhabited, but like a wilderness, full of sick and nastiness with not above 13 men in tolerable order to do their duty. All this was owning to the negligence of Captain P——ces, who commanded here. The contrast is now this: all the channels are cleaned and clean water comes in every tide, as I had the sluice repaired. The post is now forever dry, even in springtide, because the dams were heightened, which prevents the overflowing of flood waters. The hedges are now shorn round about, neat gardens begin to be planted, and all the houses and bridges have been repaired. The greatest cleanliness is also recommended. This change produced the following consequences. In the places of a handful of poor, weathered, and

---

98. This is the same Accara referenced above.

99. I.e., a slang term for a flag.

100. This line is a bit confusing, but Stedman clarified what he meant in the draft noting, "most of my Old shipmates were dead or returned to Europe. Nay, not a single officer was at this time in rank above me, except such as had formerly been inured to the West India climate" (FD, 498). He's essentially saying he was the only European officer who had survived this long and had not previously been to the West Indies.

101. I.e., some sort of broth or soup.

starved[102] scarecrows, I now have the pleasure of commanding 50 able men, all jolly and full-spirited and not a sick among them except the lieutenant and quartermaster. The duty goes like clockwork, while all is content and flowers spring at every corner.

May 28: I receive the honor of Monsieur Mondier's damned wearisome company, the very contrast of the Rietwijk director. While that man plagued me with his impertinence, this one wearied me with his damned French ceremony. I write a letter to Thomas Palmer.

May 29: My poor little boy is not well—a sore throat. I receive greens from Mondier with a letter which I return. Medicines come from Maagdenburg. I hear that Captain Bolt is at Wayampibo. I write Medlaer for medicines and provender. Jack gets hens and viands[103] for a present from the negroes around and about.

May 30: He is a deal better as the pain was occasioned by his getting teeth. Mr. Schadts and Zeelen pass. I buy two turkeys from Mr. Mercier of Hazard. Mr. Rulagh comes to dine here.

May 31: Mercier sends me a stoop of confit banana.[104] I give Corporal Kerster *straff guard* for having commanded a wrong man. I send the monthly list to Fourgeoud and send him a letter. Three free negroes pass for Poelwijk. I hear talk of a rebels' road being found behind the plantations Wayampibo, Appe-Cappe, Killenstein Nova, Cakkera, Castra, and Cemes. Distribute some old clothes to the men.

June

June 1: Get a letter from Timme. Send a letter to Appe-Cappe asking about the bush negroes. Two directors from Bethlehem and Cling from Tomasberg dine with me.

June 2: They send me herring, peppers, and greens. A boat from Maagdenburg passes for Paramaribo. I dine at new ground with Mr. Moryn, Baak, Gourlay, and Vischer. Medicines come from Maagdenburg. Had forgot that last night, about 9pm, I had made the sentry fire his musket to make a false alarm. The whole post was in the greatest readiness and the utmost regularity.

June 3: Moryn and the others come to this side and I dine with him. I receive letters from Medlaer and Bolls and provender from Maagdenburg. I intervene

---

102. "Starven" in the original.
103. I.e., an archaic term for foodstuffs.
104. I.e., preserved bananas.

in a dispute[105] about Accara with the planters. I put Accara under arrest. Poor Cabanus who relapsed last evening, this evening died at 6pm. I write to Fourgeoud, Medlaer, Seyburg, and Rulagh to send me another officer. I send Seyburg an extract out of my journal. Mr. Francen comes from Klarenbeek to serve, to make Cabanus's inventory, and bury him.

June 4: Mr. Moryn gives Cabanus a black chest[106] and the poor lad was buried with all the decency that lay in my power. The funeral procession began with Mr. Francen and a detachment of 24 men marching before the coffin. It was carried upon four muskets by eight officers, and all the burgher gentlemen and myself following. The procession was closed by the soldiers with side arms. Mr. Moryn gave the men a jug of dram. With Mr. Gourlay, I read part of my journal. My dam breaks and the post swims.[107] Moryn promises to help. At dinner, his director affronts me and Moryn takes his leave,[108] he already having affronted the men. A hot quarrel ensues. I leave the dinner, offer money for the chest, and send back the jug with dram to Mr. Moryn who was exceedingly affronted when I told him I did not want his help anymore, and drew back all my obligations. For the dirty dinners received, I send his boat negroes a piece of salt beef.

June 5: Gourlay and Vischer being gone, I give Mr. Timme and Baak with Mr. Moryn, a glass of punch to show that my anger against them was over, but not against *mijn heer* Blenderman.[109] They set off for Vlamberg before my door and the director was carried through the water like a piggy on a negro's back, who set off at once for the other side of the river well knowing what is to happen to him for I'm resolved on satisfaction. Mr. Francen and myself, as commissaries, make the inventory of the deceased, given his hens and old clothes to his man. Mossy Bruyn from Rietwijk passes, whom I remember for his former impertinence and I make him sit at the landing. Mr. Meyer comes from Maagdenburg to serve here.

June 6: I get a whole stoop of molasses from Mercier and send away a dog from a *bassia*.[110] *De Vaandrigh*[111] Francen goes to Klarenbeek. I send a man to

---

105. In the original, Stedman wrote, "am like to dispute about Accara with the planters."
106. I.e., coffin.
107. Stedman had his men construct a dam to prevent the post from being inundated with water, a problem in the riverine plains of Suriname where most of the plantations were located, but the beginning of the rainy season and spring flooding in May and June caused the dam to burst.
108. "His part" in the original.
109. Blenderman was Moryn's director referenced in the previous entry. *Mijn heer* is the Dutch equivalent of "sir," and Stedman used it sarcastically here.
110. "Bastia" in original.
111. For some reason, Stedman used the Dutch term for "ensign" here.

Klarenbeek and from there to Maagdenburg with fallen sickness. Get sailcloth from Killenstein Nova. Three negroes come from command. NB They are to repair the sluice. This was the thing that occasioned discord.[112] This evening the soldiers danced country-dances.

June 7: A patrol comes from Rietwijk with a letter from Mr. Rulagh. The boat passes with Mr. Moryn and the other gentlemen from the other side. I, and Mr. Meyer, step into Mr. Heyde's corral, and follow them over. When I address myself to Mr. Moryn, I desire to know if he is ready to give me satisfaction for his director's impertinence to me and the soldiers, yes or no. After some deliberations and giving us a decent breakfast, Mr. Blenderman the director appeared with his head uncovered and with a pale visage and trembling accent, begged my pardon before all the company. I granted it with a stern look and at the same time breaking a suppling,[113] which had been cut for his purpose, over my knee and throwing the two pieces before his shins. I told him he was pardoned so sure as this was broke. After which, Moryn, Baak, Timme, and I drunk friendship and this being done, we procured a tent boat and long pipes and returned to L'Espérance in full triumph. Romelyn was called to Klarenbeek. Patrol returns to Rietwijk. Mr. Otto Cling, director of the plantation Tomasberg, dines with me. Having ordered the cakes to be made, the surgeon called to Klarenbeek. Fish from Rulagh who buys it there for a trifle.

June 8: Send Cabanus's goods to Paramaribo and write "Shaver." A nail in my foot. The two men, Vale and Culner, play for my fiddle. It falls to Culner's share. The men dance.

June 9: Drummer Herman passes from the fort. Mr. Mewis to L'Espérance and Meyer, down. News from Paramaribo. Fowler came from ambassade[114] and the other two are expected soon; the bills of our departure were locked up; that all the freemen negroes had got new guns and shables,[115] short green mountain,[116] and capes; and that a director had hanged himself.

June 10: Get dram from Wayampibo. It is said that the late director Gramn, the Jesuit,[117] is now punished for stealing. Get a letter from Thys, at Appe-Cappe, yesterday with a complaint against my sergeant and men, who had

---

112. This sentence is in reference to the dispute between Stedman and Blenderman and Moryn. It seems Stedman requested enslaved people from plantation L'Espérance to repair the sluice, and Blenderman, the director/overseer, refused.
113. I.e., a walking stick.
114. I.e., a diplomatic mission.
115. I.e., a Scots term for a saber.
116. Unclear what Stedman meant by the term "mountain," spelled "mown taine" in the original, but it was most likely a type of footwear, given the context of the entry.
117. Gramn was not actually a Jesuit, but the label was a term of derision used by Protestants in the eighteenth century to denote duplicitousness and untrustworthiness.

passed on patrol. I correct them this day and answer the letter. Two men come from Klarenbeek and get a letter from Rulagh.

June 11: I repair the landing place with old planks that Blenderman had given me before the last quarrel. He denies it and offers to break it again, but that I prevent in spite of his teeth.

June 12: My uncle Cojo[118] shoots a baboon. I send Van der Meer and Coene to Nuten-Schadelyk. Mr. Cling dines with me. The negroes baniard.

June 13: Mewis dines with Cling. Get a fat *pingo* from Rulagh. The surgeon called to Klarenbeek. The post negroes were this day relieved by damned bad ones. I refuse three that were infamous and keep three of the old ones until better come.

June 14: Visits from Mr. Rulagh and Trebulon.

June 15: Coene comes from Nuten-Schadelyk, but Cobus was left sick at Rosenback. A letter and greens from Rynsdorp.

June 16: Having sent a boat for him, the poor devil[119] comes home. He is very sick. I send a patrol down. No news. A boat passes from Paramaribo. Letter from Sergeant Herman with some bottle of medicines. I write a letter to Major Medlaer. Romelyn called to Klarenbeek.

June 17: I receive an impertinent letter from Rulagh. Give the answer to Mr. Francen to purpose. Get letter from Timme. I discover a monstrous *wassee-wassee* nest just above the room-door which I resolve not to disturb, but will try if they attack me without offense.

June 18: Mr. Mewis to Tomasberg. Two boats and three old negroes this day are relieved. Get a visit from Fleming. Give the men a new song. Blenderman hunted[120] my negroes.

June 19: I warn him about his hogs. Joanna is sick with fever. I send for Sara, an old Indian woman. She comes to Joanna. The Fauconberg director sick and goes to town.

June 20: Mewis to Bethlehem. I form a new hospital at Klarenbeek. Some free negroes, while passing, report to have ruined, under Vinsack, 20 or 22 fields with rice and cassava.

June 21: I prigel[121] Coene. Mercier sends white bread.

---

118. I.e., Joanna's uncle. This line suggests Stedman considered Joanna his wife and her family, regardless of their race and status, his own relation.
119. I.e., Cobus from the previous entry.
120. I.e., hounded or harassed.
121. I.e., haggle with.

June 22: A punt with provender was passing and I take out 40 cheeses for the post. Get letters from "Shaver" and Hamell, who is at Java Creek. The command had been at Marowijne from May 28th until the 31st. Had no news. Mercier lends me turkey cocks.[122] Fredericy and Van Guerick, after some time passed, arrived from Owca and Saamaka. The last had sore legs.

June 23: I visit Mr. Gourlay who promises to help me in the affairs of Joanna and Jack. Receive letter from the "Shaver," to be ready the 15th of next month to come down with the troops. I write Palmer. Upon returning to the post, I find my poor boy in convulsions.

June 24: A boat from Paramaribo passes. I have Fourgeoud's letter read to the men here and at Klarenbeek. Get letter from Palmer. I write to Gourlay who sends me Rhenish and Spanish wine, white bread, and bananas.

June 25: Mewis to Hazard. I take fuel wood by force from that villain Blenderman.

June 26: I send for provender to Maagdenburg and get the fever. Rulagh passes.

June 27: The fever again. Medlaer and Noot pass. I cheat Medlaer with his girl.

June 28: Have strong fever. Poor little boy very sick.

June 29: Mantua asks for a discharge to live at Klarenbeek.

June 30: A strong fever. All the sick come from Klarenbeek.

July

July 1: Provender and dram come. A boat from the fort arrives. I take two pairs of shoes. Letters from "Shaver" and Van Coeverden. Mewis to Courlay. A dead dog is found at Blenderman's door.

July 2: Send the lists to Paramaribo. Joanna and Jack sick. Head to town. Still have a fever. Send books to Palmer.

July 3: I go to Gourlay. A favor letter from Palmer.[123]

July 4: Letter from Bolls. Three punts arrive for the troops.

July 5: Am better. Dine with Cachelieu.

July 6: Timme returns. I have a dispute with Gourlay.

---

122. I.e., male turkeys.
123. I.e., a letter of recommendation, probably related to Stedman's attempts to purchase Joanna's and Jack's freedom.

July 7: My papers come. Cachelieu dines with us. Mewis sends ammunition to Klarenbeek and water casks to town.

July 8: "Old boy" and I are good friends.[124] I send my ducks to Knoppemombo.

July 9: Give ammunition to the men at L'Espérance.

July 10: Lieutenant Meyer and Cling to Gourlay. One sergeant and 17 men of the Society soldiers come to L'Espérance. I dine at Hazard. Mr. Mercier had always treated me with the greatest civility. I hunt away Blenderman, *furia bassia*,[125] with a stick, and come to L'Espérance.

July 11: Meyer, Francen, and Cling come to see me. I go to Knoppemombo. Letter from Schadts. Send *groo-groo*[126] and pantaloons to Knoppemombo.

July 12: I go to Fauconberg and bring home one sheep. Some Society troops come. Segelar and Thys dine with me. The Society men to Klarenbeek. I write Rulagh who wrote me. I number the punts. Mewis goes to Tomasberg. Send flag and pennant onboard the punts.

July 13: Gourlay writes, can't come. Mewis returns. I kill two sheep and have eight guests. Mewis goes to Knoppemombo.

July 14: He returns. Landau goes down. Gourlay comes. Gives me rum and coffee. Ivierkant, a steersman,[127] Sara, and Cojo come. The Society men on guard. The Klarenbeek troops come before L'Espérance. I treat 12 guests. Meyer and Van Dyke drunk. Captain Elsperman comes to us.

July 15: Give the post and some materials to Mr. Meyer who stayed with 12 men. I give orders to the officers and *strimbuijde*[128] and make the post embark. Rulagh impertinent. At 10am, I fire my musket as a signal and the troops row down. Take leave of several plantations. Take in Mewis and go to Gourlay where we dine. Mewis goes back to the punts. The Maagdenburg fleet comes down. I sleep at Bergshoven.

July 16: Leave Gourlay. Pass the fleet. Stop at the Goldmine and sleep with Palmer at Fairfield.

July 17: Pass the fleet and sleep at MacNeil's. Get all my papers from Corporal Corver.

---

124. It seems that Stedman and Gourlay made up after their dispute two days prior.
125. I.e., like an angry driver. It is a play on words because Blenderman was a plantation overseer, so Stedman played the role of a slave driver in this case.
126. A type of grub that people in Suriname ate.
127. "Sturman" in original.
128. This seems to be a corruption of an older Dutch term meaning "blockhead" or "knucklehead." Stedman used it as a slang term for the regular soldiers.

July 18: Send back the six-person oar party and write to Gourlay. I go down in Captain Vinsack's sailboat. I call at Rynsdorp's. Meet the fleet at Fort New Amsterdam[129] and so we all come to Paramaribo. I go onboard the three ships hired for our departure: the first, *Paramaribo*, Captain Spruyt; the second, *Adricham*, Captain Strapp; and the third, a wherry.[130] I am to embark on the *Vrou Anna Geertruy*, Captain Hermanis Piterse. I send Mewis to ask for orders, then call on the "Shaver," who was not in, and so sleep ashore. Find Joanna well and Johnny better.

July 19: Deliver all my papers to Fourgeoud, go to arrange the places onboard the third ship, and then dine with Mr. Gordon. Several visits.

July 20: Dine with Fourgeoud. Drink Burgundy with Texier and go sleep onboard. Get drunk with gin.

July 21: With the most damnable difficulty, I receive my own money, mostly in cards, by which I must lose five percent. Receive letter from Loare, the Deventer cook, and some rarities from Roux. I dine with Mrs. Godefroy. That excellent woman stocks me with presents for Europe, too many to mention in this small journal.

July 22: Dine with Colonel de Borgnes and sleep onboard. Mijnershaaven gives me a fine pasquil.

July 23: I dine with Mrs. Godefroy. She gives me a pair of gloves. This day the colors were brought onboard in great state, the major commanding 100 men. The fort does no honors for the colors. I complain about Captain Strapp's second mate. I pay 400 guilders to worthy Mrs. Godefroy.

July 24: This day the sails are tied to the yards and the eating in cabin begins. For that paltry dinner, we must now piss at the rate of 400 guilders a year. All the doctors' and surgeons' accounts made by the officers are put on land, reckoning by the orders of His Highness the Prince, by which I profit not a farthing since, just before I heard of it, I paid about 60 guilders to the surgeon. MacNeil had a grand dinner and asked me but I refused, having not been invited the day before and dine with Mrs. Demelly.

This day, the "Shaver" and all his minions went to take leave of the governor, who gave to understand, that his fort would have paid the honors due to States troops, but having no intelligence, was ignorant. This created small debates and I'm of the governor's opinion that in that quality he might have had notice [of the colors] onboard the cabin [had been] taken in by the subalterns, who chanced to be the scum of the whole corps, and far below my notice.

Yesterday, each man received one half bottle of wine, which much surprised me until I heard today that one, Mr. Van Heyst, had given 300 bottles for that very purpose.

---

129. "The new Fortress" in original.
130. I.e., a small barge.

The whole corps was asked at the comedy and I believe all went, myself alone excepted, who preferred Joanna and poor Jackie's company to any other amusement. The poor girl is almost distracted with the thoughts of me going away and the little boy and myself have a fever every day.

I had almost forgot that all the Society officers went to Fourgeoud to wish him and his corps a good voyage. I this day send all the baggage onboard. Gourlay's not coming, which makes me low spirited. One Monsieur Jacot went around with a paper to get it signed by all the inhabitants. It was a request to Fourgeoud to make the troops stay still. However, not so many people signed it as Monsieur Jacot expected and it could not be of any purpose. NB It is said that the contents of the request were signified or composed at the "Shaver's" own house. At the rest, you can guess.

July 25: The first news I hear is that a ship is at the mouth of the river. I dine at Mr. Gordon's.

July 26: The ship was the *Anna Elizabeth*, Captain Swiertz, who brings news that we must remain once more until troops are sent to relieve us. Hard news for the poor soldiers who were all embarked and this very day appointed for the ships to go down to Braam's Point. Now nor tomorrow nor until further orders are the men to set a foot onshore. Colonel Seyburg was sent to read the Prince's intentions onboard all three vessels. The poor men were called before the quarterdeck to hear and they were much dejected at being so often disappointed. However, they were ordered to give three cheers, which they refused onboard the *Anna Geertruy*. Then the colonel made an officer, Mr. Hamer, beat the other officers and threatened to shoot the man that now refused again. Then, as the sloop set off from alongside, the sailors onboard did begin to "hooray" to save the poor soldiers' bacon, who followed them in the most melancholy tone. So they were forced to sing a *coup de bâton*, but, NB, the intention of the "hooray" was not because we stayed, but because the Prince of Orange thanked all of us for our good behavior, which the poor fellows had not taken notice of.

This day, Mr. Gourlay comes to Paramaribo. A negro of Mr. Rotarious shot one of his.

I dine with Captain MacNeil where I enter into a dispute with a damned impertinent fellow, a captain of the Owca negroes, called Fortune Dago-So. The case is that everybody dreads their prowess[131] and our "Old Shaver" spoils them by being too good to all intents and purposes. Because I said to Mrs. MacNeil the words, "Madam give that man a dram and he shall go away," he jumped up, asked if I was at my house where I had so much command. He very bluntly told me that if he had me at Owca, he would show me a trick. I was incensed to hear so much from the mouth of a bush negro and replied to him in the most threatening language he had ever heard in town before. The fellow left me

---

131. The word in the original is illegible and truncated by the edge of the page.

and I went in, ate nothing, was not pleased at Captain MacNeil's silence, and repented the dispute with Captain Fortune. After dinner I met him. We spoke together and reconciled. He kissed my hand and showed me his teeth as a token of friendship. I was much satisfied and promised him four bitts the next day. They [the maroons] are supported by Fourgeoud and exceedingly dangerous in themselves. The white people are the creation of it—for making an inglorious peace with them, now wanting to break their word in not standing to their promises, feeding them with trifling presents, and a most unmanly submission for those Black gentlemen wherever they appear. The negroes are no fools and in return presume impertinence, trying daily to keep the whites more and more in awe of their long beards and silver-headed staves, whom they will, at last and at this rate I'm afraid, try in futurity to extirpate altogether. And that will make the English American prophecy that they shall need no more to send for slaves to the coast of Guinea true. NB Their number is incredible and all are armed.

July 27: I go and breakfast with Gourlay and after giving Jock[132] Fowler the 4 bits for the Owca negro, I go home with a fever. The negro found my house. I gave him dram and he took leave.

July 28: I give myself in sick to the doctor.

July 30: The ladies, Musellious, Beugel, and Goetzee, send me some confections from Holland.

August

August 1: The colors are again fetched ashore and nine officers and upwards of 160 men are sent sick onboard the ships *Paramaribo*, Captain Spruyt, and *Anna Geertruy*, Captain Piterse. The officers were Captains Hamell and Tulling and subalterns Meyer, Hamer, Swildens, Francen, Rulagh, and Emnick. Major Medlaer takes command of both ships.

August 2: I pay 30 guilders to James[133] who goes sick to Holland.

August 3: Mr. Gourlay tells me Mrs. Godefroy refuses to be caution[134] for Joanna and Jack's liberties, which I cannot believe and makes me mad. Mrs. Tulling comes to take leave in a coach. A most scandalous burlesque[135] upon her if she has deserved it. She knows best.

---

132. "Jock" is Scots for "Jack," a diminutive of "John" or "James." In this case, it was James Fowler, one of Stedman's sergeants.

133. Unclear who this was. Stedman does not provide a first or surname.

134. I.e., post bond, which was required when enslaved people were manumitted in Suriname.

135. I.e., mockery.

By the event of the colors and Fourgeoud staying, I win a wager of 50 guilders from Mr. Rulagh. He comes and offers me a bill on another, like himself, for three months hence. I refuse it and ask the money. He insists that he has it not, and effects to cry. Seeing that cannot help him, he leaves the room in a passion muttering something and never showed his face to me after. In the afternoon, he sent Jock Fowler to offer me the line again. I refuse it knowing he wanted to play a trick on me and sent for the answer. That abrupt leave hurt me, that I could not take his bill and as long as I lived I should never ask him for the money he owed me.

August 4: Telling this adventure to Mr. De Graaff, he told me that, just before that villain mounted the staircase to come to me, he had paid him 50 guilders for the director, Van Dyck. This money was in his pocket when he told me he had no money upon him. Gourlay leaves Paramaribo. I take the air in Mr. Schouten's chaise. This day, I send under the care of Major Medlaer: a letter to General Stuart with confections and pickles, 15 stoop in a case; a letter to my mama with ditto for her and my brother also; a letter to Mrs. Vonck with a chest of confections and pickles and 15 stoop; and a letter to cousin Reygersman with a box of butterflies, two apes, two parrots that have blue and purple tops—they are very fine. James takes his leave and goes abroad.

August 5: I take leave of Jock Fowler who goes to Holland. Also, all the officers that stay still and those that go away take leave of one another at Fourgeoud's house. After the last go onboard, the two ships drop to the new fortress about 10am and they and Fort Zeelandia saluted each other with several guns. The same happened at the new fort, Amsterdam. The colors and several officers are conducted down.

August 6: I visit Mr. Schouten's cabinet of curiosities.

August 7: This day the two ships put out to sea. All the officers go to salute the "Shaver" for the birthday of Her Royal Highness. He gives them a paltry supper. I'm still sick. This is also a great fast day in the colony.

August 8: I go take a ride in Schouten's chaise. Yesterday, I had a visit from a gentleman. Mr. M———ew[136] is his name, of whom I must repeat a story between him and young Mr. R———d[137] of the Society. The last, in an unguarded frank way, happened to say he'd been a captain at such a time, he'd lay 50 guilders M———ew down[138] and thought no more about it. But this time expired, R———d was craved for money by M———ew. R———d protested to have forgot he had ever said so in earnest or said it at all. Besides, he had no money.

---

136. Unclear who this was as Stedman did not provide a full name.
137. Stedman did not provide a full name.
138. I.e., he would wager fifty guilders with M———ew.

Mr. M——ew still insisted on the money or his blood. This frightened the poor young man. He was forced to comply with one or the other. He chose the first and gave M——ew a line in which he owned the debt.[139] M——ew drew the sum of 50 guilders on R——d's account at Paramaribo. What difference betwixt this and sharping?[140] The answer? None.

August 9: News comes that in Blaaw Berg,[141] all the negro wives were taken away by the bush negroes and that, at Para,[142] Mr. Dey, his[143] director, was murdered.

August 10: I take a walk for the first time and wait on the "Old Shaver" in the cool of the evening. I am ordered to command the 1st Division. One Mr. Benelle asked me to come and keep the Feast of St. Hubert at his house. I don't. Miss Phillis was kicked by a packhouse keeper.[144] Mrs. Mewis, who lost her husband recently, died this day. It is thought to be caused by vexation after her daughter was forsaken, even after the wedding clothes were made ready, by Mr. Heemskerk, the *fiscaal*,[145] who was to have married her. At Mr. Spaan's house, where the greatest cruelties happen every day, I saw, on this day and by Mrs.'s orders, a negro woman whipped most barbarously over the breasts and nowhere else. Oh fuck.

NB I speak with Godefroy who absolutely refuses to be caution for Joanna and Jack's liberties, so I find myself worse as ever.

August 11: This day, Lieutenant Van Dale was married to one widow Van der Straaten, a d——d etc.[146] This morning saw a young negro woman fall out of a three-story window in the midst of nothing but broken bottles. All her limbs were hale,[147] but several ribs broke and sadly mangled by the glass. The free

---

139. I.e., this was an account that owed R——d money and that M——ew could draw upon to get his due.

140. I.e., swindling or fraudulent gaming.

141. Blaaw Berg was a plantation district in Suriname to the south of Paramaribo on the Suriname River. Stedman noted that it was sometimes called "Mount Parnassus" because of the bluffs overlooking the river in the region. The attack happened at plantation Bergendal. In the *Narrative*, Stedman called this the "rape of the Sabines," an allusion to the kidnapping of Sabine women to get wives for ancient Rome. See FD, 543.

142. Another plantation district to the south of Paramaribo but to the north of Blaaw Berg on the Suriname River. This region was home to Jew's Savannah, the oldest Jewish settlement in the colony.

143. Although Stedman did not note who "his" was, it was probably the person that related this information to him.

144. I.e., a person who managed a warehouse.

145. The *fiscaal* was the *Raad Fiscaal*, or attorney general, of the colony.

146. It is unclear what Stedman meant to call the widow. It might be "damned," but he usually wrote that word out. Regardless, it seems that Stedman disliked the woman.

147. Spelled "heal" in the original, this is a Scots word meaning in sound health or medically fine.

negroes ordered ready to go to Blaaw Berg. I go with one Mr. Hulser to the Graaf[148] Van Reneval's. Buy ten plates and am pretty well diverted.

August 12: I am told Mr. Perret is also married to one Mrs. Seyelle, a very fashionable woman. I hear the man in Para was murdered by a free negro inhabitant, who is now brought to town. I receive another letter from Mr. Loare, the Deventer cook, about his [illegible]. I go out for the first time and dine at Mr. Gordon's. This morning, I took a ride in a chaise. The young woman that fell yesterday is in a good way and promises to recover. I gave myself recovered to the doctor. Palmer came to town very sick. I visit him. Two Philadelphia sailors were fighting the other day on the forecastle of their vessel and both fell overboard and were drowned in the harbor.

August 13: Dine with Mrs. Godefroy.

August 14: Breakfast with Palmer. Since the major's departure, I do the major's duty and receive the daily report. I dine with the "Shaver." Seven hundred negroes begin to cut the cordon[149] that has so long been spoke of. MacNeil came to town, leaves his house abruptly. I sup with Bolls, who has forsaken Mimi and taken Mary. She upbraids him with inconstancy and makes him suffer hell torments. I'm diverted.

August 15: I dine with Rynsdorp. Took a ride in the morning. This evening, about 9pm, Mrs. Beugel, the governor's niece, died. She was married, but separated. She had sense in discoursing—more as she had in acting. Fredericy was her darling, to whom she left 5,000 guilders and 1,200 guilders per year. He generously desisted from accepting in favor of her children.

August 16: This morning, the wretch who had shot the director on Altona in Para was executed in addition to another who had shot a negro on plantation Bergshoven. This last was beheaded and one that had been his accomplice was *spanso-bocked*[150] below the gallows. But the first, who shot the white man—never did I see such a barbarous execution or did it enter in my thought that human nature could behave with so much spirit and resolution. I call it heroism in its own way. Tied on the cross, his hand was chopped off and with a large iron crowbar all his bones were smashed to splinters. And he still let his voice be heard. Receiving at least four strokes on his left leg and his arms not being well tied, he raised himself on his middle to see what was the matter. All done and the ropes slacked, he writhed himself off the cross and, when seeing the magistrates and others going off, he groaned three or four times and complained in a clear voice that he was not yet dead. He had not expected that

---

148. Dutch title of nobility equivalent of a count or earl in the British peerage.
149. I.e., a path or road.
150. A form of punishment where the victim is hogtied and flogged with tamarind branches. For a full description, see *Narrative*, 2:308–9.

he was going to be left in this condition until God showed him more mercy as his judge, but seeing it was their intention, he heartily cursed them and said they must also die once. He then begged the hangman to finish him. It was all in vain and he cursed him too. Then, seeing nothing could help and he must suffer, he said he had killed a man and deserved death, but now cared not if he must suffer 20 days. He then sung and spoke with the people with the least marks of concern, laughed and joked with the young women, asked to smoke tobacco, and craved[151] a Jew for the eight shillings he owed him. When the mob tormented him with reproaches, he called them barbarous dogs and said that all the white people ought to be damned for their cruelty to the negroes, especially the *fiscaal*, for cheating him in this way. He was a handsome young fellow of about 20. His killing of the director happened in dispute. He declared that women had been his mistake. He lived from 6:30am until about 11am when his head was chopped off.

I dine with Mrs. Godefroy.

August 17: I dine with Goetzee.

August 18: I dine with Captain MacNeil. In the morning, I took a ride in a chaise. Took Palmer along. I had Palmer to breakfast with me. This day I speak with Mistress Godefroy once more and am in good hopes of bringing matters about with her.

August 19: Mr. Roux sends me a declaration concerning Mr. Loare. I ride with the governor to his indigo plantation. This day I dined with Mr. Palmer.

August 20: I dine with the governor. After dinner walk. In the chaise with Madame Mijnershaaven. She is fond of talking about love matters. This day I wrote Loare. Enclosed Roux's declaration.

August 21: I dine on a calf's head with De Graaff. And take a walk in moonshine with Mrs. Mijnershaaven. The discourse is on the old topic. I resolve to shun.[152] This morning Joanna went to speak to Mrs. Godefroy. Seyburg comes to town and I get a furlough.

August 22: I send to ask if I can dine with de Borgnes. Refused. I pass there at midday. See the table covered and full of company. I go in, ask for a dram, and invite myself. So, I stay for dinner. They were confused and blamed the negroes. I resolved after this to never more be misled by their negroes and shall never enter the house until the ill-bred bougerers[153] ask me civilly. They go to plantation. This evening I go to the Dutch comedy, *Simer Saisons Joon de Rijk* and the comedy *Der Eyland van ver Warreling*.

---

151. I.e., begged.
152. She most likely spoke of love again, which is a topic that Stedman did not wish to discuss.
153. I.e., sodomites. Scots version of "buggerer."

August 23: I dine with Mrs. Godefroy. The *Hind*, an English man-of-war of 18 guns and her tender schooner, *18 Swivels*, is cruising the coast for American vessels.

August 24: The birthday of His Royal Highness William VI. The corps waits on Fourgeoud and there we dine today. This day, I visit Mrs. Godefroy with whom I strike a bargain, infinitely more to my advantage—and that of Joanna—as Godefroy had been the caution. I lent Joanna to herself so long as she lives, but then she is to have her liberty at Mrs. Godefroy's entire expense, which capital is her caution. I profit 900 guilders and the buying of a yard and house. Joanna is with a mother and not a mistress,[154] free from all taxes and assizes,[155] and sure of her liberty, fully at her lady's death, which was not in my power to give her. I also form a request to free Johnny. I sup with the governor. The requirements do come from Holland concerning the slaves there. They are to be slaves for the time of six months and at longest for a year. The negro, Graman Quassi, got a present from the prince.

August 25: Joanna, her mother, and myself go to Mrs. Godefroy's. The two women declare their good will to let Joanna go over in Mrs. Godefroy's hands, which makes the bargain infinitely more agreeable. The old lady gives me a present of 50 guilders and a piece of check.[156] This day, the governor gives a great dinner at his indigo plantation, where I dine, he having sent his coach for me. At 4:30pm, I leave the company and go home in the governor's coach to Mr. Goetzee's with whom I, that evening, go to plantation Catwijk. This plantation is very agreeably situated and has all the help of diversions[157] to make time short. Here one may ride on horseback or in a chaise. Here is a sailboat, a billiard table, etc.

August 26: I begin to now rig a neat model of a Dutch man-of-war[158] that hangs in the great hall of the house.

August 28: Mr. Van Peene goes away.

August 29: My good friend De Graaff comes here also. And here is lodged, Mrs. Van Eys, a gay lady. In short, we are, every day, eight or ten at the table.

August 30: ———

August 31: We all go with De Graaff to his plantation A La Bonheur.[159] There we meet more guests, now being about 16 in number. We pass the time very

---

154. This statement refers to Mrs. Godefroy and her relationship to Joanna under Stedman's new bargain—i.e., she was not going to be treated as a slave, although she was still Godefroy's property.
155. I.e., since she was not technically free, Joanna would not have to pay taxes.
156. A type of cloth.
157. "Art" in original.
158. "Model of a" added by the editor to clarify the passage.
159. The name means "good luck."

merrily and make good cheer. We had also a sailing match of four long boats. We hear that the negro Graman Quacy has come home from Holland and that His Highness should have paid all his expenses.

September

September 1: Nothing until the…

September 3: Then we returned to plantation Catwijk and Mr. De Graaff and Mr. Waring went with us.

September 7: He and Waring went to Paramaribo. This morning I saw a sight of horror. A poor, half-starved mulatto woman, having spoke thoughtlessly, was, between two whips, lashed stark naked until no skin was almost left on her thighs and legs up to above the haunches. Before the execution, she was fettered, both her feet together so that she could hardly stir. The frau Van Eys is in low spirits for the absence of her dear De Graaff. It was that bitch that gave poor Brandt's mistress a *spanso-bocko* at the fort because he would not fuck her.[160] Damn her.

September 8: Joanna's mother comes from A La Bonheur. Captains Kanz and Voss come. The last sleeps.

September 10: Mr. De Graaff comes from Paramaribo.

September 11: Mr. d'Halbergh comes here also. He showed us a snuff box he got from the empress of Russia and gold and diamonds valued at 6,000 Holland guilders. He showed us two Danish or Swedish bits set in a heart of gold, surrounded by diamonds, being all his treasure when he left his country. This is pretty singular.[161] I had forgot that Captain Kanz told us he brought over Quacy as a passenger, who also got, as a complement from His Highness, a broad gold-laced coat and hat with a white feather, a large gold medal, a gold-headed cane, and a silver gilt hanger. The fellow had two chests of wine and all for free.

September 12: By long intercession, I prevail on Mistress Goetzee to loose Jette[162] out of her irons, to which she consents with the greatest reluctance. Captain Reygers comes to dine.

---

160. I.e., Van Eys. "Herself" in original.
161. Here, Stedman described how d'Halbergh, from somewhere in Scandinavia, was poor when he arrived in Suriname and later became fabulously rich. To celebrate the newfound wealth, he embedded the two bits, or small coinage, from Denmark and Sweden that he carried to Suriname in gold and jewels.
162. Jette, spelled "Yettee" in the FD, was the mixed-race woman Stedman described as being tortured on September 7. See FD, 555 for more details of this story.

September 13: I present De Graaff with a drawing[163] of his coffee plantation A La Bonheur and Mr. Goetzee with his own picture.

September 14: Captain Tiede came here and dined with us.

September 15: Mr. and Mrs. Verul dined with us along with Captains Kanz and Reygers. In the evening, they all go away, along with De Graaff. I write a letter to Mr. Luik about my furlough.

September 16: Mrs. Van Eys goes to Paramaribo after getting the poor mulatto[164] another flogging.

September 17: I go with Goetzee's family on Perica Creek to 's-Graven-Hague, the property of his wife's mother. Captain Kanz comes to pay us a visit also.

September 18: Get a visit from Baron Ruite van Lelien Horn. Smoke a pipe at plantation Amsterdam with De Pier. At 's-Graven-Hague, I discover a son of Douglas, who was a captain in De Salve's regiment. The boy's name is David. He is a mulatto.

September 19: We go to plantation Alida on the Cottica River.

September 21: We go to Hagenbosch and back to Alida. I give a young negro child the name of Charlotte, after my brother's wife.

September 22: Seven negroes were most damnably whipped.

September 26: Give Mrs. Goetzee her handsome picture.

September 28: Leave Alida plantation and Goetzee's family.

September 29: Come to Catwijk. I visit Alkmaar and there meet Mrs. Godefroy, Mistresses Mijnershaaven, Morithus, and Stuyvesant, and Mr. Mijnershaaven. Bolls and Heersary, in the evening to the fort for news. All the Society soldiers called from plantation to do their military duty. Mr. Texier has left to march to Marowijne. The two mulatto companies have received their colors in great ceremony and 13 poor devils got the gauntlet of ours for having been a little fuddled in a change house.[165] Many were prigeled.[166]

September 30: I wait on Fourgeoud and Seyburg and dine with Captain Perret and his lady.

---

163. "Copy" in original.
164. See the end of September 7 entry.
165. I.e., a brothel.
166. I.e., robbed.

October

October 1: Dine with De Graaff. I write to Gourlay and…

October 2: …also to Colonel Dundas, my brother, James Douglas, Miss Van Calker, Mr. Van Anrae, Mr. Lagh, Mr. Geelguin, and Mr. Van Coeverden. Dine with De Graaff.

October 3: Dine at Stolker's. He shows me a two-story window, through which one of his boys jumped to escape a beating. The boy only fainted. Then, he was whipped for the supposed fault and got a *spanso-bocko* for risking himself.[167] A mulatto boy and a sailor were lately murdered. No inquiry is ever made.

October 4: I dine with Fourgeoud, who was at plantation for three days.

October 5: Dine with Rynsdorp. I was last night sadly hagridden.[168] Waked the family. Monsieur Rochetaux's cook cut his throat and died. Lately one of Charles Rynsdorp's negroes did the same.

October 6: I dine with Mr. Gordon. One of his negroes was lately sold for offering to do the same,[169] also another of his was drowned. I peruse a billet tucked on the courthouse for my little boy's liberty at the New Year. Captain Perret had a scuffle with one Mr. Monsamoy, who had challenged both him and Captain Fredericy.

October 7: They both enter a complaint with Fourgeoud and the subaltern is arrested. I dine with De Graaff. Mistress Godefroy has come to town again.

October 8: Dine with Mrs. Godefroy.

October 9: Bury Mr. Casimier, a Society officer. I make Schadts mad about his mistress. Dine with Kissam. He and Bolls pass the evening with me.

October 10: Dine with Mrs. Godefroy. Fourgeoud goes to plantation.

October 11: Dine with the governor. I give my old suit to Sergeant Sheffer. Seyburg buys that damned bitch Phillis, who used to cuckold Tulling, for about 2000 guilders. I sup with the governor.

October 12: I dine with Mrs. Godefroy. Jews and mulattoes dance.[170]

---

167. The "boy" was enslaved in Stolker's household. For a fuller story of this episode, see FD, 556.
168. I.e., had nightmares.
169. I.e., in reference to the previous entry, commit suicide.
170. This is possibly a reference to Simchat Beit HaShoeivah celebrations, which involved dancing, during the Jewish holiday of Sukkot. Sukkot occurs in the Christian months of September or October, depending on the year of the Jewish calendar.

October 13: Dine with Mr. Gordon. I correct Fredericy in friendship and ask him to breakfast with me. He is confounded. NB A damned puppy has advised them and ought to be damned for it.[171]

October 14: He breakfasts with me. He now sees his error and repents what he did to complain. I dine with Mrs. Godefroy. Joanna takes possession of her new house.

October 15: I dine with Mr. Lemmers. I get a present from the Honorable Thomas Palmer, King's Counsel of Massachusetts Bay: an old pair of silk stockings, an epaulet, and lace intended for his *valet de chambre*, but neither made use of one or the other. NB A Jew teaches[172] Lemmers's children Christianity.

October 16: I dine with the governor and give notice I want a room. [One line scribbled out.][173]

October 17: I dine with the "Shaver." Laurant died more than a month ago.

October 18: Mrs. Godefroy's birthday. The whole town and governor's family rejoice and I dine on purpose with Rynsdorp knowing full well that Fourgeoud hates her. All who know that do frequent her house since she reconciled with Jan Nepveu.[174] I cast out with MacNeil. Two bush negroes brought in from Wana Creek by the new company of free mulattoes.

October 19: I dine with the Godefroys. Hire a room on approbation. [Two lines scribbled out.][175] Mr. Monsamoy is set at liberty. By God, this is an infamous affair and may not be done. The soldiers receive new mountain,[176] the first we got in Suriname.

October 20: I dine with Mr. Rynsdorp and put on a new suit of clothes that cost 200 guilders. Sup with famous Monsieur de Borgnes.

October 21: Receive a letter from my mama that Willie is now a lieutenant of grenadiers and his wife is big with bairn.[177] The news comes that several officers are coming back with the new troops. I dine with Godefroy, sup with Spaan. This day, I enter my new quarters.

---

171. Stedman does not elaborate on this day's events elsewhere, but it seems Fredericy was receiving poor advice from someone Stedman considered a fool. Stedman offered a friendly correction to Fredericy.

172. "Learns" in original.

173. Unlike previous attempts to scribble lines out of the diary, Stedman was largely successful here. Based on previous scribbles, this line probably referred to his or others' sexual activities.

174. The governor of Suriname.

175. See note for October 16 for speculation why Stedman scribbled out these lines.

176. I.e., footwear.

177. I.e., child. She was pregnant.

October 22: Dine with Nagel. News comes that Texier met the rebels, but did nothing.

October 23: I dine at home alone with Joanna.

October 24: Dine with Fourgeoud.

October 25: Dine with Cogenas.

October 26: Dine with the governor.

October 27: Dine with Demelly.

October 28: Dine with De Graaff. By the English captains, I discover to have relations at Philadelphia and York. These, I do suppose, are the Stedmans that left Rotterdam, from Boompjes,[178] about eighteen or twenty years ago. I am informed all are merchants or ship captains.[179]

October 29: Dine with Mrs. Godefroy.

October 30: Dine with that good woman once more. This morning the divisions were reviewed to make ready to march and shables were brought. Mrs. Godefroy gives me a ham, two pounds of tea, and a double sugar loaf. I hear Fourgeoud received a copy of Lieutenant Hamer's letter from the Duke.

October 31: Dine with Mistress Godefroy. Ordered again to be ready and on call.

November

November 1: Dine at Godefroy's. My house offered to lease. News that Long Island and the town of New York are taken.[180] I received letters from Mrs. Vonck and Mr. Volkman.

---

178. Boompjes is a commercial district along the Maas River in Rotterdam.

179. One of these relatives was Charles Stedman of Philadelphia (1753–1812), who remained loyal to Britain during the American Revolution, served in the British Army during the American War of Independence, settled in England after the war, and wrote a history of the conflict, *History of the Origin, Progress, and Termination of the American War* (1794).

180. Throughout the diary and *Narrative*, Stedman expressed an interest in the American War of Independence. His interest stemmed not only from his loyalty to Great Britain and being appalled at the behavior of the Americans but also from a belief the Scots Brigade would be deployed to North America to fight the rebels. This entry referenced British general William Howe's campaign to capture New York and defeat George Washington's Continental Army from July to November 1776. New York City would remain the headquarters for the British Army for the duration of the war. In the original journal, "New York" is referred to as "the town of York," suggesting Stedman's ignorance of American geography—something not that uncommon for eighteenth-century Britons living in Europe.

November 2: Bitch de Borgnes treats her gang on her birthday.[181] I dine with Mrs. Godefroy. Captain Ingram gives me *groo-groo* with onions.

November 3: I dine with Mr. Gordon. Mrs. Godefroy gives me butter, candles, and vinegar. Jan Sheffer gives me a ham. The damned news comes that the old officers will not be coming, but instead all the new ones, except Captain Van Halm, who is good for nothing. One, Captain Van Alst, who has never been abroad, will take my rank when he arrives even though I have spent so long in the bushes.

November 4: I dine with Godefroy. The soldiers and subaltern officers sent in punts once more to the woods. We captains are to follow with a boat. Betty Medlaer's girl got a daughter.

November 5: I dine with the governor. A house damaged by thunder. Mrs. Godefroy gives me potatoes and Mrs. Rynsdorp music.

November 6: Dine with Godefroy. I give her my box with papers and a letter, sealed and addressed to General Stuart, only to be opened if I should happen to die in the colony. I give Joanna a copy of my contract to free her—the original is in the hands of Mr. Gordon—and ask Mr. Gourlay to assist the mother and take care of the boy in my absence. I write to plantations Fauconberg and Knoppemombo for a sheep and eggs for Johnny's nurse. Mrs. Van Eys gives a great dinner to "Shaver" on his birthday. De Graaff chases Jan—he is a damned rascal.[182] The Indians had a battle with *aputus*.[183]

November 7: I dine with Fourgeoud. Have meat roasted in Holland. He sometimes wears a sword and nightcap. Five or six get a new house. This forenoon, I took a ride with Mijnershaaven.

November 8: Dine with Goetzee. Smoke on the river denotes that the woods are burning on the seaside. One negro was hanged and another beheaded at the fort.

November 9: I dine with Mistress Godefroy. I give Mr. Goetzee four drawing of plantations that I drew for him. I read in the news that Willie has a company in Stuart's regiment. The paper was dated August 23, 1776. The Utrecht paper censures Fourgeoud for his embassy to the Owca. We take leave of Colonel Fourgeoud the evening.

---

181. It is unclear what Stedman meant by this statement. He obviously disliked Mrs. de Borgnes, and "gang" in this context means "clique."

182. Not clear who Jan was.

183. Spelled "potoo" in the original. An *aputu* is a type of war club used by the Amerindian peoples of the Guianas. Stedman probably witnessed a mock battle.

November 10: Seyburg, de Borgnes, Perret, and myself set out. We dine at Maas Stroom and sleep at Lavontun.

November 11: Arrive at Saardam. Seyburg to Perica Creek.

November 12: Seyburg back. Saw Texier, who took a woman and confirms the rebels are passed Marowijne.[184] Lieutenant Keen lately took two negroes and killed one. We come to Lebanon. NB At Saardam, I make them give an English sailor half jug of dram for half a bottle of the same, on the pretense that it was rum from New England.[185]

November 13: We camp near Cassipora Creek and there meet all the men and officers camped.

November 14: A most foolish order that we are to no more frequent Ensign Monsamoy, of the Society, dated November 19.[186]

November 15: ─────

November 16: ─────

November 17: Quaco beats Captain Fredericy's boy damnably. All the officers dine with Colonel de Borgnes.

November 18: I write to Alida plantation for bananas and also to Mrs. Godefroy to send me gin and shoes.

November 19: A poor man of Ranfort, going to wash, was drowned. I ducked after him and also ran some risk.[187] Dispute with Papen about making my house. He is always drunk. Divisions are visited.

November 20: I march with two subalterns, three sergeants, seven corporals, 50 men, a negro freeman, and a surgeon. I am only allowed one carrier and am ordered to set out without counting the shot. In place of the 800 shot that were supposed to be in the box, I find but 480. This infamous lie was told to me by de Borgnes and he risked a whole command. I camp at Cassipora Creek after having lost the negro Gausarie[188] for more than four hours.

---

184. I.e., they passed into the French-controlled territory of Cayenne/French Guiana.

185. Rum distilled in New England was considered to be of a higher quality than rum from other parts of the Americas.

186. It is unclear what Stedman meant by this line, but based on the soldiers' previous spats with Monsamoy, it may have been an attempt to keep them out of trouble, essentially ordering them to stay away from him.

187. In the draft, Stedman embellished this story, claiming the man, who was a marine, was "Snapt away by a Large Alligator." Had such an extraordinary thing happened, Stedman would have been sure to note it in his journal. See FD, 560, for the story.

188. He was the freeman referred to earlier in the entry.

November 21: I pass the old country, or banana ground, and camp where the bush negroes were heard the first time. The whole day, no water.[189]

November 22: Pass Myland's Swamp. Discover a *tayer*[190] ground and camp in the old ground Cofaay. This whole day found no water. Here the men only got one biscuit for five men and *caros*[191] apiece in place of an allowance.

November 23: Destroy the ground taken yesterday and follow a path due east in hopes of discovering negroes. There were *pingoes*, so return to Cofaay and rest. Then, an odd event happens. An old tall bush negro, with a white plaid[192] and long shabble[193] approaches the sentry and stands still. I gave him the best words to come into the camp, to have him alive. He shakes his head, says "no," and, in a twinkling, disappears by jumping in the shrubs. Two men fired at him and both missed at the distance of six or eight paces. In the afternoon, we destroy all the grounds. At Cofaay, we find three or four withered huts, some cotton, sugarcane, pineapples, bananas, *bacobas*, *tayers*, rice, and peas. But all this being weathered is a sign of no bush negroes. We camp in the same place, in Cofaay.

November 24: Pass marshy swamp to the burnt villages. Find nothing. We cross the *biree-biree*[194] south, which was now almost dry and camp in a dry rusk.

November 25: Pass where the second time the pallaber[195] was heard and camp soon on the Barbacoeba path. The swamps all stink of dead fish.

November 26: We arrive home at the headquarters. A letter from Jansen at Alida and bananas. We all dine with Seyburg. Captain Bolls comes. Reports the Indians beat the bush negroes on lager wall,[196] took two and killed as many.

November 27: Johnny is two years old. I drink to his health.

November 28: I give in my journal[197] to that beast de Borgnes.

---

189. November is the dry season in Suriname, making drinkable water difficult to find when away from the major rivers and creeks.
190. I.e., the Dutch word for *Xanthosoma sagitattifolia* or white yam.
191. I.e., a type of coin similar to a penny. It denotes an amount of grain, as elaborated on by Stedman in FD, 563.
192. A type of sheet tied around his body.
193. I.e., beard.
194. I.e., swamp.
195. I.e., talking or conversation.
196. Not clear what Stedman meant here. It could be a place—"Lagerwall"—or a misspelling of "walk," a term used for provision grounds. Moreover, it could refer to a type of tactic the Amerindians used to fight.
197. Most likely the log he kept while out in the field.

November 29: A quarrel with him about where to build my hut. The beast Seyburg takes his side,[198] like a false, dirty bugger. We agree again. Captain Perret goes to Jerusalem on command.

November 30: This being St. Andrew's Day and I have nothing to drink, so this is the poorest St. Andrew's that I ever kept in my whole life, always being accustomed to have treated all the officers and men of the Scots Brigade. Captain Bolls who lived in my hut since the 26th leaves me with damned little thanks.

December

December 1: I write to Gordon, Halfhide, De Graaff, and Mrs. Godefroy. Perret's command returns. Captain Fredericy goes to Paramaribo with a sore thumb. I take on a servant, Jan Kiefhaber.

December 2: Can get no house, so repair my hut.

December 5: Mr. Hesseling goes down very sick.

December 7: Being beat by the rain day and night, I resolve to build a house for myself, so Jan, Quaco, and I begin it and set the posts.

December 8: Get negroes to help me. We cut the palisades.[199] De Borgnes calls Pape a rebel, who rebukes it. I confess that he is a drunken rascal. News comes that Charles MacDonald changed with Major Small, so now is in Dundas's regiment. Mr. Hertell is at Marowijne post and has taken two negroes.

December 9: We begin to tie the palisades to my house with the help of the sent cook, who is also a seizer[200] and a steersman.[201]

December 10: He presents me with fish. We begin to cut pines to cover the house. Bolls, who lives next to me, asks me to dine with him and acquaints me that Sergeant Danneville's mother was the real sister of the late French queen and consort of Louis XV. I receive from Paramaribo 17 bottles of red wine. One was stolen. Halfhide sends me a *groo-groo* with dry biscuit, a ham, two sausages, a pair of shoes, and a small case of Jenever. Joanna sends me coffee and eggs. Also, news comes that about 350 fresh troops arrived at Braam's Point on the 6th and Paramaribo on the 8th. Their voyage lasted nine weeks and three days and they came in three ships: *Anna Elizabeth en Anna*, Captain Jan Janker; the *Hollandia*, Captain Heede Janse Bakker; and the *Jacoba Geertruyda*, Captain Wilhelm Emkes.

---

198. "Part" in original.
199. I.e., timbers for the walls.
200. Someone in charge of confiscating contraband.
201. "Sturman" in original.

December 11: We begin to thatch the house. Dine with Bolls.

December 12: Split pine and thatch. One negro taken away. I work worse than any slave myself and so does Captain Bolls. 100 negroes pass from Wana Creek. I dine with Seyburg. I treat the captains and field officers with wine for St. Andrew's. Wager with de Borgnes that we shall not sail for Europe in the spring for 12 bottles.

December 13: I get under roof, so sleep dry for the first time. Captain Bolls goes on command to cut a path. Debits and Hogeboom, a mason and wright, come to pay a visit to Colonel Seyburg....

The manuscript version of Stedman's Suriname diary held at the James Ford Bell Library at the University of Minnesota ends in the middle of the entry on December 13, 1776. A later published edition of the diary has entries through December 24, 1776, but given that edition's general unreliability, this edition ends where the Bell Library's manuscript does.

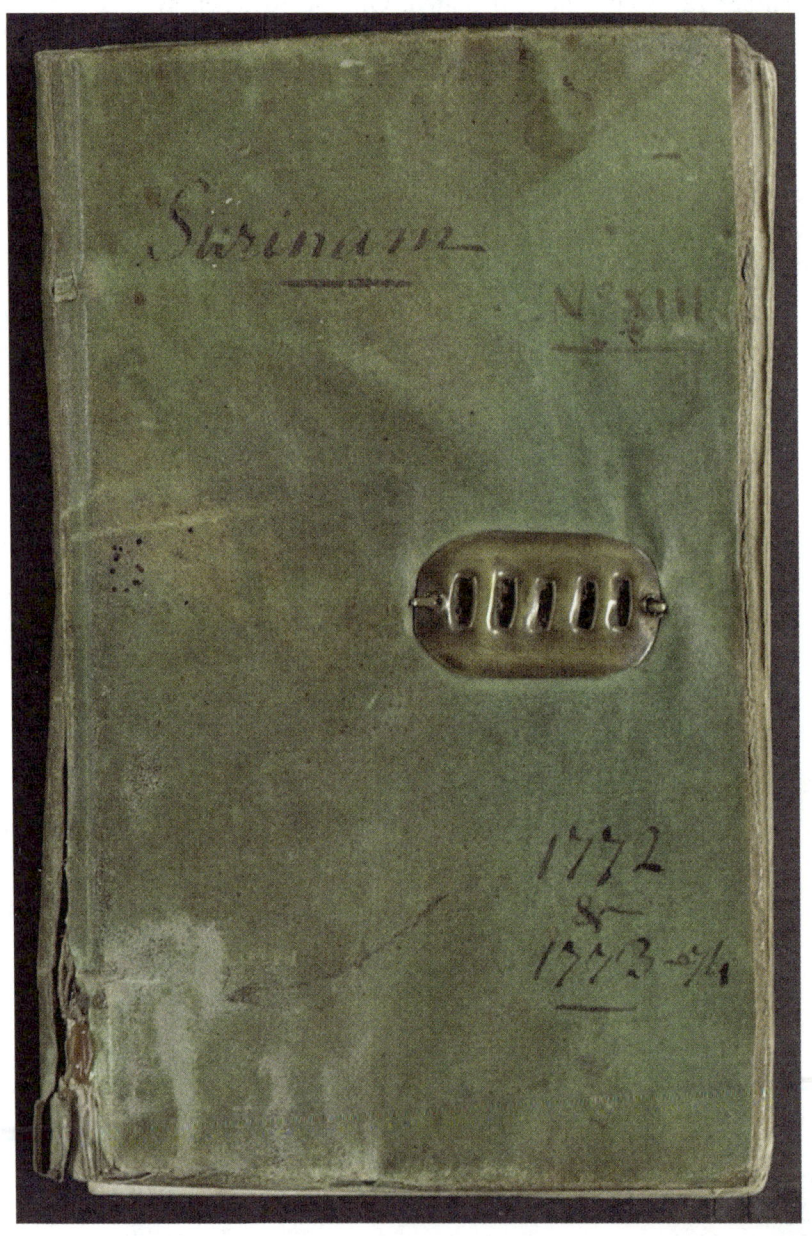

Cover of the first volume of Stedman's Suriname diary and two pages (facing page) from the time of his February 1773 arrival in Suriname. Images courtesy of the James Ford Bell Library, University of Minnesota.

25 a warm quarrel with hat:
    t — in about if the Bates you
    bate I tell the mid your funny
30 but though trying to the weather
    being heavy — we leave the line
    12 [?] [?] [?] water
31 we see a [?] ship at anchor
    from the windward we pass the
    [?] a large rock and
    several other [?] near
    and leave anchor near the
    tropic islands —
    N.B. current runs along the coast
    to the N.W. 20 leag. in 24 hours
Feb 1 we see a large turtle in sea
    leave anchor on the coast —
2 we sail up the river Vivienne
    and leave anchor at 8 o'clock
    before the new fort another [?]
    where the vigilance cap. [?]
    was arrived 3 days before us
    she [?] the ship which
    [?] which we return
    we all dress in uniform

Feb. 1 keep a guard of off. and 7 file
    on the quarter deck
    capt. beltour is dispatch in the
    sloop to Demarara to acquaint
    the governour [?]
    general colon. officers come
    to pay us a visit
3 several more join us — some
    come to see it in hot boats
    moved 3, negros (12 mules)
    we get several [?]
    [?] — is [?] [?] [?]
4 the officers are sent ashore
    to take a walk in the [?] —
    to celebrate there class [?]
    col. [?] goes to Demarara
    in cognito
7 I write to mama & col. Rogers
1 receive a kind invitation from
    Mr. Cochran to accept of his
    house at Demarara
2 I walk alone in the [?]
    where I see nothing except
    an [?]
    O tis a visit to the [?]

This picture, by famed eighteenth-century engraver Francesco Bartolozzi (1727–1815), was the frontispiece for the 1796 edition of the *Narrative* and depicts a young, defiant John Gabriel Stedman standing over a dead maroon following the battle at Gado-Saby. The poem framed the Boni Maroon War as a tragedy that profoundly shaped the lives of all those who fought in it. Image courtesy of the British Library.

One of the most enduring legacies of Stedman's *Narrative* was the graphic visualizations of violence against enslaved people. These infamous images helped to communicate the horrors of slavery and appeared throughout in the text, including this one by Francesco Bartolozzi depicting the woman who had been whipped and chained at the ankle. Image courtesy of the British Library.

Joanna by Thomas Holloway (1748–1827). Image courtesy of the British Library.

A bucolic image of Stedman, Joanna, and an infant Johnny alongside the cabin Stedman lived in while stationed at L'Espérance/The Hope. Image courtesy of the John Carter Brown Library.

Engraving of a Ranger by William Blake (1757–1827).
Image courtesy of the British Library.

Europe Supported by Africa and America by William Blake is the last engraving to appear in the 1796 edition of the *Narrative* and depicts three allegorical women representing Europe, Africa, and the Americas. It was meant to show the reader how imperialism buoyed the European economic and social system. Image courtesy of the British Library.

Original watercolor painting by John Gabriel Stedman. See Example IV in the Appendix for more information. Image courtesy of the James Ford Bell Library, University of Minnesota.

Manner of Sleeping &c. in the Forest, by Inigo Barlow (1759–?).
See Example IV in the Appendix for more information.
Image courtesy of the John Carter Brown Library.

The Narrative of a Five Years Expedition against the Revolted Negroes of Surinam (1796)

VOLUME I

The Preface

In this short preface, Stedman explained the purpose of his book, the people the reader would encounter, and why he was able to write such a narrative.

This work, being perhaps one of the most singular productions ever offered to the public, I think it right to give the reader a short sketch of what he is going to peruse. I have endeavored to arrange matters in some degree like a large garden, where one meets with the sweet-smelling flower and the thorn, the gold-bespangled fly and loathsome reptile, the richest glowing plumage and the darkest shades. The whole is so variegated as to afford, I hope, both information and amusement, without racking or depressing the spirits and damping the mind. Here one will not find the modern pomp and brilliancy of style, but rather a simple tale, where TRUTH is the chief ornament.

Here, in the different characters of a commander, a rebel negro, a planter, and a slave, not only tyranny are exposed, but benevolence and humanity are unveiled to the naked eye. Here the warrior, the historian, the merchant, and the lover of natural philosophy will meet with some gratification. Nevertheless, for having introduced my private adventures, I must make some apology. None of those apologies are for the lovely slave, who makes not the least interesting figure in these pages as female virtue in distress, especially when accompanied with youth and beauty, must ever claim protection.[1]

Upon the whole, perhaps, some allowance may be made, when the reader considers he is perusing no fictional romance, but a real history, totally unembellished with the wondrous. It is the production of an officer, whose pen and pencil have alone been employed ON THE SPOT, a circumstance but very seldom met with.[2]

---

1. Here is Stedman's first reference to Joanna, the mixed-race woman he had a relationship with. Much of the work is a celebration of their relationship, and Stedman often positions himself in the text as her protector—as he is doing here.
2. Stedman's all-caps "TRUTH" in the first paragraph and "ON THE SPOT" here are meant to build credibility with his reader. He presents himself, largely through his firsthand observations and experiences, as an authority able to tell the truth about the many subjects of his book.

As to the shocking cruelties that here are so frequently exposed, let it suffice to say that to deter others from similar inhuman practices and teach them virtue was my sole and only motive. While, on the other hand, it must be observed that LIBERTY, nay even too much lenity, when suddenly granted to illiterate and unprincipled men, must be to all parties dangerous, if not pernicious.[3] Witness the Owca and Sarameca Negroes in Suriname, the Maroons of Jamaica, the Caribs of St. Vincent, &c.[4]

While the Colony of Suriname is reeking and dyed with the blood of the African negroes, truth compels me to observe that the Dutch there are not the only guilty. Most other nations, and particularly the Jews, is owing this almost constant and diabolical barbarity.[5]

Reader, peruse the pages annexed with impartiality and with temper—sort the flowers from the weeds and divide the gold skillfully from the dross—and perhaps you may not regret the hours you have thus dedicated. A few orthographical errors and inaccuracies have been discovered, particularly in the First Volume, from my having unavoidably been prevented from superintending its progress while in the press. In a short errata after the index, to which I refer the curious, will be found properly spelled the names of men and things.[6] Let it however not be understood, that I never laid claim to excellence in writing or drawing. If the plain and MANLY TRUTH, so often spoken of, and so seldom found, are of any avail, however, I presume to hope, that these Volumes are not entirely unworthy [of] the attention of a BRITISH Public.

---

3. This passage is the first indication of one of the main tensions in Stedman's text. He wishes to expose the barbarity and inhumanity of slavery, but his deep-seated racist and classist beliefs prevent him from viewing enslaved people as capable of being free. Throughout the text, he constantly demonstrates the horrors of slavery. Yet, he also believed that people of African descent were incapable of being free responsibly, ultimately settling on advocating for a more regulated, reformed, and humane slavery.
4. The peoples Stedman named here were all free communities of African and Indigenous ancestry in the West Indies. They had largely liberated themselves from European imperial powers and negotiated their own independence, winning official recognition. Nevertheless, by the time Stedman published his narrative in 1796, these communities had run afoul of and ended up in open conflict with Europeans. And, for Stedman, that proved his point that they could not be trusted with freedom.
5. Not only was Stedman a steadfast racist and classist, he was also an anti-Semite. There was a long tradition of blaming Jews for being behind the slave trade and believing them to be particularly cruel enslavers. This trope appears throughout the diary and *Narrative*.
6. Errata are corrections for mistakes in a book that are added as a list at the end.

Chapter I

Introduction—Revolt among the Negroes in Dutch Guiana— An Expedition sets out from the Texel—Short Account of the Voyage—The Fleet arrives in the River Suriname—Reception of the Troops in that Colony—Sketch of the Inhabitants, &c.

In Chapter I, Stedman, more than twenty years after his journey to Suriname, described why the Dutch government sent soldiers to the colony, why he volunteered for the expedition, and what he encountered on his arrival. Even in the edited and published version of the Narrative, *readers can see that Stedman used the observations he recorded in his diary as the primary source for writing the book. Instead of using transitions in the text, Stedman uses dates. By writing in such a fashion, we know Stedman arrived in Suriname on February 2, 1772. Almost immediately, he entered an alien world that was alluring and foreboding at the same time. The first thing he witnessed was the brutalization and torture of an enslaved woman, demonstrating to his readers that in Suriname, slavery and the requisite violence to maintain it were inescapable. Shortly after that, he encountered the toxic social, racial, and sexual politics of the colony. At the same time, however, he became intoxicated with the beautiful scenery and enjoyed the warm welcome he received from the colony's officials and planters. He tempered his Edenic description of Suriname with a discussion of the many natural dangers, such as mosquitoes, and moral hazards, like the seemingly unlimited access white men had to liquor and women of African and Amerindian descent. By characterizing Suriname as a place at once gloriously beautiful and horrifyingly brutal and treacherous, Stedman set the tone for the rest of his narrative.*

Since stories of exploration, particularly since the recent discoveries of the immortal Captain Cook, having been so popular in recent years, I have ventured to offer such observations from a unique part of the globe, a place which few Englishmen have been thrown either by accident or curiosity.[7] The colony of Suriname, in Dutch Guiana, inhabited and cultivated by Europeans near the seacoast, has indeed been known for many years past. But deep exploration of the interior of the country has been constantly discouraged and obstructed by the impenetrable thickness of the jungle. Very little true information concerning that country has as yet been obtained, except what relates to such objects

---

7. Stedman opened the *Narrative* by indicating the English public's fascination with tales of exploration and discovery during the late-eighteenth century. Accounts of famous explorers like Captain James Cook (1728–1779) were best sellers, and there was an insatiable appetite for travel literature.

of commerce common to most of the tropical settlements. This publication, therefore, is chiefly intended to explain the circumstances and events that necessitated my penetrating into the interior parts of the country and enabled me to make these observations.

My readers, I must hope, will receive with some indulgence a work proceeding from an officer, whose military and maritime profession prevented him from acquiring perfection as a writer or a painter. I nevertheless humbly flatter myself that whatever may be found wanting in style and elegance, is in some degree compensated by that fidelity and correctness, which can alone be the work of a pen and pencil employed on the spot. With respect to a few quaint expressions, and even curses, usually spoken by common soldiers and sailors, that unavoidably occur in the narrative, I must humbly request the world not to be startled at them. Not only because these enliven the picture, but also because I am determined to write truth only, and expose vice and folly. Come then, my friends:

> "Together let us beat this ample field,
> "Try what the open, what the covert yield;
> "The latent tracts, the giddy heights, explore
> "Of all who blindly creep, or sightless soar:
> "Eye Nature's walks, shoot Folly as it flies,
> "And catch the manners living as they rise;
> "Laugh where we must, be candid where we can;
> "But vindicate the ways of God to man."
> POPE.[8]

I will now boldly launch out on the difficult task. As the nature, however, of these transactions can only be understood by a reference to the occasion which called me to Suriname, I feel myself under the necessity of still providing a few words upon that subject.

Every part of the world, where slavery is established, is prone to insurrection and disquiet, especially where the slaves constitute the majority of the inhabitants. The colony of Suriname, in Dutch Guiana, has been peculiarly unfortunate in this respect. Whether from the shelter which the immense forests that cover much of this country provide the fugitives or the government of this settlement be radically defective, it is certain that its European settlers are constantly exposed to the most violent ravages and the most desperate outrage.

---

8. These lines of poetry come from Alexander Pope's (1688–1744) *Essay on Man*, where he attempted to create a system of ethics using poetry. Pope was one of the most cited and famous English-language poets in the eighteenth century, and Stedman's readers would have been familiar with these lines, which he used to invite readers on his journey to Suriname. Stedman cited lines of poetry from Pope and others throughout the *Narrative*.

Of these circumstances, this is not the place for a minute detail. Let it suffice for the present that these repeated revolts and insurrections demanded the most vigorous measures for the restoration of a general peace. Accounts of the insurrection transmitted to Holland in the year 1772 described a considerable body of armed people who had assembled in the forests and became extremely formidable. The colony convinced their High Mightinesses the States of the United Provinces to send out a sufficient force to oppose the insurgents, and, if possible, to quell the insurrection.[9]

A career in the British navy had been my choice and ambition and I was well recommended. The small hopes of advancement in time of peace and my paternal estate being lost just after my birth by accidental misfortunes, however, induced me to relinquish the hopes of advancement in the sea service. Instead, I accepted an ensign's commission, presented me without purchase, in one of the Scots Brigade regiments in Holland, during Sir Joseph York's (late Lord Dover) time as ambassador from the British court. Before him, I had the honor to take the usual oaths of abjuration and allegiance to my KING and COUNTRY, as registered at the British War Office. I must mention this fact, as a duty owing to myself and to show the world in general that it was necessity, not choice that compelled me to enter into a foreign service. Nevertheless, a more ancient and distinguished corps does not exist than the Scots Brigade has proved to be for above two hundred years.[10]

At the time of the above insurrection, I was Lieutenant in the Honorable General John Stuart's regiment. When, desiring to traverse the sea, my favorite element, gratifying my curiosity in exploring a part of the world not generally known, and still more by believing the prospect of promotion which might come with such a dangerous expedition, I instantly solicited admission into a corps of volunteers preparing to sail for Guiana. I had the honor, by his Serene Highness William V, Prince of Orange, to be advanced to the rank of captain

---

9. At this time, the Netherlands was an oligarchic republic controlled by a legislative body called the States General, who Stedman noted took a keen interest in the slave rebellion/maroon war in Suriname and decided to send soldiers.

10. When he could not afford to purchase a commission in the Royal Navy, Stedman, like his father, joined the Scots Brigade, a long-standing mercenary brigade in the Dutch Army. It was made up of six regiments, three of which were composed mostly of Scots and their descendants. It is unclear what Stedman meant when he said his "paternal estate lost just after my birth by accidental misfortunes." However, it may be covering for the fact that Stedman was a spendthrift and deeply in debt by the time he joined the expedition to Suriname. His desire to escape creditors seems to have been a motivating factor for going to the colony.

by brevet, under Colonel Louis Henry Fourgeoud, a Swiss gentleman from the Alpine Mountains, who was appointed our commander-in-chief.[11]

Having taken the oaths of fidelity on the 12th of November to the new corps and prepared what was necessary for the voyage, I bade farewell to my old regiment, and immediately sailed to the island of Texel, where several of our gentlemen were already assembled.[12] Going ashore, I had nearly perished by the boat's shipping a sea and sinking in the surf.

The island of Wieringen was however the spot of general rendezvous.[13] Colonel Fourgeoud arrived on the 7th of December and the volunteers were all assembled to the number of five hundred fine young men. On the morning of the 8th we were formed into seven companies and embarked as a regiment of marines....

Between his embarkation and arrival in Suriname on February 2, 1772, Stedman recounted his sea voyage to Suriname. It is largely a discussion of the weather with a few accounts of marine life.

On the 2nd [of February], having hoisted our anchors at daybreak, we again set sail, keeping course along the coast. After having doubled Braam's Point with a light breeze, under top and top-gallant sails, we finally entered the beautiful river Suriname. At three o'clock pm dropped anchor before the new fortress called Amsterdam.[14] Here we were extremely happy to meet with our friends in the *Vigilance*, which vessel (as I have mentioned) had parted company with us in a gale of wind on the 2nd of January, off Cape Finisterre, and arrived two days before us in this river.

---

11. William V, prince of Orange (1748–1806), was the stadholder, or chief executive, and military leader of the Dutch Republic. The House of Orange had held the position of stadholder in the Netherlands, except from 1650–1672 and 1702–1747, since the Dutch rebelled and declared their independence from the Spanish in the 1570s. William had been ousted from power and driven into exile to England in 1795, a year before Stedman published his book. The reference to "Serene Highness" suggests the deference and affection Stedman had for William. Those feelings may have been generated in part because of the men's shared experience of exile from the Netherlands. Given his role as chief military commander, it was in William's power to issue a brevet, or commission, promoting Stedman to captain. Brevets did not often come with increased pay, however, and it is unclear if that was the case here.

12. The island of Texel sits off the northern coast of Holland at the entrance of what used to be the Zuiderzee (now the IJsselmeer). Its proximity to Amsterdam and the towns surrounding the bay had long made it a stopover for ships, especially naval vessels, preparing to depart on long sea voyages.

13. Stedman referred here to the town of Wieringen, which sits southeast of the island of Texel. Because of the construction of extensive dykes and drainage canals during the twentieth century, Wieringen is no longer an island and is now part of the mainland.

14. Fort New Amsterdam is a large fortress that was constructed between 1737 and 1747. It sits at the intersection of the Suriname and Commewijne Rivers.

Our ships' crews now were in the highest flow of spirits, seeing themselves surrounded by the most delightful greenery, while the river seemed alive by the many boats and barges passing and re-passing to see us. Groups of naked boys and girls were promiscuously playing and flouncing, like so many Tritons and Mermaids, in the water. The scene was new to all, and nothing was heard but music, singing, and cheering on deck, as well as in the rigging, from the ideas of happiness which each individual now promised himself in this luxuriant flourishing spot, while between decks the heat had become insupportable. How miserably these poor fellows were mistaken shall soon be seen.

I must indeed acknowledge that nothing could equal the delicious sensations. We seemed intoxicated by the fragrance of the lemons, limes, oranges, and flowers, wafted over from the adjoining plantations that line the banks of all the rivers in this everblooming settlement. Large amounts of fruit were sent on board our ships by Colonel de Ponchera of the colonial troops. This gentleman, being the commandant of Fort Amsterdam, also saluted the vessels with nine guns from the batteries. With an equal number, we returned the compliment. A long boat with one of our captains was afterwards dispatched to Paramaribo, to announce to the governor the arrival of the troops in the colony.

During our stay in this place, the soldiers frequently went ashore, and I accompanied them in their excursions. But the pleasure I had flattered myself with, from exchanging the confinement of a ship for the liberty of ranging over a delicious country, was damped by the first object I saw after landing. This was a young female slave, whose only covering was a rag tied round her loins, which, like her skin, was lacerated in several places by the stroke of the whip. The crime which had been committed by this miserable victim of tyranny, was the non-performance of a task to which she was apparently incapable. She was sentenced to receive two hundred lashes and to drag for months a chain several yards in length. One end of which was locked round her ankle and the other end was affixed with a weight of at least a hundred pounds. Strongly affected with this shocking circumstance, I drew the unhappy sufferer, and retained a dreadful idea of the inhumanity of the planters towards these miserable subjects.

The grass in this part of the country was very long and coarse and harbored two species of very disagreeable insects, termed *Pattat* and *Sorapat* lice by the colonists, which settled on every part of our persons. The former is so small as to be barely visible. The latter is something larger, and formed like a crab. Both adhere closely to the skin and occasioned an intolerable itching. These insects abound most during the rainy season. The best means of avoiding their attacks is allegedly by walking barefoot as they are believed to fasten more easily and consequently in greater numbers, upon the clothes. From there, however, they very speedily find their way to the skin. We did not get rid of our disagreeable companions until our return to the ship, when we washed the affected parts with the juice of limes or lemons, which considerably alleviated our troublesome sensations.

On the 3rd [of February] we received a visit from several officers of the Society and the West India Company's troops, accompanied by a number of other gentlemen, to welcome our arrival in the colony.[15] Nor were they satisfied with paying us merely a compliment in words, but regaled us with a large quantity of excellent fruits and other refreshments. They came in very elegant barges or tent-boats, adorned with flags, and attended by music. The vessels were rowed by six or eight negroes, who were entirely without clothes, except a small stripe of check or other linen cloth, which was passed between their thighs and fastened before and behind to a thin cotton string tied round their loins. As the colonists generally make choice of their handsomest slaves for rowing this purpose, the rowers were healthy, young, and vigorous and looked extremely well. Their being naked gave us a full opportunity of observing their skin, which was shining, and nearly as black as ebony. This scene was contrasted by the arrival of two canoes filled with emaciated starving wretches, who clamorously solicited relief from the soldiers and were ready to fight for the possession of a bone.

The day following our commander-in-chief was visited by a Mr. Rynsdorp, who introduced to him two Black soldiers, freed slaves, who composed part of a corps of three hundred which had been lately formed. These men were exhibited by Mr. Rynsdorp as specimens of that valiant body, which had recently most gallantly distinguished itself by offering protection to the colony.[16]

While we still remained at anchor before the fortress Amsterdam, I received a polite invitation from one Mr. Lolkens, a planter, to whom I had been recommended, to accept the use of his house and table on our arrival at Paramaribo, the capital of the colony.

On the 8th [of February] we once more went under way and, after the usual ceremonies on leaving the fortress, sailed up the river Suriname with drums beating, colors flying, and a guard of marines drawn up on the quarterdeck of each vessel. Having at length reached Paramaribo, we finally came to anchor within pistol-shot of the shore, receiving a salute of eleven guns from the citadel Zeelandia, which was returned by all the ships of our small fleet.[17] After being confined nearly sixty-three days in a small vessel, it is not easy to describe

---

15. While technically a Dutch colony, Suriname was governed by a private company, the Society of Suriname. As such, the company maintained its own army. Likewise, the three owners of the Society of Suriname, the city of Amsterdam, the Van Aerssen van Sommelsdijck family, and the Dutch West India Company were also responsible for defending the colony, thus Stedman's reference to the "West India Company's troops." The Society of Suriname governed the colony until 1795 when the Dutch government took control.

16. This is Stedman's first reference to the Rangers, freed slaves who fought for the Dutch against the maroons.

17. Fort Zeelandia still sits along the riverfront in Paramaribo. The English constructed the fort in the 1650s when they controlled Suriname. Once the Dutch captured the colony in 1667, it became Suriname's military and administrative center.

the pleasure we experienced on finding ourselves once more on land and surrounded by a thousand agreeable circumstances.

The town appeared uncommonly neat and pleasing, the shipping extremely beautiful, the adjacent woods adorned with the most luxuriant verdure, the air perfumed with the utmost fragrance, and the whole scene gilded by the rays of an unclouded sun. We did not however take leave of our wooden habitation at this time, but the next day were formally disembarked with a general appearance of rejoicing.

All the inhabitants of Paramaribo gathered to behold this splendid scene nor were their expectations disappointed. The corps consisted of nearly five hundred young men (for we had been so fortunate as only to lose one during the voyage). The oldest was scarcely more than thirty. The whole party was neatly clothed in their new uniforms and in caps ornamented with twigs of orange-blossom. We paraded on a large green plain between the town and the citadel opposite to the governor's palace. During the course of those ceremonies, several soldiers fainted from the excessive heat. The troops then marched into quarters and prepared for their reception. The officers were regaled with a dinner by the governor, which seemed decadent compared to the salt provisions to which we had so long been confined had any contrast been necessary to heighten our opinion. The choicest delicacies of America and Europe were united in this meal and served up on silver. A great variety of the richest wines were poured out with profusion and the dessert was composed of the most delicious fruits. The company was attended by a considerable number of extremely handsome negro and mulatto maids, all naked from the waist upwards, according to the custom of the country.[18] The other parts of their persons were dressed in the finest India chintzes and their entire bodies adorned with golden chains, medals, beads, bracelets, and sweet-smelling flowers.

After partaking of this superb entertainment till about seven o'clock, I set out in search of the house of Mr. Lolkens, the hospitable gentleman who had invited me to make it my own. I soon discovered the place, but my reception was so ludicrous that I must relate the particulars. On knocking at the door, it was opened by a young female negro, of a masculine appearance, whose whole dress consisted of a single petticoat. She held a lighted tobacco-pipe in one hand and a burning candle in the other, which she brought close to my face, in order to examine me. I asked if her master was home, but she replied in a language totally unintelligible to me. I then mentioned his name, on which she burst into an immoderate fit of laughter, displaying two rows of very beautiful teeth. At the same time, grabbing the breast-buttons of my coat, she made me a signal to follow her. I was much at a loss how to act, but went in and was

---

18. Stedman used the term "mulatto" here to refer to people of mixed African and European heritage. Over the course of his time in the colony, he learned more about the distinctions between mixed-race people, often dictated by the percentage of European heritage they had.

ushered by the girl into a very neat apartment. She brought some excellent fruit and a bottle of Madeira wine, which she placed upon the table. She then, in the best manner she was able, informed me that her *masera*,[19] with the rest of his family, left to spend a few days at his plantation. She was left behind to receive an English captain, whom she supposed to be me. I signified that I was and filled her out a tumbler of wine, which I had the utmost difficulty to persuade her to accept. That is the degrading light in which these unhappy beings are considered, and it is believed presumptuous for them to eat or drink in the presence of a European. I contrived for some time to carry on something like a conversation with this woman but was soon glad to put an end to it by recurring to my bottle.

Tired with the employments of the day, I longed for some rest and made a signal to my attendant that I wanted to sleep. My motion was strangely misconstrued. She immediately seized me by the neck and imprinted on my lips a most ardent kiss. Heartily provoked at this unexpected, and (from one of her color) unwelcome salutation, I disentangled myself from her embraces, and angrily flung into the apartment allotted for my place of rest. But here I was again pursued by my Black tormentor, who, in opposition to all I could say, insisted upon pulling off my shoes and stockings, and in a moment disencumbered me of that part of my apparel. I was extremely chagrined at her conduct, though this is commonly performed by the slaves in Suriname to all ranks and sexes without exception. No one should conceive that this apparently extraordinary conduct resulted from any peculiarity of the girl. Her behavior was only such as would have been practiced by the generality of female negro slaves, and what will be found, by all who visit the West India settlements, to be characteristic of the whole dark sisterhood.[20]

Finding in the morning that my friend the planter had not returned, I took leave of his mansion and very hospitable servant. After visiting the soldiers in their new abodes, the quartermaster escorted me to a neat habitation for my use. I found the house entirely unfurnished, though not destitute of inhabitants. I had left my captain's commission, which was of parchment, in the window, the first night and had the mortification to find in the morning that it was devoured by the rats.

Having taken possession of my habitation, my next wish was to furnish it properly. All concerns of this nature, however, were rendered unnecessary by the generous hospitality of the inhabitants. The ladies supplied me with tables, chairs, glasses, and even plate and china in great abundance. The gentlemen loaded me with presents of Madeira wine, porter, cider, rum, and sugar

---

19. "Master" in the local Suriname dialect. Sometimes used by enslaved and free Black people when addressing any white person in Suriname.

20. See the Appendix for a comparison of how Stedman described this encounter with the diary to how he wrote about it here.

in addition to a quantity of the most exquisite fruits. Among the latter, I was particularly struck with the *shaddock* and *awara*. The former of these is of a very agreeable flavor—somewhere between sweet and acidic—and is produced from a tree supposed to be transplanted from the coast of Guinea by a Captain Shaddock, whose name it still retains throughout the English West India islands. In Suriname, it is called *pompelmoose*. This fruit appears to be a citrus but is as large as the head of a child of eight or ten years old. The skin is extremely thick, of a bitterish taste, and a pale yellow or citron color. There are two species of the *shaddock*. The pulp of the one is white and that of the other a beautiful pale red, which may be safely eaten in considerable quantities. Indeed, it is esteemed by the natives, who are in general remarkably fond of it, as very salubrious.[21]

The *awara*, or *avoira*, which is less remarkable for the excellence of its flavor than its beautiful appearance, grows upon a species of palm tree, and is of an oval form, about the size of an Orlean plumb, and of a rich deep orange color, nearly approaching to red. It is much esteemed by the negroes, who exercise their ingenuity in forming rings out of the pits, which they decorate with cyphers, initial letters, and other devices. They then dispose of them to the Europeans, who mount them in gold. These pits are large, extremely hard, and as black as jet or ebony, but the pulp which surrounds them is very thin.[22]

This day, on examining into the state of our remaining livestock, including hogs, sheep, ducks, geese, fowls, and turkeys, we found them nearly as many in number as when we first sailed from Holland. These were all sent to the colonel's poultry yard at the headquarters. We had the additional indignity of seeing above sixty large kegs with preserved vegetables and just as many fine Westphalia hams (being perfectly rotten) thrown into the Suriname River to feed the sharks.

I now observed, on the second morning after our landing, that my face, my breast, and hands were entirely spotted over like the skin of a leopard. This was occasioned by myriad mosquitoes, which flying in clouds, had kept me company during the night. The fatigue from my voyage and the oppressive heat of the climate had sunk me into so profound a sleep that I could not feel their bites until I saw the spots. These insects are inconceivably numerous here during the rainy season, and particularly on the banks of creeks or rivers. None are secured from their attacks, but they peculiarly infest strangers in preference to the natives. Wherever they insert their proboscis and remain unmolested,

---

21. The *shaddock* or *pompelmoose* is the modern grapefruit.
22. In this paragraph, Stedman discussed the fruit of the palm tree *Elaeis oleifera*. This tree is native to equatorial Central and South America and is a cousin to the African oil palm popular today. In the eighteenth century, enslaved people in Suriname used the pits of this fruit to make jewelry.

they suck the blood till they are scarcely able to fly. Every puncture they make is succeeded by a large blotch and accompanied with an almost intolerable itch. The presence of the mosquitoes is indicated by their buzzing noise, which alone is sufficient to make one sweat. The noise is so very disagreeable to those who have suffered from their stings that they are nicknamed the *Devil's Trumpeters*. They are indeed inconceivably troublesome in every respect. The candles are no sooner lighted in an evening than they are stuck full of them. All kinds of food and drink are exposed to their disagreeable visits and even the mouth and eyes are not exempted.

The best cure for their stings is an application of the juice of lemons or limes, mixed with water, which is also a tolerable preventative against their attacks. Immediately before shutting the windows, the inhabitants commonly burn tobacco in their apartments, the smoke of which occasions the insects to fly about the room. The negro girls then unreservedly throw off their petticoats, which is the whole of their covering and run naked about the chamber, chasing the mosquitoes out the windows or killing them. The more delicate or luxurious amongst the natives still employ their slaves in fanning them during the whole night, excepting such as have green gauze doors covering their beds or pavilions. The generality of the people in Suriname sleep in roomy cotton hammocks, which are covered with a very large thin sheet, suspended from a tight line immediately over them—like the awning of a ship—which serves in some measure to deter these troublesome insects. My lack of one exposed me to be thus stung all over.

On the morning of the 22nd [of February], an elderly negro woman with a Black girl about fourteen entered my apartment. It would be difficult to express my astonishment when she gravely presented me her daughter to become what she termed my "wife." I had so little gallantry, however, and rejected the offer with a loud laugh. At the same time, I accompanied the refusal with a small but welcome present, which perfectly satisfied them. They then departed with every possible demonstration of gratitude and respect. The girls here, who voluntarily enter these relationships, are sometimes mulattoes, sometimes Indians, and often negroes. They all desire living with a European, whom in general they serve with the utmost tenderness and fidelity and tacitly reprove those numerous white women who break through ties more sacred and solemn. Young women of this description cannot be married or connected in any other way as most of them are enslaved. So little is the practice of concubinage condemned that they remain faithful and constant to the partner by whom they are chosen. The women are countenanced and encouraged by their nearest relations and friends, who call this a lawful marriage. Even the clergy avail themselves of this custom without restraint. Many of the sable-colored beauties will, however, follow their own penchant without any restraint, refusing with contempt the golden bribes of some, while bestowing their favors on others for a dram or a broken tobacco-pipe, if not for nothing.

The hospitality I had experienced on our arrival in the colony continued. I had a general invitation to visit—besides his excellency the governor, and Colonel Texier, the commandant—more than twenty respectable families whenever convenient. Though the officers of our corps had formed a regimental mess, I seldom [had] the honor of their company. One gentleman in particular, a Mr. Kennedy, carried his politeness so far, as not only to offer me the use of his carriage, saddle-horses, and table, but even presented me with a fine negro boy named Quaco to carry my umbrella as long as I remained in Suriname.[23] The other gentlemen of the regiment also met with great civilities and the whole colony seemed anxious to testify their respect by vying with each other in a constant round of festivity. Balls, concerts, card-assemblies, and every species of amusement in their power were constantly contrived for our entertainment. The spirit of conviviality next reached on board the men-of-war, where we entertained the ladies with cold suppers and dancing upon the quarter-deck under an awning until six in the morning. We generally concluded the frolic by a cavalcade or an airing in their carriages. This constant routine of dissipation, which was rendered still more pernicious by the enervating effects of an intensely hot climate where one is in a perpetual state of perspiration, already threatened to become fatal to two or three of our officers. Warned by their example, I retired from all public companies, sensible that by such means I could alone preserve my health in a country which has such a tendency to debilitate the human frame. A European, however cautious to avoid excesses, has always reason to apprehend the climate's dreadful effects.

Dissipation and luxury appear to be congenial to the inhabitants of this climate and great numbers must annually fall victims to their very destructive influence. Their fatal consequences are indeed too visible in the men, who have indulged themselves in intemperance and other sensual gratifications and who appear withered and fatigued in the extreme. Nor do the generality of the creole females exhibit a more alluring appearance.[24] They are languid, their complexions are pale, and the skin of even the young ladies is frequently shriveled. This is however not the case with all. And I have been acquainted with some who, preserving a glow of health and freshness in their lovely countenance, were entitled to contend for the prize of beauty with the fairest European. But, alas! The numbers of this last description are so small, that the colonists in their amours most usually prefer the Indian, negro, and mulatto girls, particularly on account of their remarkable cleanliness, health, and vivacity. For the excesses of the husbands in this respect and the marked neglect which they meet from them, the creole ladies most commonly, at a very early period,

---

23. This is the first appearance of Quaco, who would remain with Stedman during his entire duration in Suriname and live with him in the Netherlands for a few years after his return. In 1781, despite freeing him, Stedman gifted Quaco to the Countess of Rosendaal.

24. Stedman used the term "creole" to refer to people of European descent born in Suriname.

appear in mourning clothes.²⁵ They then have the privilege of making another choice in the hopes of a better partner. Nor are they long without another mate. Such indeed is the superior longevity of the fair females of Suriname, compared to that of the males (owing chiefly, as I said, to their excesses of all sorts) that I have frequently known wives who have buried four husbands, but never met a man in this country who had survived two wives.

The ladies do not, however, always bear with patience the slights and insults they thus meet with in the expectation of a sudden release. Mostly, they persecute their successful sable rivals (even on suspicion) with implacable hatred and the most unrelenting barbarity. While they chastise their partners not only with a show of ineffable contempt, but also with giving in public the most unequivocal marks of preference towards those gentlemen who newly arrive from Europe. That occasioned the trite proverb and observation about the colony: that the tropical ladies and the mosquitoes have an instinctive preference for a newly landed European. This partiality is indeed so very extreme and the proofs of it so very apparent and nauseous that some command of temper is necessary to prevent the disgust which such behavior must naturally excite, particularly where the object is not very inviting. Nay, it was even publicly reported at Paramaribo, that two of these tropical Amazons had fought a duel for the sake of one of our officers.²⁶

I must now mention a word or two of the Governor and Colonel Fourgeoud.... Notwithstanding the polite reception our whole corps had met with ever since we first landed in the colony, it was evident to perceive that mutual coolness which subsisted between him and our commander in chief. The colonel gave the first public cause of animosity—on the very day of our debarkation—by drawing up his regiment with their backs toward the governor's palace.²⁷

It is easy to conceive that the disgust which so early and so reciprocally manifested itself between the above two gentlemen. Both of them were our commanders, but also totally independent of each other, and made our stay at Paramaribo extremely disagreeable to all the officers in our regiment, as well as those of the Society corps. The consequence of which was, after having resided but a few weeks in the colony, it was thought proper by the governor to acquaint Colonel Fourgeoud, that, as the rebel negroes seemed no further disposed to disturb the tranquility of the settlement, the colony's own troops, and the corps of Black rangers, were deemed sufficient for its defense. In consequence, Colonel Fourgeoud, with his marines, no longer being wanted, was at liberty to return to Europe whenever he thought proper.

---

25. I.e., they are widowed at a young age.
26. Here, Stedman compared the dueling creole women of Suriname to the Amazons, a mythic race of warrior women.
27. This is Stedman's first indication of the political dysfunction that plagued the expedition for the duration of his time in Suriname.

Various were the feelings of pleasure and reluctance with which our gentlemen received this news. Preparations were made for our departure, but in a few days these were again suspended by the inhabitants, who clamorously insisted on our staying. When the wooding and watering of the vessels was provisionally stopped, the ships were still kept in commission on speculation. It was during this interval of leisure and uncertainty that I seriously thought of employing myself in writing a short history of the colony, and of drawing such objects as I thought most suitable to complete my little plan. In these designs, besides consulting the best authors on the subject, I had the honor to be materially assisted by his excellency the governor, who not only favored me with several manuscripts, but also daily furnished me with such a succession of animals, shrubs, etc. as I was desirous of being acquainted. Thus, independent of that coolness which was so evident between these two veteran officers, I made it my earnest study and endeavor, if possible, to keep friends with both parties. Independent of that duty which I owed Colonel Fourgeoud, as my commander-in-chief, to treat the governor of the colony with that respect which I thought was due to his dignity, his rank, and his conduct. In this motive (though not by all), I was steadily supported by the most respectable officers in the corps....

Chapter V

The Scene changes—Some Account of a beautiful Female Slave—The Manner of traveling in Suriname—The Colonel explores the Situation of the Rivers—Barbarity of a Planter—Wretched Treatment of some Sailors

Chapter V followed three chapters that discussed Suriname's history, geography, climate, and culture. Here, Stedman resumed narrating his experience in Suriname. Most importantly, in this chapter, Stedman introduced readers to Joanna, the mixed-race enslaved girl who became Stedman's "Suriname wife" during his time in the colony. He seems to have met her shortly after arriving and lusted after her for months until, because of her changing fortunes that Stedman related, she entered a relationship with him. To describe their connection, he used classical and contemporary allusions that would have been familiar to his readers, trying to persuade them of the legitimacy of his love and affection for a girl who was significantly younger than him, who European readers believed to be racially inferior and, being mixed-race, promiscuous and lascivious, and who, being enslaved, could never truly consent to a relationship with Stedman. By recounting some of the words Joanna spoke, Stedman also offered readers the opportunity to explore how she thought and felt about her situation. For example, Joanna's speech that Stedman recorded suggests that she understood her own value and place in the negotiations over her companionship. In addition to meeting Joanna, Stedman began describing the effect of disease, debauchery, and heat on the European soldiers sent to subdue the rebellion and the treatment of European soldiers and sailors in the colony. Both of these are subthemes of the Narrative, *which is unsurprising given Stedman was a soldier. Finally, there are further descriptions of the brutality of slavery as Stedman ventured outside Paramaribo to visit plantations.*

Having in the first chapters given some account of our incorporation, our voyage, our landing, and our reception in the colony in February 1773 and having described the colony of Suriname, its boundaries, and revolutions, from its earliest discovery, I shall now proceed in my narrative. I will connect the proceedings of our little corps with the general chain of events and write precisely what I have learned by local and ocular observation.

From our arrival until February 27th, we seemed to have traveled to Guiana for little more than idle dissipation. I shall now proceed from the same date, which was about the commencement of the rainy season, when our mirth and conviviality still continued. As a contrast to the preceding scenes of horror, I will offer a description of the beautiful mulatto maid Joanna. This charming young woman I first saw at the house of a Mr. Demelly, secretary to the court of policy, where I daily breakfasted.[28] His lady Joanna, but fifteen years of age, was a very remarkable favorite. Taller than average, she was possessed of the most elegant shape that nature can exhibit, moving her well-formed limbs with more than common gracefulness. Her face was full of modesty and the most distinguished sweetness. Her eyes, as black as ebony, were large and full of expression, bespeaking the goodness of her heart. She had cheeks, through which glowed, in spite of the darkness of her complexion, a beautiful tinge of vermillion, when gazed upon. Her nose was perfectly well formed and rather small. Her lips a little prominent, which, when she spoke, discovered two regular rows of teeth, as white as mountain snow. Her hair was a dark brown inclining to black, forming a beautiful globe of small ringlets and ornamented with flowers and gold spangles. Around her neck, her arms, and her ankles, she wore gold chains, rings, and medals. A shawl of India muslin, the end of which was negligently thrown over her polished shoulders, gracefully covered part of her lovely bosom. A petticoat of rich chintz alone completed her apparel. Bare-headed and bare-footed, she shone with double luster. She carried in her delicate hand a beaver hat, the crown trimmed round with silver. The figure and appearance of this charming creature could not but attract my particular attention as they did indeed that of all who beheld her. It induced me to enquire

---

28. Demelly was the clerk for the Court of Policy and Justice, the primary court for adjudicating civil and criminal matters in Suriname.

from Mrs. Demelly, with much surprise, who she was as she appeared to be so much distinguished above all others of her species in the colony.

"She is, sir," replied this lady, "the daughter of a respectable gentleman, named Kruythoff, who had, besides this girl, four children by a Black woman, called Cery, the property of a Mr. D. B. on his estate called Fauconberg, in the upper part of the river Commewijne.

"Some few years since Mr. Kruythoff made the offer of above one thousand pounds sterling to Mr. D. B. to obtain manumission for his offspring, which, being inhumanly refused, it had such an effect on his spirits, that he became frantic and died in that melancholy state soon after. That left in slavery, at the discretion of a tyrant, two boys and three fine girls, of which the one now before us is the eldest.[29]

"The gold jewelry, which seems to surprise you, are the gifts her faithful mother, who is a most deserving woman towards her children, and of some consequence amongst her caste, received from her father (whom she ever attended with exemplary affection) just before he expired.

"Mr. D. B., however, met with his just reward. Having since driven all his best carpenter negroes to the woods by his injustice and severity, he was ruined, obliged to flee the colony, and leave his estate and stock to the disposal of his creditors. One of the above unhappy deserters, a *sambo*,[30] has by his industry been the protector of Cery [Seerie] and her children. His name is Jolycoeur, and he is now the first of Baron's captains, whom you may have a chance of meeting in the rebel camp, breathing revenge against the Christians.[31]

"Mrs. D. B. is still in Suriname having been arrested for her husband's debts. She cannot leave until Fauconberg can be sold by execution to pay creditors. This lady now lodges at my house, where the unfortunate Joanna attends her, whom she treats with peculiar tenderness and distinction."[32]

---

29. Original footnote: In Suriname all such children go with their mothers; that is, if she is in slavery, her offspring are her master's property, should their father be a prince, unless he obtains them by purchase. [Slave societies in the Americas followed the legal principle of *partus sequitur ventrem*, often called *partus*, meaning that children followed the status of their mothers. Thus, Joanna and her siblings were, like their mother, enslaved despite their father being white and free.]

30. Original footnote: A sambo is between a mulatto and a negro.

31. The relationship between Seerie and Jolycoeur speaks to how small and intimate of a society Suriname was. Jolycoeur was a leader of the rebels, while Seerie's daughter Joanna became close with Stedman, one of the officers sent to quell the rebellion.

32. Plantation owners everywhere in the Americas, especially in Suriname, were deeply in debt. Plantations were expensive to run, requiring constant upkeep of machinery and infrastructure and purchasing enslaved laborers and provisions. Planters likewise led lavish lifestyles and borrowed heavily to acquire the latest fashions and luxury goods. These debts usually exceeded the value of their estates, meaning they were always on the cusp of financial ruin. One bad harvest, untimely death, revolt, or zealous creditor could create havoc for planters and, as one of the few forms of readily salable property planters owned, enslaved people alike.

Having thanked Mrs. Demelly for her account of Joanna, in whose eye glittered the precious pearl of sympathy, I took my leave, and went to my lodging in a state of sadness and stupefaction. However trifling and romantic this relation may appear to some, it is nevertheless a genuine account. On that score, I flatter myself that it may not entirely be uninteresting to others.

When reflecting on the state of slavery altogether, my ears were stunned with the clang of the whip and the dismal yells of the wretched negroes on whom it was used from morning until night. Considering that this might one day be the fate of the unfortunate mulatto I described, should she fall into the hands of a tyrannical master or mistress, I could not help execrating the barbarity of Mr. D. B. He withheld her from a fond parent, who, by bestowing on her a decent education and some accomplishments, would probably have produced, in this forsaken plant—now exposed to every rude blast without protection—an ornament to civilized society.[33]

I became melancholy with these reflections. In order to counterbalance, though in a very small degree, the general calamity of the miserable slaves who surrounded me, I began to take more delight in the prattling of my poor negro boy Quaco than in all the fashionable conversation of the polite inhabitants of this colony. My spirits were depressed, and in the space of twenty-four hours I was very ill indeed. When a cordial, a few preserved tamarinds, and a basket of fine oranges, were sent by an unknown person, this first contributed to my relief. Then, after losing about twelve ounces of blood, I recovered.[34] So much so that on the fifth I was able, for change of air, to accompany a Captain MacNeil, who gave me a pressing invitation to his beautiful coffee plantation, called Sporksgift, in the Matapacca Creek.

In the next three paragraphs, Stedman described tamarinds and their medicinal properties.

We now set out from Paramaribo for plantation Sporksgift, in a tent-boat or barge, rowed by eight of the best negroes belonging to Mr. MacNeil's estate. Everybody, as I have already mentioned, travels by water in this colony.

These barges I cannot better describe than by comparing them with those that accompany what is usually styled the Lord Mayor's Show on the river Thames.[35]

---

33. Here, Stedman compares Joanna to a plant. She had been carefully tended early in life and given an education, which began the process of "civilizing" her. However, because of Mr. D. B.'s cruelty and irresponsibility, her education would be neglected, and she would revert to the allegedly "savage" ways of people of African descent.

34. Stedman had been bled, a common medical practice used in the eighteenth century to treat many different disorders.

35. Stedman wrote for a largely British audience and used comparisons to Britain and the British Empire throughout the text. Here, he referenced the Lord Mayor's Show, an annual parade held in London to mark the inauguration of a new Lord Mayor. Today it is a street parade, but in the eighteenth century, it was a boat parade on the River Thames.

They are, however, somewhat smaller, though some are very magnificent, and are often decorated with gilded flags, filled with musicians, and abound in every convenience. They are sometimes rowed by ten and even by twelve oars, and being lightly built, sweep along with astonishing swiftness. The rowers never stop, from the moment they set out until the company is landed at the place of destination. They continue, the tide serving or not, to tug night and day, sometimes for twenty-four hours together, singing a chorus all the time to keep up their spirits. When their labor is over, their naked bodies still dripping with sweat, like post-horses, they headlong, one and all, plunge into the river to refresh themselves:

> The wanton courser thus, with reins unbound,
> Breaks from his stall, and beats the trembling ground;
> Pamper'd and proud, he seeks the wonted tides,
> And laves in height of blood his shining sides.[36]

We now passed a number of fine plantations, but I could not help taking particular notice of the cacao estate, called Alkmaar, situated on the right side in rowing up the river Commewijne. It is no less conspicuous for its beauty than for the goodness of its proprietor, the invaluable widow Godefroy, whose humanity and friendship must always be remembered by me with gratitude.

At our arrival on the estate Sporksgift, I had the pleasure to be the spectator of an instance of justice which afforded me the greatest satisfaction.

The scene consisted of Mr. MacNeil's firing the overseer and ordering him to immediately depart from the plantation in an inferior boat, called a *ponkee*,[37] to Paramaribo, or wherever he thought proper. The cause of his disgrace was having, by bad usage and cruelty, caused the death of three or four negroes. His departure was made completely joyful to all the slaves and celebrated with a holiday, which was spent in festivity by dancing and clapping hands on a green before the dwelling-house windows.

The overseer's sentence was the more ignominious and galling as at the time of receiving it a negro foot-boy, who was buckling his shoes was ordered back and he had to buckle them himself. The spirited conduct of this planter, the joy of his negroes, the salubrity of the country air, and the hospitable manner in which we were entertained at his estate had such an effect on my constitution and my spirits that on the ninth I returned if not recovered at least

---

36. In this poem, Stedman takes his comparison of the rowers to horses a step further, indulging his readers with a metaphorical allusion. Stedman composed poems throughout his narrative. They, like this one, are largely rhetorical flourish but were common in travel literature, and some readers may have expected them. Nevertheless, his poetry is largely superfluous to the narrative as a whole, and Stedman used it to show he was intellectual and cultured.

37. Original footnote: A ponkee is a flat-bottomed boat of four or six oars, something like a square-toed shoe: sometimes it has a tilt, and sometimes not.

greatly benefited to Paramaribo. But I should be guilty of partiality if I do not relate one instance, which throws a shade over the humanity even of my friend MacNeil.

Having observed a handsome young negro walk very lamely, while the others were capering and dancing, I inquired into the cause of his crippled appearance. I was informed by this gentleman that the negro had repeatedly ran away from his work and MacNeil had been obliged to hamstring him. This operation is performed by cutting through the large tendon above one of the heels. However severe this instance of despotism may appear, it is nothing when compared with some barbarities which the task I have undertaken will oblige me, at the expense of my feelings, to relate.

On our return to the town of Paramaribo, the only news that occurred consisted in a few shocking executions. The *Boreas*, a man-of-war under Captain Van de Velde had sailed for Holland. Colonel Fourgeoud had on the eighth, the Prince of Orange's anniversary, entertained a large company with a ball *en militaire*, in the officers' guardroom. The music on this occasion consisted of two fiddlers only, who had the conscience to make the colonel pay one hundred and twenty Dutch florins for rosin and catgut.[38]

About this time I was attacked by a distemper called the *prickly heat* (by the colonists, *rootvont*). It begins by the skin turning a color like scarlet—caused by a number of small pimples—and itching inconceivably. Under the garters or any place where the circulation is impeded, the itching is almost insufferable.[39]

With this pest all newcomers from Europe are soon infested. The cure is to bathe the parts with the juice of limes and water similar to the treatment for the bites of gnats or mosquitoes. The prickly heat is supposed to be a prognostic of good health by the inhabitants. I have reason to think this true, since from that period my health and spirits were perfectly re-established and I was once more as happy as Paramaribo could make me.

At this time Colonel Fourgeoud set out with a barge to inspect the situation of the rivers Commewijne and Cottica in case the actual service of our troops should soon be wanted. At his departure, he was saluted by the guns from Fort Zeelandia and by those of the ships in the river. This compliment I acknowledge astonished me after the coolness which took place and was now rooted between this gentleman and the governor of the colony.

As we were still in a state of inaction, I made another excursion with a Mr. Charles Rynsdorp. He rowed me in his barge to five beautiful coffee estates and one sugar plantation on the Matapacca, Paramarica, and Werapa Creeks. I must defer the description of them to another occasion. At one of them called

---

38. Stedman listed this as one of the two "shocking executions" because the fiddlers charged an exorbitant amount of money for the supplies needed for their fiddles. It added to the list of reasons Stedman believed Fourgeoud exercised poor judgment.

39. Prickly heat is a skin rash caused by sweat trapped under clogged pores.

Schovnort, however, I was the witness to a scene of barbarity which I cannot help relating.

The victim of this cruelty was a fine old negro slave. He thought he had been undeservedly sentenced to receive some hundred lashes by the lacerating whips of two negro drivers.[40] In the midst of the execution, he pulled out a knife, which, after having made a fruitless thrust at his persecutor the overseer, he plunged up to the haft in his own bowels, repeating the blow till he dropped down at the tyrant's feet. After he recovered, he was condemned to be chained to the furnace which distils the *kill-devil*.[41] There he was kept in the intense heat of a perpetual fire night and day, being blistered all over until he should expire by infirmity or old age—the latter of which however he had but little chance. He shewed me his wounds with a smile of contempt, which I returned with a sigh and a small donation. Nor shall I ever forget the miserable man, who, like Cerberus, was loaded with irons and chained to everlasting torment.[42] As for everything else I observed in this little tour, I must acknowledge it to be elegant and splendid and my reception hospitable beyond my expectation. But these Elysian fields could not dissipate the gloom which the infernal furnace had left upon my mind.

[…] We now once more, on the sixth of April, returned safe to Paramaribo […] This day, dining at the house of my friend, Mr. Lolkens, to whom I had been, as I have said, recommended by letters, I was an eyewitness of the unpardonable contempt with which negro slaves are treated in this colony. His son, a boy not more than ten years old, when sitting at table, gave a slap in the face to a grey-headed Black woman, who by accident touched his powdered hair as she was serving from a dish of kerry.[43] I could not help blaming his father for overlooking the action. Lolkens told me, with a smile, that the child should no longer offend me as he was next day to sail for Holland for education. I answered that I thought it almost too late. At the same moment, a sailor

---

40. Drivers, called *bassia* in Suriname, were enslaved men placed in charge of gangs of enslaved workers on plantations. It was their job to keep enslaved people working and maintain the peace on plantations. They were also responsible for disciplining, often using a whip, recalcitrant slaves, or those believed not to be working hard enough. It was one of the few positions of leadership that enslaved men could aspire to in a slave society and often carried prestige and respect from both the slave community and white overseers and planters.

41. Original footnote: *Kill-devil* is a species of rum which is distilled from the scum and dregs of sugar cauldrons. This is much drunk in the colony and the only spirits allowed the negroes; many Europeans also, from a point of economy, make use of it, to whom it proves no better than a slow but fatal poison.

42. Cerberus was the dog-like creature that guarded the gates of the underworld in Greek mythology.

43. It seems Stedman's reference to a "dish of kerry" refers to heavy Irish stoneware used as serving dishes in Lolkens's household.

passing by broke the head of a negro with a bludgeon for not having saluted him with his hat. Such is the state of slavery, at least in this Dutch settlement!

About this time, Colonel Fourgeoud made a second excursion and now departed with a barge to explore the banks and situation of the Suriname River, as he had before done those of Commewijne and Cottica Rivers.

At this time died Captain Barends, one of the masters of the transports, which were still kept in commission, in case they should be wanted for our return to Europe. Five or six sailors belonging to the merchant ships were now buried every day, whose lamentable fate I cannot pass by unnoticed. They are actually used worse than the negroes in this scorching climate. Besides rowing large flat-bottomed barges up and down the rivers, day and night, for coffee, sugar, etc., being exposed to the burning sun and heavy rains, and stowing the above commodities in a hold as hot as an oven, they are obliged to row every upstart planter to his estate at a call. This saves the gentleman so many negroes and for which the sailors receive in return nothing—many times not so much as a mouthful of meat and drink. They palliate hunger and thirst by begging from the slaves a few bananas or plantains, eating oranges, and drinking water, which in a little time relieves them from every complaint by shipping them off to eternity. In every part of the colony they are no better treated, but, like horses, they must (having unloaded the vessels) drag the commodities to the distant storehouses, being bathed in sweat and bullied with bad language, sometimes with blows. While a few negroes are ordered to attend, but not to work, by the direction of their masters. Many would willingly do to relieve the drooping sailors to whom this usage must be exceedingly disheartening and galling. The planters even employ those men to paint their houses, clean their sash-windows, and do numberless other menial services for which a seaman was never intended. All this is done to save the work of their negroes. By this usage thousands are swept to the grave, who in the line of their profession alone might have lived for many years. Nor dare the West India captains refuse to offer their men without incurring the displeasure of the planters and seeing their ships rot in the harbor without loading. Nay, I have heard a sailor fervently wish he had been born a negro and beg to be employed amongst them in cultivating a coffee plantation.

I now took an early opportunity to enquire of Mrs. Demelly what had become of the amiable Joanna. I was informed that her lady, Mrs. D. B. had escaped to Holland on board the *Boreas* man-of-war under the protection of Captain Van de Velde and that her young mulatto was now at the house of her aunt, a free woman. She expected hourly to be sent up to the estate Fauconberg, friendless and at the mercy of some unprincipled overseer appointed by the creditors, who had now taken possession of the plantation and stock until the whole should be sold to pay the several sums due to them by Mr. D. B. Good God! I flew to the spot in search of poor Joanna and found her bathed in tears. She gave me such a look—ah! such a look! From that moment I determined to be her protector against every insult and eventually persevered. Here, reader, let my youth, blended with extreme sensibility, plead my excuse. Yet assuredly my feelings will be forgiven me—by those few only excepted—who delight in the *prudent* conduct of Mr. *Incle*, to the hapless and much-injured *Yarico* at Barbados.[44]

I next ran to the house of my friend Lolkens, who happened to be the administrator of Fauconberg estate. Asking his assistance, I intimated to him my strange determination of purchasing and educating Joanna.

Having recovered from his surprise, after gazing at me silently for some time, an interview at once was proposed. The beauteous slave, accompanied by a female relation, was produced trembling in my presence.

Reader, if you have perused the tale of Lavinia with pleasure, though the scene admits of no comparison, reject not the history of Joanna with contempt.[45] It now proved to be she who had privately sent me the cordial and the oranges in March when I was nearly expiring. She now modestly acknowledged she "was in gratitude for my expressions of compassion respecting her sad situation."[46] With singular delicacy, however, she rejected every proposal of becoming mine upon any terms. She was conscious, she said:

> "That in such a state should I soon return to Europe, she must either be parted from me forever or accompany me to a part of the world where the inferiority of her condition must prove greatly to the disadvantage of both herself and her benefactor and thus in either case be miserable."[47]

In these sentiments Joanna firmly persisting, she was immediately permitted to withdraw and return to the house of her aunt. I could only intreat of

---

44. "Mr. Incle" and "Yarico" were the two lead characters in the popular 1787 comic opera *Inkle and Yarico*, about an English merchant, Inkle, shipwrecked in the West Indies, who is aided and falls in love with an Amerindian woman named Yarico. Musician Samuel Arnold composed the music, while dramatist George Colman wrote the libretto or text of the opera. The story is, in part at least, based on actual events. Richard Ligon, an English merchant and speculator most famous for writing an early history of Barbados, recounted the life and experiences of an enslaved Amerindian woman named Yarico, who lived in his household and was most likely his concubine. See Richard Ligon, *A True and Exact History of the Island of Barbados*, ed. Karen Ordahl Kupperman (Indianapolis: Hackett Publishing, 2011), 107.

45. Lavinia was the wife of Aeneas, the hero of the ancient epic recounting the birth of Rome, the *Aeneid*. In the poem, she had many suitors from Italy but knew she was destined to marry a stranger and for greatness. Stedman's allusion to Lavinia suggested that Joanna was likewise destined to reside with a foreigner.

46. Readers should be skeptical of Stedman's direct quotations. He rarely recorded them in his diary and often relied on his faulty memory to compose them.

47. This is the first time that Joanna rejected Stedman's advances, especially any suggestion that she would leave Suriname and reside with him in Europe.

Mr. Lolkens his generous protection for her, that she might at least for some time be separated from the other slaves, and continue to reside in Paramaribo. In this request, his humanity was induced to indulge me.

On the 30th the news arrived, that the rangers, having discovered a rebel village, had attacked it, and carried off three prisoners, leaving four others dead upon the spot, whose right hands, chopped off and barbecued or smoke-dried, they had sent to the governor of Paramaribo as a proof of their valor and fidelity.[48]

On receiving this intelligence, Colonel Fourgeoud immediately left the river Suriname, where he still was and on the first of May returned to town in expectation of his regiment being employed on actual service. There the business ended, however, and we still, to our utter astonishment, were allowed to linger away our time, each agreeably to his own peculiar fancy. On the 4th of May, the rangers were reviewed in the Fort Zeelandia, I was present at the ceremony and must confess that this corps of Black soldiers had a truly manly appearance They were warriors whose determined and open aspect could not but give me the satisfaction of a soldier in beholding them. They once more received the thanks of the governor for their manly behavior and faithful conduct, particularly at the taking of Boucou.[49] They were entertained with a feast, at the public expense, at Paramaribo, to which were also invited their families. At the feast several respectable people of both sexes made their appearance with pleasure to witness the happiness of their sable friends. The day being spent in mirth and conviviality, without the least disturbance, nay even with decorum and propriety, to the great satisfaction of the inhabitants.

The *Westellingwerf*, Captain Crass, now left the river also, bound for Holland, but first for the colony of Demerara. Thus both ships of war having sailed without us, there was some reason to suppose we were soon to be employed on actual service. There were many motives, indeed, for wishing either that this might be the case or that we might speedily be permitted to return to Europe. Not only our officers, but our privates began to feel the debilitating effects of the climate and many of that continued debauchery so common in all ranks in this settlement. And as hard labor and bad treatment constantly killed the poor sailors, so now our common soldiers fell the victims of idleness and licentiousness and died frequently six or seven in a day. Whence it is evident to demonstration that all excesses, of whatever kind, are mortal to Europeans in the climate of Guiana.

But men will give lessons which they do not themselves observe. Thus, notwithstanding my former resolution of living retired, I again relapsed into the vortex of dissipation. I became a member of a drinking club, I partook of all

---

48. To prove that they had carried out a successful attack and collected a bounty, the Rangers had to either bring captives taken in battle or the right hands of their victims.

49. Boucou was a rebel stronghold.

polite and impolite amusements, and plunged into every extravagance without exception. I did not, however, escape without the punishment I deserved. I was seized suddenly with a dreadful fever. Such was its violence that in a few days I was no more expected to recover. In this situation, I lay in my hammock until the 17th with only a soldier and my Black boy to attend me, and without any other friend. Sickness being universal among the new-comers to this country and every one of our corps having so much to do to take care of themselves, neglect was an inevitable consequence even among the nearest acquaintance. This, however, is a censure which does not apply to the inhabitants, who perhaps are the most hospitable people on the globe to Europeans. These philanthropists not only supply the sick with a variety of cordials at the same time, but crowd their apartments with innumerable condolers who from morning until night continue prescribing, insisting, bewailing, and lamenting friend and stranger without exception. This lasts until the patient becomes delirious and expires. Such must inevitably have been my case between the two extremes of neglect and importunity. Had it not been for the happy intervention of poor Joanna, who one morning entered my apartment to my unspeakable joy and surprise, accompanied by one of her sisters. She informed me that she was acquainted with my forlorn situation and that if I still entertained for her the same good opinion, her only request was that she might wait upon me until I recovered. I indeed gratefully accepted her offer. By her unremitting care and attention, I had the good fortune so far to regain my health and spirits as to be able, in a few days after, to take an airing in Mr. Kennedy's carriage.

Until this time, I had chiefly been Joanna's friend. Now I began to feel I was her captive. I renewed my wild proposals of purchasing, educating, and transporting her to Europe, which, though offered with the most perfect sincerity, were rejected once more, with this humble declaration:

> "I am born a low contemptible slave. Were you to treat me with too much attention, you must degrade yourself with all your friends and relations. The purchase of my freedom you will find expensive, difficult, and apparently impossible. Yet though a slave, I have a soul, I hope, not inferior to that of an European and blush not to avow the regard I retain for you, who have distinguished me so much above all others of my unhappy birth. You have, Sir, pitied me. Now, independent of every other thought, I shall have pride in throwing myself at your feet until fate shall part us or my conduct become such as to give you cause to banish me from your presence."

This she uttered with a down-cast look and tears dropping on her heaving bosom while she held her companion by the hand.

From that instant, this excellent creature was mine. Nor had I ever after cause to repent of the step I had taken as will more particularly appear in the course of this narrative.

I cannot omit to record, that having purchased for her presents to the value of twenty guineas, I was the next day greatly astonished to see all my gold returned upon my table.[50] The charming Joanna having carried every article back to the merchants, who cheerfully returned her the money.

> "Your generous intentions alone, sir, (she said) were sufficient. Allow me to tell you, that I cannot help considering any superfluous expense on my account as a diminution of that good opinion which I hope you have and will ever entertain, of my disinterested disposition."

Such was the language of a slave, who had simple nature only for her instructor, the purity of whose sentiments stood in need of no comment, and these I was now determined to improve by every care.

I shall now only add, that a regard for her superior virtues, so singular amongst her cast, gratitude for her particular attention to me, and the pleasure of producing to the world such an accomplished character under the appearance of a slave could alone embolden me to risk the censure of my readers, by intruding on them this subject. Let this be my apology, and if it be accepted but by few, I shall not be inclined to complain.[51]

In the evening I visited Mr. Demelly, who, with his lady, congratulated me on my recovery from sickness. At the same time, however strange it may appear to many readers, they, with a smile, wished me joy of what, with their usual good-humor, they were pleased to call my conquest. One of the ladies in company assured me, while it was perhaps censured by some, was applauded by many and, she believed in her heart, envied by all. A decent wedding, at which many of our respectable friends made their appearance, and at which I was as happy as any bridegroom ever was, concluded the ceremony. I shall beg leave to conclude a chapter, which, methinks I hear many readers whisper, had better never had a beginning.[52]

---

50. Stedman's reference to purchasing Joanna's companionship, the first mention of it in the *Narrative*, shows how he aggressively courted Joanna. Twenty guineas, or twenty-one pounds sterling, was a substantial sum of money in the eighteenth century.
51. Stedman worried about how his relationship with Joanna, a mixed-race woman, would be perceived by his readers. By transforming her into a paragon of virtue and innocence, he attempted to alleviate the audience's concerns. As his diary shows, however, Stedman's relationship was much more fraught.
52. Stedman referenced his "wedding" in his diary on May 8, 1773. Under the law, enslaved people were not allowed to marry, meaning the ceremony's purpose was to formalize the concubinage between Stedman and Joanna. The mention of the wedding here is once more trying to assuage his readers, who, as the last sentence implies, Stedman believed would judge him for his relationship with Joanna.

Chapter VIII

Three Estates burnt, and the Inhabitants murdered by the Rebels—Real Picture of Misery and Distress—Specimen of a March through the Woods of Suriname—Colonel Fourgeoud and the remaining Troops leave Paramaribo

Chapter VIII opened with Stedman in the field. More men perished while he struggled with fever and other illnesses. In this chapter, the reader learns of the difficulties of jungle combat and the terror Stedman experienced. Death and disease stalked Stedman and his men, and rumors circulated about the maroons being near, infusing the relatively mundane patrols and guard duty with paranoia and uneasiness. Moreover, adapting to fighting in the jungle required learning new tactics and maneuvers. In detail, Stedman explained how he and his men had to march through the bush while exposing its grim realities. Stedman also reported additional attacks by the maroons and demonstrated a keen understanding of their strategies, yet, at this point in the Narrative, *did not have the manpower or ability to confront them. Facing adverse conditions and frustrated by his inability to strike at the maroons, Stedman continued to be critical of Colonel Fourgeoud. Finally, toward the end of the chapter, the reader learns of Stedman's propensity for violence when he confronts one of his sergeants. His brutality is ever-present in his diary, but Stedman only intermittently detailed it in the* Narrative.

On the 27th of August, I relieved Captain Orzinga with his men and took the command of Devil's Harwar. Having been on board the *Charon* exactly fifty-six days,[53] in the most wretched condition that can be described, I now hoped to get better with the help of a few refreshments, such as milk, etc., which could not be obtained in our former situation. The Society troops (above one hundred in number) were going to set off next day with my empty barges to La Rochelle in Patamacca. I reviewed my marines and I found I only had left two officers (out of five), who were both sick, the three others being dead. I had also only one sergeant, two corporals, and fifteen privates, out of fifty-four healthy men, who embarked with me on the 2nd day of last July. This army was not more than sufficient to defend the hospital (which was crowded with sick), the ammunition, and victualling magazine on a spot where lately had been kept three hundred soldiers, particularly while the enemy were certainly lurking not far off. In consideration of which, the Society captain reinforced

---

53. Stedman commanded two fortified barges, the *Charon* and *Cerberus*, which sailed the rivers and creeks in eastern Suriname hunting the maroons. Because of conditions on shore and the terrible state of military bases in the colony, Stedman and his men often lived onboard these barges for extensive amounts of time.

me with twenty of his men. The next evening, he entertained me and my two subalterns with a supper of fresh meat, roasted and boiled, to our great comfort and surprise. But which, to my unspeakable mortification, proved to be the individual poor cow with her calf on whom we had built all our hopes for a little relief. It appeared that one of his sentinels, as concerted between them, had shot it by a willful mistake.[54] Thus did Captain Orzinga, for the sake of a momentary gratification, deprive us all of that lasting comfort on which we had so much depended and of which we had so much need being altogether emaciated for want of wholesome and nutritive food.

On the morning of the 28th, the Society troops rowed to Patamacca. When examining the twenty soldiers they had left me, I noticed they proved to be the refuse of the whole part with agues, wounds, ruptures, and rotten limbs and most of them next day were obliged to enter the hospital.

On the 29th, having bastinadoed my late pilot for stealing from the soldiers, I dispatched the information to Colonel Fourgeoud that I had taken post and, acquainting him with my weak situation, requested a proper reinforcement. In the evening, two of my men died.

All things now being regulated and settled, I thanked heaven in the expectation of getting some rest, being still extremely weak. With these cheering hopes retired at 10 o'clock at night to my hammock, but this tranquility was again of short duration. Having scarcely closed my eyes, I was awaked by my sergeant, and the following letter put into my hand, sent by an express from the captain of the militia in Cottica.

> Sir,
>
> This is to acquaint you that the rebels have burnt three estates on your side: Suyingheyd, Peru, and L'Espérance. The ruins of which are still smoking and they have cut the throats of all the white inhabitants that fell in their way. As on their retreat, they must pass close by where you are posted, be on your guard. I am in haste.
>
> Your's, &c.
> (Signed) STOELMAN

Conscious of my defenseless situation, I immediately started up. The express who brought the letter having spread the news the moment of his landing, there was no necessity for beating to arms since not only the few soldiers who were well, but the whole hospital burst out. Several of them, despite of my opposition, crawling on their hands and feet to their arms, dropped dead upon the spot. May I never behold such another scene of misery and distress! Lame,

---

54. It is unclear what Stedman meant by "willful mistake," as the phrase is an oxymoron. Perhaps the soldier intended to slaughter the cow for meat, not knowing that Stedman and his men wanted her as a dairy cow.

blind, sick, and wounded, in the hope of preserving a wretched existence, rushed upon certain death! They could only, in a word, be compared to the distressed army and navy at Cartagena, commanded by the British Admiral Vernon, whom Thomson describes:

> "You, gallant Vernon, saw
> The miserable scene, you pitying saw,
> To infant weakness sunk, the warrior's arm;
> Saw the deep-racking pang, the ghastly form,
> The lip pale quivering, and the beamless eye,
> No more with ardor bright."[55]

For my own part, I was in a very weak condition indeed. However, we continued to lie all night on our arms, during which I pressed the messenger to stay in order to add one to our miserable number [...] But no enemy appearing in the morning, we buried the dead in their hammocks, not having a board to make a coffin on the whole post. In this situation, I lost all patience, and had the audacity to write to my commander. I told him that besides what had happened, my last men stood upon the brink of the grave from hardships and for want of being properly supported. The very waiters of the hospital having deserted on the moment of my arrival here, and gone to Paramaribo. Our whole number, indeed, was now melted down to twelve men, who were to protect twelve buildings with no more than two very small chests of ammunition. There was no retreat for the sick as the barges went to Patamacca and the last canoe dispatched with my letter to Colonel Fourgeoud. I had set adrift the canoe when the messenger, who was a bookkeeper of a neighboring plantation, arrived in order to prevent him or any other from making their escape. In this situation, I was now obliged to convert the slaves into soldiers. These I armed with a hatchet, not daring to trust them with a firelock.[56] For this whole night we again watched under arms and in the morning found two more of our little party dead on the ground.

---

55. This is an excerpt from Scottish poet James Thomson's (1700–1748) *Summer*. Thomson composed *Summer* as part of his larger series of poems entitled *The Seasons*. Although originally published in 1727, Thomson edited and expanded *Summer* throughout the rest of his life. The version Stedman quotes is most likely from the 1744 edition, the final one Thomson published. The excerpt refers to the Battle of Cartagena de Indias in 1741 during the War of Jenkin's Ear (1739–1748) between Great Britain and Spain. During that battle, a British military expedition commanded by Admiral Edward Vernon (1684–1757) attempted to capture Cartagena de Indias (in modern Colombia) from the Spanish. Between March and May 1741, nearly 30,000 British army and navy personnel attempted to take the city but had to withdraw due to a particularly severe outbreak of yellow fever. The British reading public would have been familiar with Stedman's references to Vernon, Cartagena, and Thomson's poetry.

56. Stedman used the term "firelock" to describe the flintlock rifles he and his men carried.

I now began really to think we were all devoted to destruction, while the men, regardless of all order (self-preservation excepted), threw out the most bitter invectives against their persecutor Fourgeoud, which I could not prevent. Nor can I help remarking the generalship of the rebel negroes, who had kept quiet until the removal of the Society troops from Devil's Harwar and seized the very first day of their departure, convinced of its being guarded only by my sick and emaciated soldiers, in order to commit their depredations on the Cottica estates. They well knew that my force was not sufficient to pursue them, nay, hardly to stand in my own defense. All this, however, was but according to my expectation. On the contrary, had my strength been sufficient, they could never have escaped at least from being cut off in their retreat, especially if the troops at Perica Creek had acted conjointly with those in Cottica by patrolling the path between the two rivers, across which the rebels were twice unavoidably obliged to pass.

On the 1st of September, we waited once more until morning and then buried another of my poor men. While I still cannot conceive how anyone was able to survive such toil in such a debilitated state and in a tropical climate, yet a few did. At length, being persuaded that the rebels must have passed the Cordon—without having thought proper to pay us a visit on their retreat—I determined to let the remaining few watch no longer, but permit them to die a natural death.[57] In the evening, when all was too late, there came down by water from the post La Rochelle to our assistance, one officer and ten men. I had but nine left to do the duty at the time of their arrival.

On the 2nd, another man died. I once more reviewed my forces, which now amounted exactly to seven marines (the few scarecrows of the Society excepted). Nevertheless, the chance of being massacred by the rebels was at this time over thanks alone to their pusillanimity or rather their hurry!

I now received a letter from Colonel Fourgeoud condoling me on the loss of so many good officers and acquainting me that I was to be reinforced. On my recommendation, my sergeant, Mr. Cubanns, was appointed an ensign, which gave me pleasure. It also took place at a very suitable time since this day my poor Ensign MacDonald was sent down very sick to Paramaribo. I answered to all this that I was obliged to the colonel adding that, while I remained without reinforcement, I could not be accountable for what consequences might happen in a place where I was left to defend a whole river with none but sick people. And even they did not have sufficient ammunition and hourly expired for want of proper medicines or a surgeon to attend them....

On the 4th, we buried another of my marines and on the following day another died. I now had not one remaining who was not ill, including one rendered unserviceable by his feet being swelled with the insects called

---

57. The "Cordon" referred to in this sentence was a footpath used by the military in Suriname for communication. It ran between the Cottica River and Perica Creek.

chigoes.[58] These poor men were mostly Germans, who had been accustomed to a healthy climate in their own country.[59] I began now to be reconciled to putting my last man underground and almost wishing to leap into the grave after him myself. Then, a barge arrived from Paramaribo with the proper reinforcement, ammunition, provisions, medicines, a surgeon, and an order from my chief to trace out the track of the rebels immediately on the former path of communication between Cottica and Perica and to write him the result of my discoveries. He intimated also that he intended to keep his magazines at Devil's Harwar and that I was not to make use of the spot I had found out for that purpose at Barbacoeba Creek....

As the manner of marching in this country is so very different from that in Europe, I shall, before we set out, endeavor briefly to describe the nature of these expeditions.

In the first place, in Suriname marching in ranks is impractical. Thus, there is no marching by divisions or platoons. Rather, the whole party being dressed in one rank, face to the right, and every man follows his leader with the negro slaves interspersed between the men in order to guard their persons as well as what they carry. This manner of marching is called Indian file. For a detachment of sixty men, consisting of one captain, two subalterns, two sergeants, four corporals, one surgeon, and fifty privates, twenty negro slaves at least ought to be employed. For their use, their masters are paid at the rate of two shillings sterling a day by the colony. This is a much greater expense than wagons and horses would be, but in this country those cannot be employed for military service.

The manner of interspersing the slaves and the troops is as follows. The foremost are generally two negroes with billhooks to cut a way and make a practicable path. One corporal and two men to reconnoiter the front, and, in case of necessity, to give the alarm. One subaltern,[60] six privates, and a corporal form the vanguard. Then follows, at some distance, the corps in two divisions. In the first, one captain, one corporal, twelve privates, one surgeon, and two negroes to carry the powder. In the second is one sergeant and twelve privates. And then again follows, at some distance, the rear guard consisting of one subaltern, one sergeant, one corporal, and eighteen privates with sixteen negroes to carry the medicines, beef, bread, spades, axes, rum, etc. The sick also are carried. The three last of all being one corporal and two men at a distance to give the

---

58. Chigoes, also known as jiggers and sand fleas, are a type of parasitic flea native to Central and South America. An infestation by female chigoes causes tungiasis, an inflammatory skin disease that is exceptionally painful. Given that chigoes often live on the ground, tungiasis commonly afflicts the foot, which is what happened to Stedman's marine.

59. Throughout the sixteenth, seventeenth, and eighteenth centuries, the Dutch recruited large numbers of Germans for their armed forces, and their inclusion among Stedman's troops is unsurprising.

60. A noncommissioned officer such as a sergeant.

alarm in case of an attack as the others had orders to do in the front, which ends the train.

Everything being ready, according to the above rules, for my small party, which consisted of myself, an officer of the Society, Mr. Hertsbergh, one surgeon's mate, one guide, two sergeants, two corporals, forty privates, and only eight negro slaves to cut open the passage and carry the baggage. We faced to the right at six o'clock in the morning and sallied forth into the woods, keeping our course directly for the Perica River. Having marched until about 11 o'clock on the Cordon, I discovered, as I had expected, the track of the rebels by the marks of their footsteps in the mud, by the broken bottles, plantain peels, etc., and found that by appearance it bore towards Pinenburgh, already mentioned.

I had now indeed found the nest, but the birds had flown. We continued our march until eight o'clock when we arrived at the Society post Scribo in Perica in a most shocking condition. We had waded through water and mire above our hips, climbed over heaps of fallen trees, and crept underneath on our bellies. This, however, was not the worst, for our flesh was terribly mangled and torn by the thorns and stung by the patat lice, ants, and *wassee-wassee*, or wild bees....

The worst of our sufferings, however, was the fatigue of marching in a burning sun and the last two hours in total darkness, holding each other by the hand. We ended up having to leave ten men behind, some with agues, some stung blind, and some with their feet full of chigoes. Being in the most hospitable manner received at Scribo by the commanding officer, I went to my hammock very ill of a fever.

On the following morning, I felt myself better for my night's rest. Neither myself nor my men, however, were able to march back. The other captain sent a small party of his soldiers to pick up the poor marines I had lost the day before and of whom they brought with them seven, carried in hammocks tied to poles, each by two negroes, the other three having scrambled back to Devil's Harwar.

During our stay here I wrote a letter to Colonel Fourgeoud, couched in such terms as few people in their full senses would do to their commanders. I told him I had found the path, that if I had had support in time I might have cut off the enemy's retreat, but instead found their foot-steps only. But now it was all too late and the party all knocked up to no purpose. This letter, I have been since told, incensed him as it is easy to suppose in the highest degree. Being sufficiently refreshed to renew my march, we left Scribo on the 9th at four o'clock in the morning and at four o'clock PM arrived, after indescribable sufferings, at Devil's Harwar. We were covered over with mud and blood, and our legs and thighs cut and torn by the thorns and branches. Most of the men did not have shoes and stockings, while I, who had gone this march in the same condition from choice, had absolutely suffered the least of the whole party by having inured myself gradually by walking barefooted on the barges.

At Devil's Harwar, I now found Lieutenant Colonel Westerloo and a quartermaster arrived to take the command.[61] His troops were not expected until the next day. I was by this circumstance, however, made exceedingly happy and hoped at last to meet with some relief. Having ceded him my written orders, the magazine, hospital, etc., I stripped and plunged into the river to wash myself and take a swim. Being before much over-heated, I found myself greatly refreshed. I also received a quantity of fine fruit, Jamaica rum, wine and sugar, from Joanna. But how did my blood chill when the quartermaster told me a secret. My sergeant, one Fowler, having first got drunk with my wine, offered violence to this poor woman.[62] He was to be at Devil's Harwar the next day and I would see the marks of her just resentment on his face!

The reader will, I trust, excuse my violence, when I tell him, that I vowed immediate destruction to the villain. I ordered a negro to cut twelve bamboo canes, and retired like a person deprived of his senses, determined to punish him according to his supposed crime.

On the 10th there arrived two subalterns, with a second barge full of men, ammunition, medicine, and provisions. After having the men marched into quarters and the goods stowed, I sent for the hapless Fowler, whose face was in three places wounded, I locked him up in a room, and, without asking one question, broke six of the bamboos over his head until he escaped all bloody out at the window and my resentment gradually abated.

He certainly had suffered much, but nothing equal to what were my sensations after being further informed that Colonel Fourgeoud had seized all my effects. He had sealed and locked them up in an empty storeroom in expectation of my decease, which, according to all appearances, might be looked for. My house was given to another by which means I could not procure so much as a clean shirt to relieve me from my disgraceful tatters. Nevertheless, by the hope of going down myself, my spirits were supported.

The other news of more importance was that the hero in person—with most of the troops—had at last left Paramaribo.[63] He had quartered them at Devil's Harwar in Rio Cottica, the estate Bellaiz in Rio Perica, and at the estates Charenbeck and Crawassibo in Rio Commewijne. Conjunctly with the troops of the Society and the Rangers, he intended to move in quest of the rebels. He had also ordered all the barges to be relieved at last and their remaining troops to reinforce the above-mentioned posts, which I must remark was a very wise and well-planned regulation.

From Patamacca, we were informed that the rebels, on their repassing the river above La Rochelle, had again destroyed a small estate and murdered its proprietor, a Mr. Nyboor.

---

61. A quartermaster was the officer in charge of supplies and logistics.
62. I.e., Joanna.
63. Stedman used the phrase "hero in person" to describe Fourgeoud.

It was either about this time, or very shortly after, that an overseer escaped by the assistance of a negro boy, who, desiring him to leap into a canoe and lie down flat upon his belly, leaped himself into the water. By swimming with one hand and guiding the canoe with the other, he ferried his master safe over Patamacca Creek through a shower of musket bullets. The rebels fired upon them all the while, but without execution. However, for this material piece of service, he was recompensed the week after with three hundred lashes by the same master for having forgotten to open one of the sluices or floodgates.

On this act of inhumanity, I shall make no comment, but proceed to my own miserable situation. Having remonstrated with Lieutenant Colonel Westerloo on the state of my health, which disabled me from joining the corps on their march, I requested that I might be removed to Paramaribo for the chance of recovery. He peremptorily refused to allow me by Colonel Fourgeoud's express command. The refusal of such a reasonable a request made me almost distracted and agitated my spirits so much that on the morning of the 12th, I determined to exchange my wretched existence one way or other. I insisted on being immediately removed or wished for *death*, which the surgeons declared must be the consequence soon if I was not permitted to go down. In the meanwhile, I vowed that I should attribute my decease to their unprecedented barbarity. A consultation was now held on the subject and, at last, not without great difficulties, a boat was ordered to row me down to Paramaribo, but no white servant was permitted to attend me.[64] Thus leaving the Lieutenant Colonel employed in fortifying Devil's Harwar with palisades and where there was also now a numerous garrison. At noon, I walked to the waterside, supported by a negro, on whose shoulder I rested, until I at length stepped into the boat, followed by my Black boy Quaco, and finally left the diabolical spot where I had buried so many brave fellows.

On the 14th, having rowed day and night, we arrived in Paramaribo at two o'clock in the morning. I was extremely ill indeed. Having no residence of my own, I was hospitably received at the house of a Mr. de la Marre, a merchant. This gentleman not only received me, but immediately sent a servant for poor Joanna, who was at her mother's, and another for a physician to attend me as my weak and hopeless condition now required every assistance that the town of Paramaribo could afford.

---

64. Not being allowed the use of a white servant, who would have most likely been a soldier, was a sign of Westerloo's discomfort with disobeying Fourgeoud. Traveling without other soldiers offered evidence to show Stedman acted alone. It also meant that his absence would not take other soldiers out of the field.

Chapter XIII

A Sugar Plantation described—Domestic Happiness in a Cottage—Further Account of Fourgeoud's Operations—Dreadful Cruelties inflicted by some Overseers—Instance of Resentment in a Rebel Negro Captain

Chapter XIII took place during what Stedman called "the golden age of my West India expedition." In Chapters IX–XII, he largely recounted more troop movements and some minor successes the soldiers had against the maroons. Chapter XIII details Stedman's stay at L'Espérance ("The Hope," in English), a sugar plantation on the upper Commewijne River. Despite Stedman's personal happiness in this chapter, he included vivid, horrifying descriptions of the brutalities and abuses of slavery, especially those inflicted by plantation overseers. Stedman also described how a sugar plantation operated and offered a more nuanced picture of Colonel Fourgeoud. That said, Stedman himself is fairly content throughout the chapter. He had a comfortable home built for himself and Joanna at Hope, and she was able to join him. This was their first time living together in their own space. He was also optimistic about the potential of purchasing her out of slavery. All of these factors insert some happiness and levity into an otherwise bleak and difficult story. Nevertheless, if this was the moment when Stedman was happiest, the graphic depictions of violence he included foreshadow the horror, disappointment, and sadness to come.

I have already said that I was happy at the Hope, but how was my felicity augmented when Mr. and Mrs. Lolkens came to visit me one evening. They not only gave me the address of Messrs. Passalage and Son at Amsterdam, the new proprietors of my mulatto, but even desired me to take her to the Hope where she would be more agreeably situated than either at Fauconberg or Paramaribo. This desire was unquestionably most readily complied with by me and I immediately set my slaves to work to build a house of manicole trees for her reception.[65]

In the meantime, I wrote the following letter to Messrs. Passalage and Son:

GENTLEMEN,

BEING informed by Mr. Lolkens, the administrator of the estate Fauconberg, that you are the present proprietors and being under great obligations to one of your mulatto slaves named Joanna, who is the daughter of the late Mr. Kruythoff, particularly for having attended me during sickness, I, in gratitude, request of you, who

---

65. This was one of the few instances in the *Narrative* where Stedman mentioned owning slaves.

are her masters, to let me purchase her liberty without delay. That favor shall be ever thankfully acknowledged and the money for her ransom immediately paid, by

Gentlemen,
Your most obedient servant,
JOHN GABRIEL STEDMAN,
Captain in Colonel Fourgeoud's
Corps of Marines

This letter was accompanied by another from my friend Lolkens, who much cheered my prospects by the assurance of success.

Having dispatched these letters to Holland, I had now the opportunity of observing the whole process of a sugar plantation and shall endeavor to give an accurate description.

The buildings usually consist of an elegant dwelling house for the planter, outhouses for the overseer and bookkeeper, a carpenter's lodge, kitchens, storehouses, and stables—if the sugar mills be wrought by horses or mules. At Hope, these are not requisite as the wheels move by water, stored in canals during the spring tide by means of sluices, which are opened at low tide and pour out like a deluge, setting the machinery in motion. A sugar mill is built at the expense of four thousand, nay, sometimes seven or eight thousand pounds.

A particular description of its construction might be too tedious. I shall only observe that the large waterwheel moves perpendicularly, corresponds with another large wheel placed in a horizontal direction, and this again acts upon three cylinders or rollers of cast iron supported underneath by a strong beam. These cylinders are so close together that when the whole is in motion, they draw in and squeeze as thin as paper whatever comes between them. In this manner the sugarcane is ground to separate the juice, called liquor, from the trash.

Those mills that are wrought by cattle are constructed upon the same principles, only the horses or mules answer the purpose of the horizontal wheel by dragging round a large lever. If the watermills work the fastest and are the cheapest, they must wait for the tides and can only work part of the day. Whereas the cattle mills are always ready whenever the proprietor finds it convenient to use them. Adjoining to the millhouse is a large apartment, also built of brick, in which are fixed the coppers or large cauldrons to boil the liquid sugar. These are usually five in number. Opposite to these are the coolers, which are large square flat-bottomed wooden vessels into which the sugar is put from the cauldrons to cool before it is put into hogsheads. These are placed near the coolers upon strong channeled rafters that receive the molasses as it drops from the sugar and convey it into a square cistern placed underneath to receive it. The distillery joins this apartment, where the dross or scum of the boiling sugar is converted into a kind of rum, mentioned before, and known by the name of *kill-devil*. Every estate in Suriname keeps a tent-boat and several other craft for the conveyance of their produce. They have also a covered dock to keep them dry and repair them.

The sugar estates in this colony contain five or six hundred acres. The parts for cultivation being divided into squares, where pieces of cane, about one foot long, are stuck into the ground in an oblique position in rows straight and parallel. They usually plant them in the rainy season when the earth is well soaked and rich. The shoots that spring from these joints are about twelve or sixteen months in arriving at maturity. When ripe, they become yellow, of the thickness of a German flute, from six to ten feet in height, and jointed, forming a very beautiful appearance. Pale green leaves like those of a leek, but longer and denticulated, hang down as the crop becomes ready for cutting. The principal business of the slaves during the growth of the canes is pulling up the weeds, which would otherwise impoverish them.

Some sugar estates have above four hundred slaves. The expense of purchasing these, and erecting the buildings frequently amounts to 20 or 25 thousand pounds sterling, exclusive of the value of the ground.

We shall now examine its progress through the mill. Here it is bruised between the three cylinders or rollers through which it passes twice—once it enters and once it returns—when it is changed to trash and its pithy substance into liquid. The latter, after extraction, is conducted through a grooved beam from the mill to the boiling-house where it is received into a kind of wooden cistern.

So very dangerous is the work of those negroes who attend the rollers, that should one of their fingers be caught between them, which frequently happens through inadvertency, the whole arm is instantly shattered to pieces—if not part of the body.[66] A hatchet is generally kept ready to chop off the limb before the working of the mill can be stopped. Another danger is that should a poor slave dare to taste that sugar which he produces by the sweat of his brow, he runs the risk of receiving some hundred lashes or having all his teeth knocked out by the overseer. Such are the hardships and dangers to which the sugar-making negroes are exposed.

From the above wooden cistern the liquor is let into the first copper cauldron, filtering through a grating to keep back the trash that may have escaped from the mill. After having boiled some time and been skimmed, it is put into the next cauldron and so on until in the fifth or last it is brought to a proper thickness or consistency to be admitted into the coolers. A few pounds of lime and alum are thrown into the cauldrons to make it granulate. Thus, it is boiled gradually stronger and stronger until it reaches the last cauldron. When

---

66. While this accident could and did certainly occur, by the time Stedman published his *Narrative*, this way of describing the danger posed by the sugar mill was a well-worn trope in the literature about slavery and sugar plantations in the Caribbean.

it is put into the wooden coolers the sugar is well stirred and scattered equally throughout the vessels. When cold, it has a frozen appearance, being candied, of a brown glazed consistency, not unlike pieces of high polished walnut tree. From the coolers it is put into the hogsheads, which, upon an average, will hold one thousand pounds weight of sugar. There it settles and through the crevices and small holes made in the bottoms, it is purged of all its liquid contents, which are called molasses. That, as I have said, is received in an under-ground cistern. This is the last operation after which the sugar is fit for exportation to Europe where it is refined and cast into loaves. I shall only further observe that the larger the grain, the better the sugar.

No soil can be more proper for its cultivation than Guiana, the richness of which is inexhaustible and produces upon an average three or four hogsheads *per* acre. In 1771, no less than 24 thousand hogsheads were exported to Amsterdam and Rotterdam only, which, valued at six pounds per hogshead, though it has sometimes sold for double, returned a sum of near 150 thousand pounds sterling. That is in addition to the vast quantity of molasses and *kill-devil*. The first is computed at seven thousand hogsheads and sold to the North Americans for 25 thousand pounds. The second, which is distilled in Suriname and used chiefly by the negroes is valued at as much more, which produces no less than 200 thousand pounds *per annum*.[67]

> *Two strange, meandering paragraphs follow. In them, Stedman discussed who drank* kill-devil, *the utility of sugarcane trash, wild deer, and how the Dutch were probably the only group to make Suriname profitable. It seems that Stedman's editor intervened here, cut large amounts of text, and pushed what remained into two paragraphs.*

And now once more to resume my narrative. I have already mentioned that my slaves were employed in preparing a house for the reception of my best friend, which was about six days in completing. It consisted of a parlor, which also served for a dining room, a bed chamber where I also stowed my baggage, a piazza or shed to sit under before the door, a small kitchen detached from the house, and a poultry house. The whole was situated on a spot by itself, commanding an enchanting prospect on every side and surrounded with fencing to keep out the cattle. My tables, stools, and benches were all made of manicole boards. The doors and windows were guarded with ingenious wooden locks and keys that were presented me by a negro and were the work of his own hands. My house being thus far finished and furnished, my next care was to lay in a stock of provisions from Paramaribo: a barrel of flour, another of salted mackerel (which in this country are delicious—they are imported from North America), hams, pickled sausages, Boston biscuit, wine, Jamaica rum, tea, sugar, and a box of spermaceti candles. In addition, there were two charming foreign

---

67. Original footnote: The first sugar was refined in anno 1659.

sheep and a hog sent me by Mr. Kennedy from his estate Vriedyk and two dozen of fine fowls and ducks presented me by Lucretia, my Joanna's aunt. Fruit, vegetables, fish, and venison flowed upon me from every quarter as usual.

On the 1st of April 1774, Joanna came down the river in the Fauconberg tent-boat, rowed by eight negroes, and arrived at the Hope.[68] I communicated to her immediately the contents of my letter to Holland, which she received with that gratitude and modesty in her looks which spoke more forcibly than any reply. I introduced her to her new habitation, where the plantation slaves, in token of respect, immediately brought her presents of cassava, yams, bananas, and plantains, and never two people were more completely happy. Free like the deer in the forest and disencumbered of every care and ceremony, we breathed the purest ether in our walks and refreshed our limbs in the limpid stream. Health and good spirits were now again my portion, while my partner flourished in youth and beauty, the envy and admiration of all the colony.

Colonel Fourgeoud was now intending to quit the woods and encamp at Maagdenburg, a post near the source of the Commewijne. I sent a large barge with provisions, escorted by an officer and 20 men to that place. Upon reviewing my remaining marines, I found that they did not amount to 20 men besides a small detachment at Callis near the mouth of Cassiwinica Creek. Higher up the same creek at an estate called Cupy were also posted an officer and a few soldiers....

On the morning of the 8th, between six and seven o'clock while we were interring one of my sergeants, we heard the report of gunshots near the Perica River.[69] In consequence, I immediately detached an officer and twelve men to give assistance. They returned next day with an account that the rebels had attacked the estate of Kortenduur where, despite the rebels pillaging some powder, the plantation slaves, being armed by their master, had bravely beaten them back before my assistance could be of use.

A small detachment from Colonel Fourgeoud at Wana Creek arrived at the Hope on the 11th with September, the negro prisoner.[70] He related that the rebels had spoken to Fourgeoud—and even laughed at him—having overheard him giving his orders not to fire on them, but to take them alive. That amongst those lost in the woods was the unlucky Schmidt, who had lately been so unmercifully beaten and of which he had never yet recovered.

About the 13th, the spring floods broke down the dams and laid our whole post under water except the spot where I had pitched my cabin, which remained dry. Unfortunately, by this accident, the officers and men were up to the knees

---

68. Describing Joanna's arrival in this way seems to have been for dramatic effect. In his diary, Stedman noted that he went to Fauconberg, retrieved Joanna, and brought her to Hope on March 22, 1774.
69. By "report," Stedman meant that he heard gunshots.
70. Stedman recounted the capture of September in Chapter X.

in water. My worthy friend Mr. Heneman, the volunteer, arrived at this time from Colonel Fourgeoud's camp at Wana Creek with a barge full of men and ammunition and was now entered as a lieutenant in my company. He informed us that the remaining troops were marching for Maagdenburg in Upper Commewijne to go into quarters. This poor young man was much emaciated with misery and fatigue. I therefore introduced him at his first landing to the care of Joanna, who was a most incomparable nurse and under whose care he felt himself extremely happy.

On the 14th, Colonel Fourgeoud with his troops being arrived at Maagdenburg, the officers and privates of the Society and the rangers amounting to nearly 200 men were sent down in barges to be stationed on different parts of the river Perica. Some landed at the Hope to refresh and behaved so very disorderly as to oblige me and my officers to knock them down by half dozens to keep the peace until they departed the same day....[71]

Over the next four paragraphs, Stedman described some of the animals and food crops raised at Hope.

I have for some time been happily silent upon the subject of cruelty. I am sorry, at a time when all appeared harmonious and peaceable, to be under the necessity of relating some instances which I am confident must inspire the most unfeeling reader with horror and resentment. The first object which attracted my compassion during a visit to a neighboring estate. There was a beautiful sambo girl of about eighteen tied up by both arms to a tree, as naked as she came into the world. She had been lacerated in such a shocking manner by the whips of two negro drivers, that she was from her neck to her ankles literally dyed over with blood. It was after she had received two hundred lashes that I perceived her, with her head hanging downwards, a most affecting spectacle. When, turning to the overseer, I implored that she might be immediately unbound since she had undergone the whole of so severe a punishment. The short answer which I obtained was that to prevent all strangers from interfering with his government, he had made an unalterable rule to always to double the punishment. He instantaneously began to put his rule into execution. I endeavored to stop him, but in vain. He declared the delay should not alter his determination but make him take vengeance with double interest. Thus, I had no other remedy but to run to my boat and leave the detestable monster, like a beast of prey, to enjoy his bloody feast until he was glutted. From that day, I determined to break off all communication with overseers and could not refrain from bitter imprecations against the whole relentless fraternity. Upon investigating the cause of this matchless barbarity, I was credibly informed that her only crime consisted in firmly refusing to submit to the loathsome

---

71. In his diary, Stedman noted breaking his sword on one of the laborers traveling with the disorderly group. See entry for April 14, 1774.

embraces of her detestable executioner. Prompted by his jealousy and revenge, he called this the punishment of disobedience and she was thus flayed alive....

At my return to the Hope, I was accosted by Mr. Ebber, the overseer of that estate. With a woeful countenance, he informed me he had just been fined in the sum of twelve-hundred florins—about one hundred guineas—for having exercised cruelty on a male slave and the victim had died during the execution.[72] In answer to his complaint, so far from giving him consolation, I told him his distress gave me inexpressible satisfaction.

The particulars of this murder were as follow. During the time that Captain Tulling commanded here, which was a little time before I came to the Hope, it happened that a fugitive negro belonging to this estate had been taken upon an adjoining plantation, and sent home, guarded by two armed slaves, to Mr. Ebber. The fugitive, during the time Ebber was reading the letter that accompanied him, found means to again escape into the forest. This incensed the overseer so much that he instantly took revenge upon the two poor slaves that had brought him, tying them up in the carpenter's lodge. He continued flogging them so unmercifully that Captain Tulling thought proper to interfere and beg for mercy. But, as in my case, his interference produced the opposite effect. The clang of the whip mixed with their dismal cries and heard to continue for above an hour until one of them expired under the cruel lash. That put an end to the inhuman catastrophe. A lawsuit was instantly commenced against Ebber for assassination. He was convicted but condemned to no other punishment than to pay the aforementioned hundred guineas, the *price of blood* which is always divided between the fiscal and the proprietor of the deceased slave. It being a rule in Suriname that by paying a fine of five hundred florins, not quite fifty pounds per head, any proprietor is at liberty to kill as many of his own negroes as he pleases. If he kills those of his neighbor, however, he is also to pay him for the loss of his slave once the crime has been first substantiated. That is very difficult in this country where no slave's evidence can be admitted. Such is the law in Dutch Guiana in regard to negroes.

The above-mentioned Ebber was peculiarly tyrannical. He tormented a boy of about fourteen called Cadetty for the space of a whole year by flogging him every day for one month. He tied him down flat on his back with his feet in the stocks for another month. He put an iron triangle[73] or pot-hook round his neck for a third month, which prevented him from running away among the woods, or even from sleeping, except in an upright or sitting posture.

---

72. A guinea was a British gold coin worth 1.05 pounds sterling or 21 shillings, minted between 1663 and 1814. Its name was derived from gold acquired in West Africa or Guinea, as it was generically known. One hundred guineas was a very large sum of money in the eighteenth century, suggesting the severity of the overseer's crime and fine.

73. Original footnote: These triangles have three long barbed spikes, like small grapplings, projecting from an iron collar.

In the fourth month, he chained the boy to the landing-place, night and day, to a dog's kennel with orders to bark at every boat or canoe that passed. And so on, varying his punishment monthly until the youth became insensible, walking crooked, and almost degenerated into a brute. The wretch Ebber was, however, very proud of his handsomest slaves and, for fear of disfiguring their skins, he has sometimes let them off with twenty lashes when, for their robberies and crimes, they had deserved the gallows. Such is the state of public and private justice in Suriname.

Ebber left the Hope upon this occasion and his *humane* successor, a Mr. Blenderman, commenced his reign by flogging every slave belonging to the estate, male and female, for having overslept their time in the morning about fifteen minutes.[74]

The reader will, no doubt, imagine that such cruelties were unparalleled, but this is not the case. They were even exceeded and by a female too.

A Mrs. S——lk——r going to her estate in a tent-barge, a negro woman, with her sucking infant happened to be passengers, and were seated on the bow or fore-part of the boat.[75] The child crying from pain or some other reason could not be hushed. Mrs. S——lk——r, offended with the cries of this innocent little creature, ordered the mother to bring it aft and deliver it into her hands. Then, in the presence of the distracted parent, she immediately thrust it out one of the tilt-windows. She held it under water until it was drowned and then let it go. The fond mother, in a state of desperation, instantly leapt overboard into the stream, where floated her beloved offspring. She was determined to finish her miserable existence. In this, however, she was prevented by the exertions of the negroes who rowed the boat and was punished by her mistress with three or four hundred lashes for her daring temerity.

Colonel Fourgeoud moved on the 20th, with all his troops, from Maagdenburg in order to establish his headquarters nearer the infirmary. His army being in a very sickly condition, he fixed upon the estate called New Rosenback situated between the Hope and the hospital for his encampment. Thither I immediately repaired to pay my respects to the chief. I then saw the remainder of his miserable army landed and received a further detail of the campaign:...Captain Fredericy's being wounded; one man was lost by neglect and another cut and disarmed; the captives running away, chains and all; and the hero scoffed at and ridiculed by his sable enemies. I shall now add that a sick marine was left to die or recover by himself and that one of the slaves, by bad usage, had his arm broke. A captive

---

74. As in this sentence, Stedman often used italics to emphasize sarcasm.

75. It was common for eighteenth-century books to redact the names of people, especially if the content could be in any way interpreted as libelous. In the draft of the *Narrative*, Stedman wrote the woman's surname in full. It was Stolker. See Richard Price and Sally Price, eds., *Narrative of a Five Years Expedition against the Revolted Negroes of Surinam: Transcribed for the First Time from the Original 1790 Manuscript* (Baltimore, MD: Johns Hopkins University Press, 1988), 267–68.

negro woman was also gone, never more to return to her conqueror, considerably increased in size from her connection with the troops, and likely to present a new recruit to her dusky monarch....[76]

In justice to Colonel Fourgeoud, I must say that upon such expeditions and in such a climate, many of these accidents cannot be prevented. While he killed his troops by scores without making captures on the enemy, he nevertheless did the colony considerable service by disturbing, hunting, and harassing the rebels and destroying their fields and provisions. For it is certain that no negro will ever return to settle in those haunts from which he has been once expelled. Colonel Fourgeoud's partaking personally in every danger and fatigue at his age must make some amends for the other faults that stained his character and may even serve, in some measure, to establish his reputation as a man of patience and fortitude. It would give me infinitely more pleasure to write nothing but in his praise. But truth—and the general benefit of mankind—requires that whilst I display his good qualities, I also point out his failings as they may serve to correct others and by these means even his vices may be rendered useful....

On the 21st, several officers came to visit me at the Hope, whom I entertained with a fish dinner....We were very happy and my guests perfectly satisfied with their entertainment. But on the morning of the 22nd, my poor Joanna, who had been our cook, was attacked with a violent fever. She desired to be removed to Fauconberg to be attended by one of her female relations, which I complied with. By the evening of the 25th, she was so extremely ill that I determined to visit her myself but as privately as possible. Fourgeoud was to visit me at the Hope the next day and his satirical jokes upon such an occasion I could very well dispense with. I knew the most laudable motives were no protection against the ungovernable sallies of his temper.

It was a difficult undertaking to see Joanna, especially considering I had to pass close to Fourgeoud's post....I set out about eleven at night in my own barge, when coming opposite New Rosenback, I heard Fourgeoud's voice very distinctly as he walked on the beach with some other officers. Immediately, my boat was hailed by a sentinel and ordered to come ashore. I now thought all was over but persisting to the last I told the negroes to answer "Killenstein Nova"—the name of an adjoining plantation—and thus got leave to proceed unmolested. Soon after I arrived safe at Fauconberg and found my dearest friend much better.

But on the morning of the 26th, I mistook the daylight for moonlight, overslept, and knew not how to return to the Hope as my barge and negroes could now not pass without being well known to the colonel. Delay was useless, so out I set trusting entirely to the ingenuity of my slaves, who put me ashore just

---

76. Here, Stedman implied that Fourgeoud's soldiers raped a captive rebel woman and that she was pregnant.

before we came in sight of the headquarters. One of them escorted me through the woods and I arrived safe at the Hope. But here my barge soon followed under a guard and all my poor slaves prisoners with an order from Fourgeoud for me to flog every one of them as they had been apprehended without a pass, while their excuse was that they had been out fishing for their *masera*.[77]

Their fidelity to me upon this occasion was truly astonishing. They all declared they would have preferred being cut in pieces rather than betray the secrets of so good a master. However, the danger was soon over as I confirmed what they had said and added that the fish were intended to *regale the hero*. After which, I made a donation of two gallons of rum among my sable privy counselors.[78] This passage, however trifling, may serve as a sample not only of European weakness, but of African firmness and resolution.

Notwithstanding my preparation, Colonel Fourgeoud did not visit me on the 27th. The next morning, however, Joanna arrived accompanied by a stout Black man, who was her uncle and whose arm was decorated with a silver band. On it was engraved these words: "True to the Europeans." This man, who was named Cojo, voluntarily fought against the rebels before his companions, because the inhuman treatment of Mr. D. B. and his overseer, had been forced to join them. Holding a little girl, called Tamera, by the hand, he related to us a remarkable story:

> "This child's father," said Cojo, "is one whose name is Jolycoeur, the first captain of Baron's men.[79] And, not without cause, he is one of the fiercest rebels in the forest, which he has lately shown on the neighboring estate of New Rosenback where your colonel now commands. On that estate, the rebels suddenly appeared and took possession of the whole plantation, seizing one Schults, a Jew, being the manager at that time and who formerly was the manager of Fauconberg. Having tied the hands of Schults and plundered the house, they next began feasting and dancing before they thought proper to end his miserable existence. In this deplorable situation now lay the victim only waiting Baron's signal for death when his eyes chancing to catch Captain Jolycoeur's, Schults addressed him nearly in the following words: 'O Jolycoeur, now remember Mr. Schults, who was once your deputy-master. Remember the dainties I gave you from my own table when you were only a child, and my favorite, my darling, among so many others. Remember this,

---

77. I.e., master, in this case, Stedman himself.

78. This is a play on words. A privy councilor was an advisor, usually to the monarch in Britain. Here, using the spelling "counselor" as in "helper" and "privy," meaning "having access to information," Stedman showed how the enslaved rowers helped him keep his secret.

79. Baron was one of Boni's chief lieutenants.

and now spare my life by your powerful intercession.' The reply of Jolycoeur was memorable and I remember it perfectly well: 'But you, O tyrant, recollect how you ravished my poor mother and flogged my father for coming to her assistance. Recollect that the shameful act was perpetrated in my infant presence—recollect this—then die by my hands and next be damned.' Saying this, he severed his head from his body with one blow of a hatchet. With his head, Jolycoeur played at bowls upon the beach and he next cut the skin from his back with a knife, which he spread over one of the cannon to keep the priming dry."

Thus, ended the history of Mr. Schults. When Cojo and young Tamera departed, I grew impatient to receive the news that I soon was to expect from Amsterdam, i.e., when the deserving Joanna should be free from the villainy of such pests of human nature.

On the 28th, Colonel Fourgeoud arrived about 10 o'clock with one of his officers, and with the very devil painted in his countenance, which alarmed me much. I, however, instantly introduced him to my cottage where he no sooner saw my mate than the clouds (like a vapor by the sun) were dispelled from his gloomy forehead. I must confess that I never saw him behave with more civility....

Having entertained him in the best manner we were able and relating the story of sneaking around him, he laughed heartily at the stratagem and giving us both a shake by the hand departed to New Rosenback in good humor and perfectly contented. From all the preceding circumstances, the above chapter may be styled the golden age of my West India expedition.

VOLUME II

Chapter XX

A Rebel Negro described—Bush-fighting—Sentimental Expressions of the African Blacks—The Town of Gado-Saby taken by Colonel Fourgeoud—Superstition—Wonderful Expedients—Great Generalship in the Enemy

In Chapter XX, Stedman recounted the experience of jungle warfare, recorded the appearance of a captured maroon, and described the habits and living conditions of the maroons. He detailed combat strategies and the tactics employed by both sides. Readers learn of the comradery between soldiers and the respect European soldiers had for the Black Rangers. Compared to other chapters in the book, it is action-packed and fast-paced with little distraction. To keep the story moving, Stedman deployed several tropes common in narratives of war and combat, such as recounting brave deeds, tragic deaths, and harrowing moments of battle. Also significant about this chapter is that it documented a rare victory for the colonial forces in Suriname. After months of chasing the maroons, being ambushed, or arriving too late to engage the enemy, there is finally an open, pitched battle. And the European soldiers triumphed in taking the village of Gado-Saby. After winning, Stedman described the maroon village and their way of life, ultimately humanizing his enemy. They were no longer a faceless adversary but real people trying to resist colonial authorities and survive the best they could. Beneath all his bigotry, Stedman acknowledged that he faced a formidable, capable enemy. Ultimately, by revealing their ingenuity, Stedman expressed a begrudging admiration for the maroons, which became a key theme in the rest of the Narrative.

On the 15th of August 1775, the rebels, flushed with their late victory over Captain Meyland and his party, whether with a design to brave Fourgeoud or to intimidate his troops, being well apprised by their spies that he was at Barbacoeba, had the assurance to set fire to all the huts in two different camps which had been left standing by his patrols. They continued shouting and hallooing the whole night within our hearing. This only proved an incentive to action, however, and enraged our veteran commander so much that he now declared he would have ample revenge at all hazards....

An hour before daybreak next morning, Colonel Fourgeoud, with his troops, were ready to march and immediately entered the woods. They now amounted exactly to two hundred Europeans fit for service, the rest being ill and unfit for service. No rangers had yet arrived, though they had been expected. The fact was that they were so much disgusted with Fourgeoud's command that they did not appear at all, which afforded this gentleman for once an opportunity of stigmatizing them as a band of pusillanimous rascals. I confess I was myself extremely astonished at this willful absence of my Black favorites, who were at other times so eager to rush upon the enemy and had declared their satisfaction at the hopes of a decisive engagement with their sable countrymen.

This whole day our course was due east and, after proceeding about eight miles (which is a great distance in this country, where the pioneers with billhooks must constantly open a path), we erected huts and encamped. Having frequently mentioned the rebel negroes with whom we were now certain to have a recounter, I present the reader with the figure of one of these people upon his guard as alarmed by a rustling among the bushes. At a distance are a couple of our rangers awaiting the moment to take him by surprise. This rebel negro is armed with a firelock and a hatchet. His hair, though woolly, may be observed to be plaited close to his head, which distinguishes him from the rangers or any other straggling negroes who are not yet accepted amongst [the maroons]. His beard is grown to a point—like that of all the Africans—when they have no opportunity of shaving. The principal dress of this man consists of a cotton sheet, negligently tied across his shoulders, which protects him from the weather and serves him also to rest on—he always sleeps under cover in the most obscure places he can find when detached from his companions. The rest of his dress is a camisa tied around his loins like a handkerchief, his pouch, which is made of some animal's skin, a few cotton strings for ornament around his ankles and wrists, and a superstitious *obia* or amulet tied about his neck in which he places all his confidence. The skull and ribs are supposed to be the bones of his enemies scattered upon the sandy savannah.

The two rangers who make their appearance at a distance may be distinguished by their red caps. Here I must observe, that the rebels have many times availed themselves of seizing one of these scarlet distinctions, which, by clapping on their own heads in an engagement, has not only saved their lives but given them an opportunity of shooting their enemies.

Another stratagem of theirs has also been discovered. Since firearms are scarce among them, some intermixed in the crowd with a *crooked stick* shaped something like a musket. This appearance has more than once had the effect of preventing a proper defense by the plantation slaves when the rebels came to ransack the estates. While with this show of armed numbers they have often struck such a panic and so damped the courage of the former that they have been calmly permitted, after burning their houses, to carry away wives and daughters.

On the 16th, we continued our march due east upon a ridge or elevated ground. These ridges, if I am not mistaken, run generally in this country east and west as do also most of the marshes and swamps. Having advanced a shorter distance than we did the day before, we were ordered early to sling our hammocks and to sleep without any covering to prevent the enemy from hearing the sound of cutting the trees. Nor were any fires allowed to be lighted or a word to be spoken and a strict watch was kept round the camp. These, in fact, were all very necessary precautions. If we were not discovered by the enemy, we were almost devoured by the clouds of gnats or mosquitoes, which arose from a neighboring marsh. For my own part, I suffered more here than I had even done on board the fatal barges in the upper Cottica as we could make no smoke to drive them away. In this situation, I saw the poor men dig holes with their bayonets in the earth. They thrusted their heads into the holes, stopping the entry and covering their necks with their hammocks while they lay with their bellies on the ground. To sleep in any other position was absolutely impossible.

By the advice of a negro slave, I, however, enjoyed my rest. "Climb," he said, "massera with your hammock to the top of the highest tree that is in the camp and there go sleep. Not a single mosquito will disturb you. The swarm will be sufficiently attracted by the smell of the sweating multitude below." This I immediately tried and slept exalted near one hundred feet above my companions, whom I could not see for the myriads of mosquitoes below me nor even hear them from the incessant buzzing of these troublesome insects....

On the 17th, we continued our march still due east until nine o'clock when we altered our course to the north and had to scramble through great quantities of those mataky roots, or trumpeters already described. This proved that we were descending into the low grounds and indeed the soil soon became very marshy. Fortunately, however, though it was now the wet season, we had as yet very little rain.

This evening we encamped about four o'clock, Colonel Fourgeoud being seized with a cold fit of the ague....[In] my hammock reflecting on all the wonders of nature, while the silver moon glittering through the verdure added beauty to the scene, I fell into a profound sleep. I enjoyed this until near midnight when we were all awaked in pitch darkness and a heavy shower of rain by the hallooing and shouting of the rebel negroes, who discharged several muskets; but as the shot did not reach our camp, we were extremely astonished, the darkness rendering it impossible to form any just idea of their meaning. This disturbance continuing till near daybreak, made us expect every moment to be surrounded and keep a very sharp look out.

In the early morning, we unlashed our hammocks and marched due north towards the place whence we conjectured the hallooing noise to have proceeded, being all much fatigued for want of rest, especially Colonel Fourgeoud, who could hardly support himself he was so weakened by the ague. We had not marched above two miles, I having the vanguard, when a rebel negro sprang up at my feet from under a shrub where he had been asleep. We had orders not to fire upon stragglers and he escaped, running with almost the swiftness of a stag amongst the brambles. I no sooner made report to the old hero than, swearing [the maroon] was a spy, which I believe was true, he shook off his illness and quickened his pace with redoubled vigor. Our pursuit was to no purpose, at least this day. At about one o'clock we got into a bog from which we could hardly extricate ourselves and were forced to return to our last night's encampment, missing two privates of the Society troops, whom we supposed to have perished in the marsh....

On the 19th, we again left our encampment and after keeping a little sound, we marched east until ten o'clock. Then, we were overtaken and joined by a party of one hundred rangers with their conductor, Mr. Vinsack, to my great satisfaction. At this period, we mustered three hundred men. However little Colonel Fourgeoud was affected, at other times to value these Black soldiers, he was not at all displeased with their company upon our near approach to an enemy with whom the rangers were well acquainted and knew how to engage much better than the marines. It will ever be my opinion that one of these free negroes is preferable to half a dozen white men in the forest of Guiana. It indeed seems their natural element while it is the bane of the Europeans.

Colonel Fourgeoud now issued orders for our little army to march in three lines or columns, his own regiment in the center, the Society troops on the right, the rangers or Black soldiers on the left all within hearing of each other with a few flankers or riflemen outside the whole. Thus formed, we advanced until about noon when we changed our course from east to northeast and continued our march over a swamp or quagmire. These are very common and dangerous in this country. They are a deep soft miry bog covered over with a thin crust of verdure sufficient in most places to bear the weight of a man and quaking when walked over. Should this crust give way, whoever breaks it is swallowed up in the chasm where he must inevitably perish if not immediately extricated. It has frequently happened that men have been seen to sink and have never more been heard of.

Quicksand is quite different as it overwhelms by a gradual suction whereas the effects of a quagmire are instantaneous. To avoid accidents, we opened our files as much as possible, which occasioned a very long rear. Even with this precaution, however, several men sunk through it as if the ice had broken under their feet and some in my presence up to the armpits, but were fortunately, though with much difficulty, extricated.

In the afternoon we passed through two old cassava fields, which indicated our near approach to the rebel settlement. We afterwards fell in with Captain Meyland's path, which we knew by the marks cut upon the trees. The evening being too far advanced to attack the enemy, we once more encamped a few miles from the swamp in which Captain Meyland and his party had been defeated.

Having had a long march and the men being much fatigued, Colonel Fourgeoud allowed during this night both huts and fires, which surprised me greatly since we were so near the rebels and though he had forbidden these comforts when we were at a very considerable distance from them. I, however, availed myself of his bounty and having got some *pigeon-peas* from my sergeant, which he had picked up in the old cassava grounds, and laid hold of one of the kettles, I invited him and a captain of the Black corps called Hannibal to share. They threw their salt-beef and rusk-biscuit into the mess with mine and stirred it round with a bayonet. We made a very excellent supper, though in a sad dreary night and heavy rain....

Hannibal now observing that we should certainly see the enemy tomorrow, asked me if I knew in what manner negro engaged against negro. Having answered in the negative, he gave me the following relation, while smoking his pipe under my hammock: "Massera," said he, "both parties are divided in small companies of eight or ten men commanded by a captain with a horn, such as this (showing me his) by which they do everything and fight or run away. When they fight, they separate immediately, lie down on the ground, and fire at the flash of each other's pans through the trees. Each warrior is supported by two negroes unarmed, one to take his place if he is killed and the other to carry away the dead body to prevent its falling into the hands of their adversaries."[1]

...Captain Hannibal also informed me, that the famous chief Boni was supposed to be in person amongst the neighboring rebels. He was born in the forest amongst them, despite being a mulatto, which was accounted for by his mother escaping to the woods from the ill treatment of her master by whom she was then pregnant.... This sable warrior also acquainted me with the names of several other rebel commanders, against whom he had frequently fought for the Europeans. These included Quammy, who was the chief of a separate gang and had no connection with the others and Coromantyn, Cojo, Arico, and Jolycoeur, the two last being celebrated captains, whose revenge was insatiable against the whites.... The noted rebel negro Baron, he believed, was now serving also under the great chief Boni.

He next proceeded to tell me the names of the principal rebel settlements, some of which were already destroyed, some now in view, and some of these were only known to us by name. These appellations were all very expressive indeed. And since they may serve in some measure to elucidate our enquiries

---

1. Original footnote: The negroes have a savage custom of mangling and tearing the dead bodies of their enemies; some even devouring part of them with their teeth, like the Caribbee Indians.

concerning the negro nations, I have thought proper to give them a place in this narrative, with their meaning in an English translation:

Boucou	I shall moulder[2] before I shall be taken.
Gado-Saby	God only knows me, and none else.
Cofaay	Come try me if you be men.
Tessee See	Take a tasting if you like it.
Mele me	Do disturb me if you dare.
Busy-Cray	The woods lament for me.
Me Salasy	I shall be taken.
Kebree me	Hide me, O thou surrounding verdure.

The others were:

Quammy Condre	From Quammy, the name of the chief.
Pinenburgh	From the pines or manicole-trees which formerly surrounded it.
Caro Condre	From the quantity of maize it afforded.
Reisee Condre	From the quantity of rice it produced.

Such were the names of the negro warriors and their settlements.

I now shook hands with Captain Hannibal and while my mind being occupied with the hopes of victory unstained by cruelty and being very much fatigued, I soon fell profoundly asleep.

On the morning of the 20th, no one could awake in a more beautiful day and better spirits than I did until they were damped by observing that at so critical a time, and even in the moment before the conflict, instead of that kind treatment which it would have been prudent to have shown to those from whose exertions we were to expect a happy period to our sufferings, there was even then such discouragement of the subaltern officers and private men. This involuntarily drew from me the reflection that (if possible to avoid it) princes and ministers should never invest any one individual with unlimited authority, especially in a foreign country, without being perfectly well acquainted with the rectitude of their moral principles and disposition. No men being fit to command but those who are possessed of manly feelings and whose valor is tempered with humanity since this is a truth that sterling bravery is incompatible with a cruel heart.

At six o'clock we advanced northeast by north towards the marsh, my melancholy evaporating with the rising sun.

About eight o'clock we entered this formidable swamp and soon found ourselves above our middle in water, well prepared nevertheless for the warm reception we expected from the opposite shore as the former party had so fatally experienced. After wading above half a mile, our grenadiers rapidly mounted

---

2. I.e., decay or crumble away.

the beach with cocked firelocks and bayonets fixed. The main body instantly followed and also mounting the beach, the whole formed without the smallest opposition. We now beheld a spectacle sufficient to shock the most intrepid, the ground strewed with skulls, bones, and ribs still covered with human flesh, and besmeared with the blood of those unfortunate men who were killed with Captain Meyland. That officer had indeed found means to bury them, but the rebels had dug them up for the sake of their clothes and to mangle the bodies, which, like ferocious animals, they had torn limb from limb. Among these, the fate of Meyland's nephew, a promising young man, was peculiarly affecting. He came from the mountains of Switzerland in quest of military preferment and met his fate in a marsh of Suriname just after his landing. His bravery was equal to that of his uncle, his intrepidity, voluntarily exposing himself to danger, knew no bounds. Such is the enthusiasm of military ambition....

This being the second or third heap of human bones we had met with in our march, I frankly acknowledge did not operate upon me as a stimulative to engage with negroes. Yet these awful relics spurred on the common soldiers to take revenge for the loss of their massacred companions....

We now followed a kind of footpath made by the enemy, which after a little turning led us in a westerly direction. Sergeant Fowler, who preceded the vanguard, came to me pale, declaring that the sight of the mangled bodies had made him extremely sick. He felt himself completely disarmed, being that moment, as it were, riveted to the ground without the power of advancing one single step or knowing how to conceal his tremor. I damned him for a pitiful scoundrel and had only time to order him to the rear....

At ten o'clock we met a small party of the rebels each with a green hamper upon his back.[3] They fired at us, dropped their bundles, and took to their heels ran back towards their village. These we later learned were transporting rice to another settlement for their subsistence because they believed they would be expelled from Gado-Saby (the name of this settlement). They daily expected this after they had been discovered by the gallant Captain Meyland. The green hampers, which they call *warimbos*, were very curiously plaited with the manicole leaves. And when our men cut them open with their sabers, there burst forth the most beautiful clean rice that I ever saw, which was scattered and trampled underfoot as we had no opportunity of carrying it along. A little after this we perceived an empty shed where a picquet had been stationed to give notice of any danger, but they had precipitately deserted their post. We now vigorously redoubled our pace until about noon when two more musket shot were fired at us by another advanced guard of the enemy meant as a signal to the chief, Boni, of our approach. Major Medlaer and myself with a few of the vanguard and a small party of the rangers rushed forward and soon came to a

---

3. "Hamper" in this context referred to a basket woven with manicole palm leaves carried on the back.

fine field of rice and Indian corn. We here made a halt for the other troops, particularly to give time for our rear to close up, some of whom were at least two miles behind us. Had we not, we might have been cut to pieces as the enemy, unknown to us, surrounded the field in which we were.

In about half an hour, the whole body joined us and we instantly proceeded by cutting through a small defile of the wood. We had no sooner entered when a heavy fire commenced from every side, the rebels retiring. We advanced until we arrived in the most beautiful field of ripe rice, in the form of an oblong square, from which the rebel town appeared at a distance in the form of an amphitheater sheltered from the sun by the foliage of a few lofty trees. The whole presenting a coup d'oeil romantic and enchanting beyond conception.[4] In this field, the firing was kept up like one continued peal of thunder for above forty minutes. During this time, our Black warriors behaved with wonderful intrepidity and skill. The white soldiers were too eager and fired over one another at random, yet I could perceive a few of them act with the utmost coolness and imitate the rangers with great effect. Amongst these was now the once-daunted Fowler, who being roused from his tremor by the firing at the beginning of the onset had rushed to the front and fully reestablished his character, fighting like a brave fellow by my side until the muzzle of his musket was split by a shot from the enemy, rendering it useless. A ball passed through my shirt and grazed the skin of my shoulder. Mr. Decabanes, my lieutenant, had the sling of his fusee[5] shot away. Several others were wounded, some mortally, but I did not, to my surprise, observe one instance of immediate death—for which a seeming miracle, however, I shall presently account.

This whole field of rice was surrounded and interspersed by the enemy with the large trunks and roots of heavy trees in order to make our approach both difficult and dangerous. Behind these temporary fortifications, the rebels lay lurking and fired upon us with deliberate aim. While their bulwarks certainly protected them in some measure from the effects of our fire and we had vast numbers of these fallen trees to scramble over before we could reach the town. We still advanced in defiance of every obstacle, however, and while I admired the masterly maneuvers of their general, I could not help pitying them for their superstition. One poor fellow in particular, trusting to his amulet or charm, fancied himself invulnerable. He mounted frequently upon one of the trees that lay near us, discharged his piece, descended to reload, and, then, with equal confidence and the greatest deliberation, returned to the charge in my full view. At last, a shot from one of my marines, named Valet, broke the bone of his thigh and he fell crawling for shelter under the very same tree which had supported him just before. The soldier instantly advanced, put the muzzle of his

---

4. I.e., a glimpse that provides a view of the entire scene.
5. "Fusee" was a slang term for a flintlock rifle or pistol.

musket to the rebel's ear, and blew out his brains. Several of his countrymen, in spite of their spells and charms, shared the same fate.

When we were about to enter the town, a rebel captain, wearing a tarnished gold-laced hat, bearing in his hand a torch of flaming straw, and seeing their ruin inevitable, had the resolution to stay and set the town on fire in our presence. The dryness of the houses instantly produced a general conflagration just as the firing from the woods began gradually to cease. This bold and masterly maneuver not only prevented that carnage to which the common soldiers in the heat of victory are but too prone, but also afforded the enemy an opportunity of retreating with their wives and children and carrying off their most useful effects. Our pursuit—and seizing the spoil—were at once frustrated both by the ascending flames and the unfathomable marsh, which we soon discovered on all sides to surround us....

I must indeed confess that within this last hour the continued noise of the firing, shouting, swearing, and hallooing of Black and white men mixed together; the groans of the wounded and the dying, all weltering in blood and in dust; the shrill sound of the negro horns from every quarter and the crackling of the burning village; and if we add the clouds of smoke that everywhere surrounded us, the ascending flames formed, on the whole, such an uncommon scene as I cannot describe, and would perhaps not have been unworthy of the pencil of Hogarth....[6]

In short, having washed off the dust, sweat, and blood and having refreshed ourselves with a dram and a bit of bread until the flames subsided, we next went to inspect the smoking ruins. We found the above town to have consisted of about one hundred houses or huts, some of which were two stories high. Among the glowing ashes, we picked up several trifles that had escaped the flames, such as silver spoons and forks, which we supposed, by the marks "BW" to have been pillaged from the Brunswick estate in Rio Cottica. We found also some knives, broken china, and earthen pots. Among the latter, one filled with rice and palm tree worms fell to my share.[7] As this wanted no fire to dress the contents and as my appetite was very keen, I emptied it in a few minutes and made a very hearty meal. Some were afraid this mess had been left behind with a view to poison us. This suspicion, however, proved, fortunately for me, to be without foundation.

I also purchased the silver plate from the men that picked it up, who had been determined to carry it off as a trophy, and I have used it ever since. Here, we likewise found three skulls fixed upon stakes, the mournful relics of some

---

6. William Hogarth (1697–1764) was one of eighteenth-century Britain's foremost engravers, painters, and cartoonists and famous for his satirical imprints of everyday life.

7. "Palm tree worms" are the larvae of the *Rhynchophorus palmarum* or South American palm weevil. They live in and feed off the hearts of palm trees and are, as Stedman attested here, consumed as food.

of our own brave people who had been killed. But what surprised us most were the heads of two young negroes, which seemed as if fresh cut off. We later learned they had been executed during the night of the 17th when we heard the hallooing and the firing for speaking in our favor.

Having buried all these remains promiscuously in one pit, we returned to sling our hammocks under those beautiful and lofty trees which I have already mentioned. Here I am sorry to add, we found the rangers shockingly employed in playing at bowls with those very heads they had just chopped off from their enemies.... They also related that upon reconnoitering the skirts of the surrounding forest, they had found quantities of human blood in different places, which had flowed from the dead and wounded bodies the rebels had carried away during the action.

To reprimand them for this inhuman diversion would have been useless. They assured us it was *condre fassee*—the custom of their country—and concluded the horrid sport by kicking and mangling the heads, cutting off the lips, cheeks, ears, and noses. They even took out the jawbones, which they smoke dried, together with the right hands, to carry home, as trophies of their victory to their wives and relations. That this barbarous custom prevails among savages is a well-known fact that originates from a motive of insatiable revenge. And though Colonel Fourgeoud might have prevented their inhumanity by his authority, in my opinion, he wisely declined it. He observed that he could not do it by persuasion and if he did it by power, he might break their native spirit and produce no other effect than alienating them from the service. They were necessary to us despite being so savagely revengeful and so bloody.

About three o'clock, while we were resting from our fatigue, we were once more surprised by an attack from a party of the enemy, but after exchanging a few shots, they were repulsed. This unexpected visit, however, put us more upon our guard during the night. No fires were allowed to be lighted and double sentinels were placed around the camp. Thus situated, being overcome by excessive toil and heat, I after sunset leapt into my hammock and soon fell fast asleep. In less than two hours, however, my faithful Black boy Quaco roused me, in the midst of pitch darkness, crying, *Massera, massera! boosee negro, boosee negro!* ("Master, master! The enemy, the enemy!") Hearing, at the same moment, a brisk firing with the balls whistling through the branches, I fully concluded that the rebels were in the very midst of our camp. Surprised, and not perfectly awake, I suddenly started up with my fusee cocked. And without knowing where I ran, I first threw down Quaco and then fell down myself over two or three bodies that lay upon the ground, and which I imagined to be dead. One of them, damning me as a "son of a bitch," told me if I moved, I was a dead man. Colonel Fourgeoud had issued orders for the troops to lie flat on their bellies all the night, and not to fire as most of their ammunition had been expended the preceding day. I took the man's advice and soon discovered him by his voice to be one of our own grenadiers named Thomson. In this situation, we lay prostrate on our arms until sunrise.

During this time, a most abusive dialogue was carried on between the rebels and the rangers. Each party cursed and menaced the other at a very terrible rate. The former reproached the rangers as *poltroons*[8] and traitors to their countrymen. The rebels challenged them the next day to single combat, swearing they only wished to wash their hands in the blood of such scoundrels who had been the principal agents in destroying their flourishing settlement. The rangers damned the rebels as a parcel of pitiful skulking rascals whom they would fight one to two in the open field if they dared but to show their ugly faces and swore they had only deserted their masters because they were too lazy to work. After this, they insulted each other by a kind of war whoop, sung victorious songs on both sides, and sounded their horns as signals of defiance. When the firing commenced once more from the rebel negroes and continued during the night, accompanied by their martial voices at intermissions resounding through the woods, which echo seemed to answer with redoubled force.

At length, poor Fourgeoud took a part in the conversation. Sergeant Fowler and I acted as his interpreters by hallooing, which created more mirth than I had been witness to for some time. Fourgeoud promised them life, liberty, victuals, drink, and all they wanted. They replied with a loud laugh and said that they wanted nothing from him, characterized him as a half-starved Frenchman who had run away from his own country, and assured him that if he would venture to pay them a visit, he should return unhurt and not with an empty belly. They told us that we were to be pitied more than they and that we were white slaves, hired to be shot at and starved for four pence a day. They scorned to expend much more of their powder upon such scarecrows, but should the planters or overseers dare to enter the woods not a soul of them should ever return. And of the perfidious rangers, they said that some of whom might depend upon being massacred that day or the next. They concluded by declaring that Boni should soon be the governor of the colony.

After this, they tinkled their billhooks, fired a volley, and gave three cheers. After being answered by the rangers, the clamor ended and the rebels dispersed with the rising sun.

Our fatigue was great, but, notwithstanding the length of the contest, our loss by the enemy's fire was very inconsiderable and this mystery was now explained. When the surgeons dressed the wounded, they extracted very few leaden bullets, but many pebbles, coat-buttons, and pieces of silver coin, which could do us little mischief by penetrating scarcely more than skin deep. We also observed that several of the poor rebel negroes who were shot had only the shards of water cans, instead of flints, which could seldom do execution. It was

---

8. I.e., cowards.

certainly owing to these circumstances that we came off so well. Nevertheless, we were not without a number of very dangerous scars and contusions.

Inconceivable are the many expedients which these people employ in the woods where in a state of tranquility, they seemed, as they boasted, to want for nothing, being plump and fat, at least such as we had an opportunity of observing. It should be noticed that they catch game in great abundance using artificial traps and springs and preserve them by barbecuing.[9] Their fields are even overstocked with rice, cassava, yams, plantains, etc. They make salt from the palm tree ashes…or frequently supply the want of it with red pepper.

We here found concealed near the trunk of an old tree a case bottle[10] filled with excellent butter, which the rangers told me they made by melting and clarifying the fat of the palm tree worms. It fully answers all the purposes of European butter and I found it in fact even more delicious to my taste. They also convert the pistachio or pinda nuts into butter…and frequently use them in their broths. The palm tree wine they have always in plenty. They procure it by making deep incisions of a foot square in the fallen trunk where the juice collects. It soon ferments by the heat of the sun. It is not only a cool and agreeable beverage, but sufficiently strong to intoxicate. The manicole or pine tree affords them materials for building. They fabricate pots from clay found near their dwellings. The gourd or calabash tree procures them cups. The silk grass plant and *maurecee* tree supplies materials for their hammocks and even a kind of cap grows naturally upon the palm-trees as well as brooms. The various kinds of vines to supply rope. Fuel they have for cutting and a wood called "bee-bee" serves for tinder by rubbing two pieces on each other. It is also elastic and makes excellent corks. Candles they can make, having plenty of fat and oil. And the wild bees afford them wax as well as excellent honey.

Clothes they scorn to wear, preferring to go naked in a climate where the warmth of the weather renders every kind of covering a useless encumbrance.

They might breed hogs and poultry and keep dogs for hunting and watching them, but this they decline from the apprehension of being discovered by their noise, as even the crowing of a cock may be heard in the forest at a considerable distance.

The rebels of this settlement being apparently subdued and dispersed, Colonel Fourgeoud made it his next business to destroy the surrounding harvest. I received orders to begin the devastation with eighty marines and twenty rangers. Thus, I cut down all the rice that was growing plentifully in the two above-mentioned fields. This being done, I discovered a third field south of the first, which I also demolished and made my report to Fourgeoud with which he appeared highly satisfied. In the afternoon, Captain Hamell was detached

---

9. "Barbecuing" in this context means preserving meat and fish by using smoke to dry it.
10. These are square-shaped glass bottles with flat sides designed to be packed into wooden crates or cases, thus the name.

with fifty marines and thirty rangers to reconnoiter behind the village and to discover, if possible, how the rebels could pass to and fro through an unfathomable marsh while we were unable to pursue them. This officer at length perceived a kind of floating bridge amongst the reeds…but so constructed that only one man abreast could pass it. On this were seated astride a few rebels to defend the communication, who instantly sired upon the party. They were soon repulsed by the rangers who shot one of them dead, but he was carried away by his companions.

On the morning of the 22nd, our commander ordered a detachment to cross the bridge and go on discovery at all hazards. Of this party, I led the van.[11] We now took the pass without opposition and having all marched—or rather, scrambled—over this defile of floating trees, we found ourselves in a large oblong field of cassava and yams in which were about thirty houses, now deserted. These were the remains of the old settlement called Cofaay. In this field, we separated into three divisions to better reconnoiter. One marched north, one north-west, and the third west. And here, to our astonishment, we discovered that the reason of the rebels shouting, singing, and firing on the night of the 20th was not only to cover the retreat of their friends…but also by using the unremitting noise to prevent us from discovering that they were employed, men, women, and children, in preparing *warimbos* or hampers filled with the finest rice, yams, and cassava, for subsistence during their escape. Of this, they had only left the chaff and refuse for our contemplation.

This was certainly such a masterly trait of generalship in a savage people, whom we affected to despise, as would have done honor to any European commander and has perhaps been seldom equaled by more civilized nations.

Chapter XXIV

Two Volunteer Companies raised, of free Mulattoes and Negroes—Description of the Arrowouka Indian Nation—Colonel Fourgeoud's Regiment receives orders to sail for Europe—Countermanded—Re-enter the Woods—Trade of the Colony—Description of a Cacao Estate—Sample of Sable Heroism

Chapter XXIV offers insights into how Stedman understood race and, by extension, reflects how many Europeans in the late-eighteenth century conceived of racial difference and the racist ideology underpinning those

---

11. I.e., the vanguard or at the head of the party.

ideas. Readers encountered free people of color, Amerindians, enslaved Africans, and enslaved Native Americans. Yet, Stedman's discussion of these people was heavily influenced by racist, albeit popular, stereotypes of the time. He described Amerindian swimmers as "amphibious," suggesting they were not fully human. Other Native peoples were depicted as peaceful and ignorantly happy, indulging his readers' belief in the "noble savage." And Stedman sexualized women of color, both Indigenous and African, by describing their naked bodies as they swam and bathed. Although Stedman was the one who gawked and spied on these women, they are the ones depicted as uncouth and licentious. Many of these ideas and stereotypes, whether Stedman acknowledged them or not, drew from larger discussions about human difference. Indeed, he cited numerous philosophers and their racist work on biological differences, such as Jean-Jacques Rousseau's Second Discourse, in the body of the text. While reflecting on his own understanding of this racist discourse, Stedman pushed the narrative forward and, although not actively fighting the maroons, he faced other issues. He received land from the governor but did not have the resources to develop it into a productive plantation, revealing, at the same moment, his commitment to using enslaved labor, but also his limited prospects if he remained in Suriname. As he began thinking about returning to Europe, a new problem arose: Joanna seemed increasingly reluctant to leave with him.

The chapter opened with Stedman receiving leave and heading from deep in the jungle to Paramaribo to see Joanna.

…I arrived once more at Paramaribo and found Joanna with her little boy perfectly well after having both been blind for above three weeks.[12] We were invited to lodge at the house of my friend Mr. De Graaff and I was completely happy.

The following day I dined with Colonel Fourgeoud, who now also was as sound as ever and who gave me a very indifferent meal of salt provisions[13] but an uncommonly hearty welcome. He acquainted me that: two new companies of free mulattoes and two of free negroes, all volunteers had just been raised; the Saamaka and Owca negroes encouraged and favored the rebels and were deceitful rascals; a few rebels had been killed in the Cassiwinica Creek; he was in hopes of rooting out Fissy-Hollo; Boni and his people were almost starving in the forest, notwithstanding their late depredations which could not last much longer; and he was fully determined, if he should lose his last man, to make this rebel surrender or harass him until he and his gang, through hunger

---

12. "Her little boy" referred to the child Joanna and Stedman had together. His name was John, affectionately called Jack or Johnny.

13. Original footnote: This he absolutely held as the best regimen for health, notwithstanding he had brought three cooks from Europe.

and distress, should be obliged to quit the colony. I learned further from him that a Frenchman had just escaped hanging for betraying the state of the fortifications to the governor of Cayenne.[14] He also pardoned Captain Tulling for his clandestine marriage and informed me that Lieutenant Colonel de Borgnes just entered into matrimony with a rich widow, Mrs. Crawford.…

I was also present at a mulatto ball composed not of slaves, but of free, independent settlers. Here, the music, lights, country dances, supper, and, above all, dresses were so superb, and their behavior so decent and genteel that the whole might serve as a model for decorum and etiquette to some of the fairer and more polished inhabitants.

On the 20th, observing a number of Indians and Black people of both sexes swimming at the back of Fort Zeelandia, young Donald MacNeil and myself completed the group by stripping and getting in among them. I must confess I never beheld more surprising feats of activity in the water than were performed by the negroes. They fought a sham battle by plunging—or rather tumbling—like porpoises and struck each other with their legs, never using their hands. The Indians, who were of the Arrowouka [Arawak] nation, swam and dived like amphibious animals.[15]

Being sufficiently refreshed, we sat down upon the beach near the twenty-one gun battery. I had an opportunity of examining the features and figure of one of their [the Arawak's] young females. She approached us like Venus rising out of the sea.[16] These people are very different from all the other Indian nations that I have already described.…In the first place, the skin of the young woman, who was now emerging clean from the river and divested of annatto-paint,[17] appeared much fairer than the copper-color of the other Indians. Her limbs were not deformed by those strait-laced bracelets or cotton-bands.…Nor did her hair hang down, but was neatly plaited[18] close round the crown of her head and fastened in the center with a broad silver plate.[19] Her only dress consisted, both during the time she bathed and after, of a small square apron made of beads…in every other respect she was perfectly naked. A finer figure cannot be

---

14. Cayenne was the capital city of, and eighteenth-century name for, French Guiana, the colony that neighbored Suriname to the east.
15. The "Arrowouka" or Arawak is one of the main Amerindian ethnicities in northern South America and the southern Caribbean. The Arawak encountered by Stedman were most likely of the Lokono nation, who still inhabit the Guianas today.
16. Venus was the Roman goddess of love, beauty, and sex. By referring to the young woman in such a way, Stedman further sexualized her for his readers.
17. This is a skin paint colored with annatto, a red-orange dye derived from the achiote plant native to Central and South America. Amerindians in the Guianas wear annatto paint to decorate their bodies, block the sun, and repel insects.
18. Braided.
19. Original footnote: This, at other times, they supply by a shell, a fish-bone, or the tooth of a tiger, &c.

imagined—erect, vigorous, active, young, and healthy—which convinced me that when the body is exposed as it certainly was ordained by nature, the face is but little noticed....

In her features was displayed that beautiful simplicity—that native unsuspecting innocence—which cannot be put on where there is the slightest consciousness of guilt. Nor is the olive color incompatible with beauty. It is certainly the standard complexion of the human race, while the black and white are supposed to be only gradations, produced probably by the extremes of heat and cold.[20] As this Indian girl was perfectly handsome, so she seemed to be perfectly happy....To be sure, a European woman would blush to her fingers, ends at the very idea of appearing publicly stark naked, but education and prejudice are everything. It is an axiom that where there is no feeling of self-reproach there can assuredly be no shame.

I remember having seen an Indian youth, whose name was Weekee, at Bergen-op-Zoom.[21] He was brought over from the colony Berbice with General De Salve,[22] who clothed and partly civilized him. Among other things, he learned cookery and to be something of a tailor at his own request, so that he might be enabled to provide both for his back and his belly. After some time, however, he expressed a desire to return to the colony. He no sooner touched American ground than stripping himself of his clothing, he launched naked into his native woods where he ended his days as he had begun them, among his beloved countrymen and companions, similar to the Hottentot mentioned by Rousseau, in his celebrated *Discours sur l'Inegalité & Conditions, &c.*[23] But to return to the girl. She had with her a live parrot, which she had stunned with a blunt arrow from her bow and for which I gave her a double-bladed knife.[24] So wonderfully expert are the Arawak Indians at this exercise that they frequently bring down a macaw in full flight or even a pigeon.

---

20. In his assessment of human coloration, Stedman drew from eighteenth-century racial theorists such as Johann Friedrich Blumenbach (1752–1840).

21. Bergen-op-Zoom is a city in the province of Zeeland in the southern Netherlands.

22. Jan Marcus De Salve was one of the Dutch military officers sent to suppress the Berbice slave rebellion.

23. In his *Discourse on Inequality* (1755), Genevan-French philosopher Jean-Jacques Rousseau (1712–1778) recounted the story of a "Hottentot"—a generic term for a person of African descent from what is today South Africa. In the story, a Hottentot man had lived with the governor of Cape Colony in South Africa, became a Christian, and learned European ways, but upon reencountering his own people, renounced all things European, including his adopted faith, and returned to his people.

24. Original footnote: The general traffic carried on between all the Indian nations and the Europeans consists in balsam, arrococerra, oil of carrabba, arnotta, and bees-wax, besides pieces of Brazil and ebony; the roots hiaree and varnillas, canoes, hammocks, slaves, monkies, parrots, and paroquets; for which they receive firearms, knives, hatchets, fish-hooks, combs, coral and glass beads, blue cotton, looking-glasses, &c.

I cannot conclude these remarks without adding a few words concerning the unspotted moral character of these people, who not only live in peace with most of the other Indian nations, but are peculiarly attached to the Europeans, while these in return profess for them the strongest esteem.

As a proof of their gratitude, I will only relate one instance. Some years ago, an Indian woman being at Paramaribo and far advanced in a state of pregnancy, a Mr. Van der Meij humanely ordered his servants to conduct her and her husband into his house. After giving them a private apartment and every other conveniency, he wished them goodnight. Before the next morning, the woman was delivered. When the servants went in to renew their offers of friendship, however, neither man, wife, nor child were to be found as they had before daybreak quietly marched into the forest.[25] Various were at this time the conjectures concerning the boasted integrity of the Arawak Indians, until, no less than eighteen months after, the same Indian returned to Mr. Van der Meij with a charming captive boy of the Accawau nation that he had taken in battle.[26] Presenting the boy to his benefactor, he only said, "That's yours" and without waiting for any answer disappeared. For this slave, the above gentleman was offered £200, which he refused and treated him as well as if he had been free.

The education these people receive in their infancy being according to the dictates only of simple nature, their minds or their bodies are very seldom deformed while a too nice attention to either is possibly as detrimental as a total neglect.... Though the Arawak Indians live in perfect friendship and harmony with us—and indeed with most of their neighbors—they yet sometimes go to war when provoked. In these combats, they use bows and arrows, and the club called *abowtow*, but they do not eat their prisoners like the Carib Indians, who even devoured the negroes whom they killed at the insurrection in Berbice.[27] Notwithstanding these people live at a greater distance from the sea than the Warrows yet they have canoes, sometimes fourscore feet in length, in which they paddle down the rivers. The Arawak Indians particularly are great herbalists and for all external accidents have recourse to simples, with which the woods of all Terra Firma abound....

---

25. Original footnote: I have mentioned before that the Indians are exempt from pain in labor.

26. Original footnote: This is however extremely uncommon, as a more peaceable people does not exist in the universe.

27. Europeans often accused Amerindians, especially the Carib peoples of the Caribbean and South America, of being cannibals. Indeed, the term "cannibal" derives from the Spanish name for the Carib. While there was some ritualistic cannibalism, accusations of the practice were exaggerated, overblown, and hung around for centuries—and are repeated by Stedman here.

In the following three paragraphs, the reader learns that the soldiers received orders from the Netherlands to depart Suriname and return home immediately. That sent Stedman into a frenzy of preparations, thinking he would be leaving soon.

On the 14th of February, ill as I was with a bad foot, a sore arm, the prickly heat, and all my teeth loose with the scurvy, I found means to scramble out on crutches with a thousand florins in my pocket. I divided them between Fourgeoud and Mrs. Godefroy for the redemption of the Black boy Quaco and my mulatto[28] and I returned borne without a shilling in my purse. Yet for this small sum of 500 florins, so inadequate to the 1800 which I owed Mrs. Godefroy, she was induced generously to renew her persuasions of carrying Joanna and the boy with me to Holland. This, however, Joanna as nobly as firmly refused, declaring, "that, independent of all other considerations, she could never think of sacrificing one benefactor to the interest of another. And that her own happiness or even mine, which was dearer to her than life, should never have any weight, until the debt of her liberty was paid by me, or by her own industry, to the utmost fraction and which she did not despair to see one day completed." She added, "our separation should only be for a time and that the greatest proof I could ever show her of my real esteem was now to undergo this little trial of fortune like a man without so much as heaving a sigh in her presence" which last she spoke with a smile, next embraced her infant, then turned suddenly round, and wept most bitterly. At this moment, I was called to Mr. de la Marre's, who had just died, where my melancholy having surpassed all description. I at last determined to weather one or two painful years in her absence and in the afternoon went to dissipate my mind at a Mr. Roux's cabinet of Indian curiosities....[29]

Stedman spent the next four paragraphs describing the dead snakes and insects in Roux's cabinet of curiosities.

I have just said that we were ordered to leave the colony and that all were overjoyed with the news, myself excepted. But on the 15th, by letters from Holland to our chief, our *return* was again countermanded for six months. My companions were therefore suddenly cast down with disappointment, while I was as suddenly revived and now determined to save all my pay until Joanna's redemption should be fully accomplished. But what grieved me very much was the other news from Europe that the Scots Brigade had been invited to England by his Britannic Majesty, while I was lamenting that I could not possibly be one of the number.[30] I, at the same time, had the offer of an American

---

28. I.e., Joanna.
29. A "cabinet of curiosities" referred to a small, privately owned collection of artifacts popular in the eighteenth century and was the precursor to modern museums.
30. Original footnote: The King's demand was negatived by the States of Holland.

company under General Washington, but this I refused without any hesitation as may be supposed.

In short, on the 18th of February, the poor dispirited men were again sent up to Maagdenburg, a large party still remaining at the Java Creek. The temper of the officers was now so ruffled that a Mr. Fisher of our corps fought no less than two duels in two succeeding days, dangerously wounding both his antagonists who were officers of the Society regiment.

As I was not yet recovered, I stayed some time longer at Paramaribo. At the house of a Mr. Rynsdorp, I saw a Portuguese Jew teaching his children the Christian religion, while the pious mother of the charity house kept flogging the poor slaves daily because they were, as she said, unbelievers. To one Black woman in particular she wantonly gave four hundred lashes, who bore them without a complaint.

But to change the disagreeable subject, while I have the leisure and the opportunity, I feel the inclination to state to the public a short account of the trade and intrinsic value of this blood-spilling colony. It might be richer still if they did not follow the example of the woman in the fable with her golden eggs.

On the 21st of February, Mr. Rynsdorp, the son-in-law of Mrs. Godefroy, took me in his sail barge for change of air to Nuten-Schadelyk, one of his own coffee estates. I saw a white man who had lately lost both his eyes in one night by the bats, or vampires as they are called. The following day, sailing up Commewijne River, we proceeded to the delightful cacao plantation Alkmaar, the property of the above lady [Mrs. Godefroy]. The negro slaves are treated like children by the mistress to whom they all look up as to their common parent. Here were no groans to be heard, no fetters to be met with, nor any marks of severity to be seen—all was harmony and content. The superb house and other offices of this charming estate, where pleasure and hospitality ever reign.… The fields and gardens, nay, even the negro houses, bore all the marks of perfect peace and plenty.

In the next three paragraphs, Stedman described cacao trees.

On the 27th, we returned to town.… At this time, the celebrated free negro Qwasi, who was the prophet, priest, and king of the rangers went to Holland on a visit to the Prince of Orange with letters of recommendation from Fourgeoud, whose praises he was to resound—as well as to complain of the Governor for not treating him with due respect. This being the period for the sessions,[31] a negro's leg was cut off for skulking from a task to which he was unequal while two more were condemned to be hanged for running away. The heroic behavior of one of these men before the court deserves particularly to be

---

31. "Sessions" referred to when the Court of Policy and Justice, Suriname's criminal court, met, adjudicated cases, and sentenced those found guilty.

noticed. He begged only to be heard for a few moments, which, being granted, he proceeded thus:

> "I was born in Africa, where, defending my prince during an engagement, I was made a captive, and sold for a slave on the coast of Guinea by my own countrymen. One of your countrymen, who is now to be one of my judges became my purchaser, in whose service I was treated so cruelly by his overseer that I deserted and joined the rebels in the woods. Here again I was condemned to be a slave to Boni, their chief, who treated me with even more severity than I had experienced from the Europeans until I was once more forced to elope, determined to shun mankind forever and inoffensively to end my days by myself in the forest. Two years had I persevered in this manner quite alone, undergoing the greatest hardships and anxiety of mind, preserving life only for the possibility of once more seeing my dear family, who were perhaps starving on my account, in my own country. I say two miserable years had just elapsed when I was discovered by the rangers, taken, and brought before this tribunal, who are now acquainted with the history of my wretched life, and from whom the only favor I have to ask is that I may be executed next Saturday, or as soon as it may possibly be convenient."

This speech was uttered with the utmost moderation by one of the finest looking negroes that was perhaps ever seen. His former master, who, as he observed, was now one of the judges, made the following laconic reply: "Rascal! That is not what we want to know, but the torture this moment shall make you confess crimes as black as yourself as well as those of your hateful accomplices." The negro, who now swelled in every vein with indignation and ineffable contempt, said "Massera, the tigers have trembled for these hands." Holding them up, he continued, "and dare you think to threaten me with your wretched instrument? No, I despise the utmost tortures you can now invent as much as I do the pitiful wretch who is going to inflict them." Saying which, he threw himself down on the rack where amidst the most excruciating torments he remained with a smile, without uttering a syllable. Nor did he ever speak again until he ended his unhappy days at the gallows....

Having dined with Colonel Fourgeoud on the 8th of March when we celebrated the Prince of Orange's birthday, Mr. Rynsdorp gave a treat to all the soldiers. He acquainted me: that the rangers were now alone encamped at the Wana Creek; that the pestilential spot Devil's Harwar was at last entirely forsaken; and that the two lately raised companies of sable volunteers had taken a few prisoners and killed others on the Wanica Path behind Paramaribo. I was at this time a good deal better, but still not being quite recovered....At this time Colonel Fourgeoud and myself were daily visitors of the ladies in whose company no man could behave better. I could often not avoid disgust, however.

Indeed, so languid were many in their looks and so unrestrained were some in their conversation, that a Mrs. N—— even asked me, *sans ceremonie*, to supply the place of her husband. She might as well have asked me to drink a tumbler of salts.

On the 17th, however, my eyes were better feasted when, going to dine with Colonel Texier of the Society troops, I first took a walk in the orange grove and the governor's gardens. Here, peeping through the foliage, I soon discovered two most elegant female figures after bathing. One was a fine young sambo and the other a blooming quadroon. The latter was so very fair complexioned that she might have passed for a native of Greece, while the roses that glowed in her cheek were equal to those that blossomed in the shrubbery.[32] They were walking hand-in-hand and conversing with smiles near a flowery bank that adorned the side of a crystal brook in which they plunged the instant they heard me rustling amongst the verdure, like two mermaids....

Leaving them to enjoy their innocent amusement of bathing, I spent the remaining hour before dinner among the shady fruit trees, blooming bowers, and serpentine gravel walks. Indeed, I saw greater variety of European plants than I imagined were produced in a tropical climate, such as mint, fennel, sage, rosemary, golden-rod and jessamine, the sensitive plant, pomegranates, roses, figs, and even some grapes....

> *Over several paragraphs, Stedman describes various fruits, such as pineapples and melons, which grew in Suriname, and the butterfly specimens he sent to Europe for study.*

Captains Van Guerick and Fredericy, along with Sergeant Fowler, were sent on an embassy to the Owca and Saamaka free negroes to procure, if possible, their assistance against the rebels. They always promised while Colonel Fourgeoud gave them presents, but never yet performed. A few of the other officers still stayed with us gallanting at Paramaribo, among whom were Major Medlaer and Captain Hamell,[33] who had both been with General De Salve regiment, in the colony Berbice and, previous to that, the first was in the Prussian service. It was no small change for us who had so little a time before appeared like wild men now strut through Paramaribo dressed like so many French marquees.

---

32. Original footnote: It is to be remarked, that though Europeans look pale under the torrid zone, the native inhabitants have often a freshness peculiarly engaging, particularly mulattoes and quadroons.

33. Original footnote: The latter gentlemen, in the year 1783, sailed from the Texel to the Molucca islands; where, as commander in chief, he killed the king of Pongue, with his three sons, and 600 men; and dethroned also the king of *Solangoo*, whose land he captured for the Dutch East-India Company, besides taking 127 pieces of cannon, &c. [In the original 1796 edition, Stedman or the printer named this man "Captain Hemmet" but corrected it in the errata, or corrections, section at the end of Volume II.]

Being a particular favorite of Governor Nepveu, I one day was induced to ask him for a piece of uncultivated forest ground and he readily granted me 400 acres. But when I inconsiderately asked it of him, I had not calculated how large a capital it required to clear away woods, purchase negroes, and provide other necessaries for such an undertaking. A little reflection convinced me how difficult it would be to find a partner of abilities to assist me, so I declined accepting this mark of the governor's regard.

Having on the 26th once more saved a poor Black girl from receiving some hundred lashes by replacing a dozen pieces of china which she had broken by accident. Another was stabbed by a Frenchman, who immediately cut his own throat from remorse and his companion, an overseer, hanged himself. Having visited the poor negro whose leg had lately been cut off by law, I packed my boxes to set out next morning on my sixth campaign and once more take the command of the Commewijne River. At that moment arrived at my lodgings six negro slaves loaded with presents from my hospitable friends, of every kind that Guiana could produce and the colony of Suriname could afford me.

Chapter XXVII

The Rape of the Sabines—Shocking Execution, and African Fortitude—Description of an Indigo Plantation—The Spanso Bocko, a Punishment—The Troops again re-enter the Woods—The Expedition draws to a Conclusion

Chapter XXVII opens with renewed maroon attacks on plantations, specifically the kidnapping of enslaved women. The chapter quickly becomes morose as Stedman continued to seek freedom for Joanna and Johnny. Without the funds to do so, however, Stedman was at the mercy of Mrs. Godefroy to take care of Joanna and the government to free Johnny. Stedman's melancholy shines throughout the chapter as he engaged in long discussions of the violence that occurred every day in Suriname, including acts against free people of color and working-class whites, such as soldiers and sailors. That said, as throughout the entirety of the Narrative, *enslaved people faced the most extreme and gratuitous violence. Stedman's description of this violence reveals a desire to elicit strong emotional reactions and empathy from his reader.*

Nevertheless, while Stedman humanized victims, he also once again equivocated on the question of slavery. Besides the horrible treatment of enslaved people, Stedman provided not only examples of benevolent enslavers but also the inhumane treatment of others in Suriname. In doing so, he largely erased the particular horror and moral abomination of slavery and instead transformed violence and callousness into an ever-present, nondescript force. Slavery was just one of many forms of inhumanity, different in degree rather than kind. And, if slavery was part of a larger world of violence, the solution to slavery was not a political process of abolition but rather more humane behavior by those who wielded power. Stedman concluded the chapter by heading back into the jungle for a final campaign against the maroons.

Notwithstanding the successive defeats and repeated distresses of the rebels, news was brought to Paramaribo on the 12th of August that they had fallen upon estate Bergendal, also called the Blue Bergh or Mount Parnassus, situated in the higher parts of the River Suriname, and carried away all the Black women.[34] They did this without committing any kind of cruelty (as too generally had been their custom) and despite a military post stationed near the above place. Upon this intelligence a party of the rangers was instantly detached thither to assist in pursuing them. About this same time the long-projected cordon, or path of circumvallation,[35] around the colony was also began to be cut by seven hundred negro slaves. The path was henceforth to be manned with military piquets at proper distances, to defend the estates against any farther invasions from without, and to prevent desertion to the enemy from within....

If, as I have just mentioned, cruelties became less common in the rivers by the rebels, barbarities still continued in a shocking degree in the metropolis. My ears were deafened with the clang of the whip and the shrieks of the negroes. Among the most eminent of these tyrants was a Miss Sp———n, who lived next door to Mr. De Graaff, and who I saw with horror from my window give orders that a young Black woman should be flogged principally across the breasts at which she seemed to enjoy peculiar satisfaction. To dissipate the impression this scene had left on my mind, I got into whiskey, and rode out. The first thing I saw was a negro girl fall naked from a garret window on a heap of broken bottles. This was indeed an accident, but she was so mangled, though not dead, that she exhibited a spectacle nearly as wretched as the other. Cursing my unlucky fate, I turned the horses and drove to the beach as the only place to avoid every scene of cruelty and misery. Here I had the mortification to see two Philadelphia sailors (while they were fighting on the forecastle of their vessel) both fall over the ship's bow into the stream where they sunk and were no more seen. On board another American brig, I discovered

---

34. Since most maroon communities tended to be majority male, they often raided plantations to seize enslaved women as wives and concubines.

35. A military term for a defensive line of fortifications encircling a piece of territory.

a little tar[36] defending himself from the crosstrees with a hatchet against a sergeant and four armed men for a considerable time. When they threatened to shoot him out of the rigging, he at last surrendered, and, being brought ashore, was dragged to Fort Zeelandia in company with two others by a file of musketeers. The latter, for having been drunk on duty, received a *fire-cant* each at the captain's request. That is, they were bastinadoed or beaten on the shoulders by two corporals with bamboo canes until their backs were black and swelled like a cushion. However arbitrary this mode of correction, the captain endeavored to explain the necessity of it. The private American sailors are of a turbulent spirit indeed when drunk, although when sober they may be fairly classed among the best seamen in the world.

Early the next morning, while musing on all the different dangers and chastisements to which the lower class of people are exposed, I heard a crowd pass under my window. Curiosity made me start up, dress in a hurry, and follow them when I discovered three negroes in chains, surrounded by a guard, going to be executed in the savannah. Their undaunted look, however averse I may be to the fight of cruelties, so attracted my attention as to determine me to see the result, which follows. The sentence being read in Low Dutch[37] (which they did not understand), one was condemned to be flogged below the gallows and his accomplice to have his head struck off with an ax for having shot a slave who had come to steal plantains on the estate of his mistress. The truth, however, was that this had been done by that lady's absolute command. The murder being discovered, she, in the hopes of saving her character, besides the expense of paying the penalties, gave up her valuable slave and permitted the unhappy man to be thus sacrificed. He laid his head upon the block with great indifference, stretching out his neck. Then, with one blow of the ax, it was severed from his body.

The third negro, whose name was Neptune, was no slave, but his own master[38] and a carpenter by trade. He was young and handsome but having killed the overseer of the estate Altona in Para Creek, in consequence of some dispute, he justly forfeited his life. The particulars, however, are worth relating. Neptune stole a sheep to entertain a favorite young woman. The overseer, who burnt with jealousy, wanted to see Neptune hanged. To prevent this from happening, the negro shot him dead among the sugarcane. For these offences, of course, he was sentenced to be broken alive upon the rack, without the benefit of the *coup de grace* or mercy stroke. Informed of

---

36. Sailor.

37. I.e., formal Dutch. Most people in Suriname, enslaved and free, spoke a creole language called Sranan Tongo. The language is still spoken in Suriname today and, as a mixture of English, Dutch, Spanish, Portuguese, and West African languages, reflects Suriname's history as a plantation colony.

38. I.e., he was a free Black man.

the dreadful sentence, he composedly laid himself down on his back on a strong cross on which, with arms and legs expanded, he was fastened by ropes. The executioner, also a Black man, chopped off Neptune's left hand with a hatchet. Next, the executioner took up a heavy iron bar with which, by repeated blows, he broke Neptune's bones to shivers[39] until the marrow, blood, and splinters flew about the field. But the prisoner never uttered a groan nor a sigh. The ropes being next unlashed, I imagined him dead and felt happy. When the magistrates stirred to depart, he writhed himself from the cross, fell on the grass, and damned them all as a set of barbarous rascals. At the same time removing his right hand by the help of his teeth, he rested his head on part of the timber, and asked the by-standers for a pipe of tobacco, which was infamously answered by kicking and spitting on him until I, with some American seamen, thought proper to prevent it. He then begged that his head might be chopped off but to no purpose. At last, seeing no end to his misery, he declared that though he had deserved death, he had "not expected to die so many deaths." "However," he continued, "you Christians have missed your aim at last and I now care not were I to remain thus one month longer." After which he sung two extempore songs with a clear voice. The subjects of these songs were to bid adieu to his living friends and to acquaint his deceased relations that in a very little time he should be with them to enjoy their company forever in a better place. This done, he calmly entered into conversation with some gentlemen concerning his trial relating every particular with uncommon tranquility. "But," he said abruptly, "by the sun it must be eight o'clock; and by any longer discourse I should be sorry to be the cause of your losing your breakfast." Then, casting his eyes on a Jew, whose name was De Vries, "A-propos, sir," Neptune asked, "won't you please to pay me the ten shillings you owe me?" "For what to do?" replied De Vries. "To buy meat and drink, to be sure—don't you perceive I am to be kept alive?" Which speech, on seeing the Jew stare like a fool, this mangled wretch accompanied with a loud and hearty laugh. Next, observing the soldier that stood sentinel over him biting occasionally on a piece of dry bread, he asked him "how it came to pass, that he, a *white man*, should have no meat to eat along with it?" "Because I am not so rich," answered the soldier. "Then I will make you a present, sir," said the negro. "First, pick my hand that was chopped off clean to the bones, next begin to devour my body, until you are glutted. When you will have both bread and meat, as best becomes you." This piece of humor was followed by a second laugh and thus he continued until I left him, which was about three hours after the dreadful execution.

    Wonderful it is indeed that human nature should be able to endure so much torture, which assuredly could only be supported by a mixture of rage,

---

39. I.e., splinters.

contempt, pride, and the glory of braving his tormentors from whom he was so soon to escape....[40]

Stedman wrote a summary of an image he drew of the execution, followed by a long passage about the vultures and eagles that inhabit Suriname.

On the 24th, being the Prince of Orange's birthday, the whole corps of officers were entertained with salt beef, salt pork, barley puddings, and hard peas by Colonel Fourgeoud. And this day (poor Joanna being inflexible in her resolutions) I ratified the agreement with the good Mrs. Godefroy in presence of her mother and other relations, whereby the above lady bound herself never to part with Joanna except to myself alone as long as she lived. Upon Mrs. Godefroy's death, Joanna would receive not only her full liberty, but also a spot of ground for cultivation and a neat house built upon it that would be Joanna's forever and to dispose of as she pleased. After this, she returned my remaining bond of 900 florins and gave Joanna a purse with gold containing near twenty ducats besides a couple of pieces of East India chintz. At the same time Mrs. Godefroy advised me to give a request to the court for little Johnny's immediate manumission....

Having both of us thanked this most excellent woman, I went to sup with the Governor where, being transported with joy, I gave him my request in full form, which he coolly put in his pocket with one hand, while he gave me a hearty squeeze with the other. Shaking his head, he told me frankly that he would lay it before the court but at the same time was perfectly convinced my boy must die a slave unless I could find the necessary bail, which he was at the same time well persuaded very few people would wish to appear for. Thus, after spending so much time and labor, besides the expense of above a hundred guineas already paid, I had still the inexpressible mortification to see this dear little fellow, of whom I was both the father and the master, exposed to perhaps eternal servitude. As for Joanna, she was now perfectly safe to my heartfelt satisfaction....

On the 25th, the Governor of the colony gave a very sumptuous feast to several of his friends at his indigo plantation, which was situated but a few miles at the back of his palace. I had the honor to be invited as one of the party and had the pleasure of inspecting the process of making indigo....

The next four paragraphs describe the process of making indigo and the man who brought the commodity to Suriname.

Dinner being over at the Governor's indigo plantation, I now departed in his excellency's coach to the waterside where a tent barge and eight oars lay in

---

40. Original footnote: At Demerara, so late as October, 1789, thirty-two wretches were executed in three days, sixteen of whom suffered in the manner just described, with no less fortitude, and without uttering one single complaint.

waiting to row me down to estate Catwijk on the Commewijne River. There, I was invited by Mr. Goetzee, a Dutch naval officer, who was the proprietor of this beautiful country seat. In this charming situation, no amusements were wanting. There were carriages, saddlehorses, sailboats, billiard tables, etc., all ready for immediate use. But what embittered the pleasure was the inhuman disposition of Mr. Goetzee's lady, who flogged her negro slaves for every little trifle. For instance, she ordered one of the footboys, called Jacky, whipped the next morning for not having rinsed the glasses according to her mind. But the unfortunate youth soon put himself beyond the reach of her resentment. Having taken farewell of the other negroes on the estate, he went upstairs and laid himself down upon his master's own bed where he placed the muzzle of a loaded fowling-piece in his mouth. By the help of his toe, he drew the trigger and put an end to his existence. A couple of stout negroes were now sent up to see what was the matter. Finding the bed all over bespattered with blood and brains, they received orders to throw the body out of the window to the dogs, while the master and mistress were so very much alarmed, that they never got the better of it.[41] Nor would any person consent to lie in the same apartment until I chose it in preference to any other, being assuredly the most pleasant room and the very best bed in the house. What added much to the alarm of the family was the circumstance of a favorite child lying fast asleep in the same apartment where this shocking catastrophe happened. They were, however, relieved from their alarms on this score by being informed that it had not received the smallest injury.

I had not been fourteen days on this plantation when a female mulatto slave, called Yettee, jocosely[42] said "her mistress had some debt as well as herself," was stripped stark naked, and, in a very indecent as well as inhuman manner, flogged by two stout negroes before the dwelling house door (while both her feet were locked to a heavy iron bolt) until hardly any skin was left on her thighs or sides. Five days after this, I had the good fortune to get her relieved from the iron bolt, which was locked across her shins. A Mrs. Van Eys alleging Yettee had affronted her also by her saucy looks, however, prevailed on Mrs. Goetzee to renew the punishment the same week. Then, she was so cruelly beaten that I expected she could not have survived it.

Disgusted with this barbarity, I left Catwijk, determined never more to return to it. Nevertheless, I still accompanied Mr. Goetzee to visit some of his other plantations in the Cottica and Perica Rivers out of curiosity. At one of these, called the Alida, a newborn female infant was presented me, by way of

---

41. Original footnote: The above unhappy people were poisoned by their slaves about six years after this happened.
42. I.e., jokingly or in jest.

compliment, to give it a name, which I called Charlotte.⁴³ But the next morning during breakfast, seven negroes were here again tied up and flogged, some with a cow-skin, which is very terrible. Hence, I made my retreat to the estate 's-Graven-Hague and there meeting a mulatto youth in chains, whose name was Douglas, I with horror recollected his unhappy father who had been obliged to leave him a slave and was now dead. Heartily tired of my excursion, I was now glad to make haste back to Paramaribo. As soon as I arrived, the first news I heard was that Colonel Fourgeoud's French valet-de-chamber, poor Monsieur Laurant, had actually been buried before he was quite dead and that, for having been found drunk in an alehouse, no less than thirteen of our men had most severely run the gauntlet and as many been terribly bastinadoed, the greatest number of which no more saw Europe.⁴⁴ Likewise, a quadroon youth and a Dutch sailor were found murdered on the beach. I was now proceeding to take a walk on the plain or esplanade, but here I was called in by Mr. St———k———r, who conducting me three stories high and told me "From this window a few days since, leaped one of my Black boys, to escape a gentle flogging. However, having only fainted in consequence of his fall, we soon brought him to life again by a hearty scouring on the ribs, so he did not escape. After which, for having risked himself, that is to say his master's property and frightened my wife, she ordered him to be sent to Fort Zeelandia, where he received the interest, that is a most confounded *spanso-bocko*."

The punishment called spanso-bocko is extremely severe indeed, and is executed in the following manner. The prisoner's hands being lashed together, he is laid down on the ground on one side, with his knees thrust between his arms, and these confined by a strong stake, which separates them from his wrists, and is driven perpendicularly into the ground, insomuch that he can no more stir than if he was dead. In this locked position, trussed like a fowl, he is beaten on one side of his breech by a strong negro with a handful of knotty tamarind branches until the very flesh is cut away. He is then turned over on the other side where the same dreadful flagellation is inflicted until not a bit of skin is left and the place of execution is dyed with blood. After which, the raw lacerated wound is immediately washed with lemon juice and gunpowder to prevent mortification and he is then sent home to recover as well as he can.

The above cruel and indecent punishment is sometimes repeated at every street in the town of Paramaribo to men and women indiscriminately, which is a severity absolutely beyond conception. However, it is never thus inflicted without a condemnation from the court. But a single spanso-bocko, without regard to age or sex, may be ordered by any proprietor, either at home or by

---

43. Stedman does not explain where the name came from, but the child may have been named after the queen consort of Britain's King George III, Charlotte of Mecklenburg-Strelitz (1744–1818).
44. I.e., they died.

sending the victim to the fortress with a note to the public executioner to whom some trifle in money is paid as a fee of office.

I next was addressed by a Monsieur Rochetaux, whose Coromantyn cook, having spoiled his ragout had just cut his own throat to prevent a whipping and Mr. Charles Rynsdorp's lately did the same.

After these facts, can it be a matter of surprise, that the negro slaves rise up in rebellion against masters who treat them with so very much severity?

As I do not recollect that I have described in what manner these insurgents generally attack the estates, I cannot introduce it on a more proper occasion.

Having laid during the night lurking in the bushes that surround the estate, they always appear a little before daybreak when they unexpectedly fall on and massacre the Europeans. They plunder the dwelling house, which they next set on fire, and then carry off the negro women, whom they load with the spoil and treat with the utmost insolence should they make opposition.[45]

And now farewell, I hope, ye wretched objects, who have not made the least conspicuous figure in these bloody pages! for which I should be more ready to apologize to the reader had I not been induced to make cruelty ashamed of itself and humanity gain ground. That at last, in some measure, my motive may be crowned with success, I most sincerely wish, abhorring every act of barbarity from the very bottom of my soul....

I have already stated that on the 24th of August I gave in a hopeless request to the Governor for my boy's emancipation. On the 8th of October, I saw with equal joy and surprise the following advertisement posted up, "That if anyone could give in a lawful objection why John Stedman, a quadroon infant and the son of Captain Stedman, should not be presented with the blessing of freedom, such person or persons to appear before January 1st, 1777." I no sooner read it than I ran with the good news to my good friend, Mr. Palmer, who assured me, that the above was no more than a form, put in practice on the supposition of my producing the bail required, which undoubtedly they expected, from my having so boldly given in my request to the governor of the colony. Without being able to utter one syllable in reply, I retired to the company of Joanna, who, with a smile, bid me "never to despair, that Johnny certainly one day would be free." Nor did she ever fail in giving me some consolation whatever desperate were my expectations.

About this time, we were informed that in the Utrecht paper an impertinent libel had appeared against the good Fourgeoud that ridiculed him for his embassy to the Owca and Saamaka negroes. That gentleman, though he had no assistance from these allies to expect and his troops now melted down almost to nothing nevertheless scorned to keep those that could stand upon

---

45. Original footnote: For minute particulars I cannot do better than refer the curious to Mr. Belknap's *History of New Hampshire*; where he describes the insurrection of the American Indians, which are almost perfectly similar to those of the African negroes.

their feet inactive. Thus, having provided the few remaining privates with new clothes (the first they had received since 1772) besides new sabers, bill-hooks, etc., he sent them all once more up, accompanied only by the subalterns to be encamped at the mouth of Cassipora Creek in the upper parts of the Cottica River. The staff officers and captains were ordered soon to follow....

Having now prepared myself once more for actual service and again received a profusion of wine, spirits, and refreshments of every kind to carry with me to the woods from different friends in Paramaribo, I left my dear mulatto and her boy to the care of that excellent woman Mrs. Godefroy. The following day, I set out on my seventh campaign to help, if possible, to complete that business we had so long and so ardently undertaken for the safety and welfare of this valuable colony and its lawful inhabitants of every denomination. Happily, my health and my spirits were at this time once more just as vigorous and strong as the very first day that I landed with Colonel Fourgeoud and his regiment of marines in Suriname.

Chapter XXIX

Some Account of a remarkable Negro—The Troops prepare for Europe—Description of a Coffee Plantation—Plan of Reform for the Increase of Population, and universal Happiness—One more Instance of horrid Barbarity; and Example of Humanity—The Regiment embarks

Chapter XXIX is the penultimate chapter of Stedman's Narrative *and the final chapter included in this edition. The chapter opens with Stedman back in Paramaribo from his final campaign and preparing to depart Suriname once and for all. He attempted to cover many topics in the chapter, including describing Graman Quassi, a famous free Black man in Suriname, and the end of the campaign against the maroons. Mostly, however, the chapter revolves around three topics. First, throughout the chapter, Stedman described his reconciliation with Colonel Fourgeoud. Second, Stedman laid out his vision for a more humane, reformed system of slavery. While certainly utopian and probably impossible to implement, Stedman still attempted, in typical fashion, to create a system that helped enslaved people and kept their enslavers content. To formulate this argument, the author indulged in a number of stereotypes about Africans, such as arguing they were ultimately better off being enslaved in the Americas than living in Africa, revealing Stedman's bigotry and belief in European supremacy. Nevertheless, Stedman did offer some insights into the status of enslaved people, such as calling them, in their current condition, "dead-alive." Stedman understood that enslaved people effectively had no legal existence outside their owner's. His reformed slavery sought to correct that issue. Finally, much of the chapter focuses on Stedman's continued tribulations with Joanna and Johnny. Joanna ultimately refused to leave with Stedman, and the chapter concludes with an emotional, if overwrought, farewell.*

Being now once more arrived in town and wishing to be no longer troublesome to anybody, I hired a very neat small house by the waterside. We lived nearly as happy as we had done at the Hope.

The first person that visited me here was the American Captain Lewis, of the *Peggy*, who, to my great concern, told me, that poor MacDonald, the grateful sailor, had died on the homeward passage after being twelve days at sea. In his last words, he desired to return to me, with his good wishes, the mother-of-pearl corkscrew I had formerly given him. He further acquainted me also, to my sorrow, that three English vessels had been captured by the *American Revenue* privateer sloop,[46] which lay at this time, with her prizes, in the road before Paramaribo. One of them, belonging to Ireland, was valued at above £50,000 sterling.

Having been waited on by a number of planters and others with congratulations on our success against the rebels, among the rest appeared the celebrated Graman Quassi, who came to show me his fine coat, gold medal, etc., which he had received as a present from the Prince of Orange in Holland. This man, being one of the most extraordinary characters of all the negroes in Suriname or perhaps in the world, I cannot proceed without giving some account of him.... This African who was born on the coast of Guinea, by his insinuating temper and industry, not only obtained his freedom from a state of slavery, but also by his wonderful ingenuity and artful conduct found the means of procuring a very competent subsistence.

Quacy is known as a *lockoman*, or sorcerer, among the lower slaves. Whenever a crime of consequence was committed, especially on the plantations, Graman Quassi, which means "Great-man Quacy" was instantly sent for to discover the perpetrators, He so very seldom missed, owing, in fact, to their faith in his sorceries, his penetrating look, and authority among them, that he has often prevented further mischief to their masters. These services occasionally received monetary rewards. The corps of rangers, and all fighting free negroes, are under his influence. He sells them his *obias* or amulets in order to make them invulnerable and, of course, to engage without fear. By this deceit,

---

46. A privateer was a privately owned ship with a license, called a letter of marque, issued by a government to raid enemy shipping during wartime. In this case, the revolutionary government of the United States extensively used privateers to attack British shipping during the War of Independence.

he has most certainly done much good to the colony and at the same time filled his pockets with no inconsiderable profit to himself. All the while, his person by the Blacks is adored and respected like a God. The trash of which his amulets are made costs him in reality nothing. They are mostly a collection of small pebbles, seashells, cut hair, fish-bones, feathers, etc., sewed up together in small packets, which are tied with a string of cotton round the neck or some other part of the bodies....

But besides these and many other artful contrivances, he had the good fortune in 1730 to find out the valuable root known by the name of *Quaciae bitter*,[47] of which he was actually the first discoverer and from which it took its name. Although this medicine is now less in repute in England than formerly, it is highly esteemed in many other parts of the world for its efficacy in strengthening the stomach and restoring the appetite. It has, besides this valuable property, that of being a powerful febrifuge....[48]

This very same week we had indeed a fresh proof of the good effects of Graman Quassi's animating obias or amulets. A captain of the rangers named Hannibal brought in the barbecued hands of two rebel negroes, which he had himself encountered and shot. One of these hands proved to be that of the noted rebel Cupido, once captured in 1774, and brought to Colonel Fourgeoud in the forest, but from whom he had since that time, though loaded with chains, found means to run away.

In returning the visits of my friends, I paid one to Mr. Andrew Rynsdorp, who showed me the loop and button of his hat, which being diamond, had cost him two hundred guineas—such is the luxury of Suriname! But even this is exceeded by the magnificence of M. d'Halbergh, who, when I waited on him, besides owing a gold snuff box set with brilliants,[49] valued at 600 pounds sterling, made me remark at two silver bits (small pieces of money) set in gold, and surrounded with diamonds with this inscription: *Soli Deo Gloria. Fortuna Beaticum.*[50]

Having signified my surprise at this peculiar attention and respect to two sixpences, he declared to me that they were all the money he had in the world when he first came to Suriname from his own country, Sweden. "Did you work?" said I. "No," he replied. "Did you beg?" I inquired further. "No," was his answer again. "You did not steal, sir?" I asked. "No, but, *entre nous*,"[51] he continued, "I whined and acted the enthusiast, which sometimes is very necessary, and I found preferable to the other three." To which I answered, "Sir, your

---

47. Its actual scientific name is *Quassia amara*, a small shrub that grows in tropical regions of the Americas. It has many uses, including as medicine.
48. I.e., a medicine used to reduce fever.
49. I.e., a type of cut diamond.
50. "Glory only to God. Fortune Blesses Us."
51. "Between us."

candid confession brings back to my remembrance your usage of your negro slave, Baron, after having promised him his manumission in Amsterdam and fully proves what you have just asserted." One instance more of the extravagance and folly of the inhabitants of this colony and I am done. Two of them had a dispute about a most elegant and expensive carriage that was imported from Holland. A lawsuit ensued immediately to determine who was to possess it, during which time the coach was left uncovered in the street till it fell to pieces and was totally destroyed.

On the 10th of February, most of our officers being now arrived at Paramaribo from the camp, Colonel Fourgeoud entertained the whole with a feast, as he was pleased to call it, at the headquarters. An old stable lantern, with broken panes of glass, hanging over our heads, which I expected every moment to drop into the soup. And here he acquainted us, with evident marks of satisfaction, that he had at last put a final end to the expedition. Notwithstanding there was so little bloodshed, he perfectly accomplished his aim in rooting out the rebels by destroying TWENTY-ONE TOWNS or VILLAGES and demolishing TWO HUNDRED FIELDS with vegetables of every kind on which they depended for subsistence. Also, the intelligence was now confirmed that the negroes were to a man fled over the River Maroni where they and their friends were settled and protected by the French colony of Cayenne. The French not only gave them shelter, but supplied them with everything they wanted. On this good news, we all heartily congratulated him and drank further prosperity to the colony of Suriname with three cheers. The future safety of which now depended on the new cordon or path of circumvallation, defended by the troops of the Society and the corps of Black soldiers or rangers.

…And what cannot but redound to [Colonel Fourgeoud's] honor is that at the time he imposed such hardships on his own troops, he never deliberately put a rebel negro captive to death nor even, if he could avoid it, delivered them into the hands of justice. He knew well that while it was his duty to expel them, nothing but the most barbarous usage and tyranny had driven these poor people to this last extremity. Indeed, I myself, whom during the first three years he persecuted with unremitting severity, must do him the justice to say that he was indefatigable in doing his duty and that, though confused, I believe him at bottom to have been an undaunted and very BRAVE OFFICER.…

After providing a lengthy discussion of coffee production in Suriname, largely drawn from secondary sources and not his own observations, Stedman made some general observations about plantation production in the colony.

…I cannot have a fairer opportunity of fulfilling my promise of submitting to the reader a few considerations, by an attention to which I cannot help thinking that not only Suriname, but also the West Indian colonies in general, might accumulate wealth to themselves. These would promote the permanent happiness of the slaves that are under their subjection without having recourse to the Coast of Guinea to supply the almost hourly consumption of that unfortunate people....I shall endeavor to point out how, in my opinion, they *ought* to be distributed and treated, according to the laws not only of humanity but of common sense....

> *Stedman explored the demography of Suriname's enslaved population before moving into a discussion of his own ideas.*

Having thus at an average demonstrated how they are distributed, I must briefly observe, that while full 30,000 live better than the common people of England and near 30,000 are kept in idleness and do no work in the fields, the remaining 20,000 may be classed (that is in general) among the most miserable wretches on earth. They are worked, starved, insulted, and flogged to death without being so much as allowed to complain for redress, without being heard in their own defense, and without receiving common justice on any occasion. Thus, they may be considered as "dead-alive," since they are cut off from all the common privileges of human society.

I will now proceed, by candidly asking the world, if the above is not an improper and senseless misapplication, not only of wealth, but of human life and labor? And, by a proper distribution and management, might accumulate the one and relieve the other?

Now would this inconsiderate colony but give up their habits of pride and luxury even in a moderate degree, 20,000 negroes at least might be added to those now laboring in the fields. Provided the whole were treated with less severity, at the same time it would keep the superfluous number of idlers employed. And, by assisting the others in their necessary occupations, could not but tend greatly to prevent that shocking mortality to which they are at present exposed by unbounded ill-usage and barbarity.

But every reform must begin at that which is the source of *manners* as well as of *justice*. Those therefore who are entrusted with the executive government should have no temptation to overlook the breaches of a law, while it ought to be a sacred and invariable rule never to allow either the governor or the magistrates of such a colony to be the proprietors of more slaves than merely a limited number to attend on their persons, according to their ranks. More than once, even to *my* observation, it has occurred that those who made and those who were appointed to enforce the laws have been the first that *broke them* for the paltry benefit of causing their negroes to work on a Sunday or to follow the bent of their unbounded passions. From such a shameful example from the magistrate, the contagion must necessarily spread among the individuals.

Let the *governor* and principal *magistrates*, therefore, be sent out from Europe. Let them be gentlemen of fortune and education. And, above all, they should be men of liberal minds, who are firm against the allurement of a bribe or the glittering of gold and whose passions are restrained by sentiment and manly feelings. Let these men be handsomely rewarded by that nation whom they so materially serve and the colony which they so conspicuously protect, but let their salaries be ascertained, without depending on the blood and sweat of the miserable Africans. Then let such men enact impartial regulations by which the negro slaves are to perform no more than their fair task and labor a reasonable number of hours. Let these be followed by protecting laws and let them be no longer racked, tormented, wantonly murdered, or infamously robbed of all that is dear to the human affections, their wives and daughters. Let regulations be adopted by which they may be properly fed and attended to when sick or indisposed. And, above all, let equal justice be administered. Suffer them, when outraged or plundered, to obtain a hearing. Permit them to complain and enable them to prove by *evidence* the grievances by which they are oppressed. Even give them what we so much value ourselves, AN INDEPENDENT JUDGE and AN IMPARTIAL JURY, nay, partly composed of their own sable companions. Thus, would you have them work and act like *men*, first suffer them to be *such*.

When regulations conform to these shall be adopted and enforced, I venture to say that nations will feel the benefit of their colonies: planters will become rich and their overseers become honest. Slavery will be little more than a name and subjects will, with pleasure, fulfill their limited task. Then, and not until then, will population sufficiently increase for the necessary work and the execrable Guinea trade be *totally* abolished, which is now too frequently carried on with barbarity and unbounded usurpation. Then, the master will with pleasure look on his sable subjects as on his children and the principal source of his happiness, while the negroes will bless the day their ancestors did first set foot on American ground.

Having thus, according to my opinion, pointed out the way—and the only way (if well considered)—to redress the grievances of this and many other colonies, I would also recommend to planters and overseers in general to…take an example by that incomparable woman Mrs. Godefroy, by Mr. Thomas Palmer, and a few others, who consider their slaves as their fellow creatures without paying the smallest regard either to their paganism or complexion. And who increase both their wealth and their happiness by their humanity.…

On the 16th, being invited to dine with his excellency the governor, I laid before him my collection of drawings and remarks on the colony of Suriname, which I had the satisfaction to see him honor with the highest approbation. I then returned him my thanks, not only for the material assistance he had afforded me in completing this work, but for the unlimited marks of regard and distinction with which he had treated me from first to last during the whole time I resided in Guiana.

Availing myself of his friendship, I ventured, two days after, to give him the following very uncommon request, praying him to lay it before the court. With a smile on his countenance and a hearty shake by the hand, he actually promised me to perform:

I, the under-subscribed, do pledge my word of honor (being all I possess in the world besides my pay) as bail, that if my late ardent request to the court for the emancipation of my dear boy JOHNNY STEDMAN be granted, the said boy shall never to the end of his life become a charge to the colony of Suriname.

(Signed) JOHN G. STEDMAN
Paramaribo,
Feb. 18th, 1777

Having now done the utmost that lay in my power, I for several days waited the result with anxiety, but without meeting with the smallest hopes of success. Thus, with a broken heart, I was obliged at last to give him (sweet fellow) over for lost or take him with me to Europe, which must have been plunging a dagger in the bosom of his mother.

While I remained in this situation, the transport ships were put in commission on the 26th for our departure and I myself ordered as one of the commissaries to see them wooded and watered. The officers were also cleared their arrears and thirteen men discharged at their own desire to push their fortune at Paramaribo. I ought here not to omit that the industrious Colonel Fourgeoud once more paid us all in paper, by which, as usual, we lost 10 percent. By letting the Jews have the gold and silver, he prudently lodged in his own pocket.[52] Meanwhile, the many hundreds of florins allowed us by government to defray excise duties, taxes, etc., were never brought to account or, rather, we were forbidden to enquire after them at all. These were trifles indeed, when divided among so many gentlemen, but in one solid mass, they were no contemptible picking.

On the 1st of March, a sergeant arrived from the camp at the Cassipora Creek, where the recently-arrived troops were hourly dying away and brought the almost incredible account. The man I mentioned to have been lost in the woods on the 10th of February was actually returned, after having been missing 26 days, nine of which he subsisted on a few pounds of biscuit and seventeen on nothing at all but water. He added that he had entirely lost his voice and was reduced to a perfect skeleton. However, by the care taken of him by the officers, there were still hopes of his life....

On the 3rd of March, my friend De Graaff sailed for Holland, but first stopped in St. Eustatius[53] where his brother was governor. To my great satisfaction, he took with him Joanna's youngest brother, Henry, for whom he has

---

52. Here, Stedman described how Fourgeoud exchanged the gold and silver coinage provided to pay the soldiers to Jewish moneylenders, who paid Fourgeoud in paper money. Since paper money was only worth 90 percent of the value of coinage, Fourgeoud would have only had to exchange that amount of coinage and kept the remaining 10 percent for himself.

53. An island in the eastern Caribbean that is still an overseas territory of the Netherlands. In the eighteenth century, St. Eustatius was an important trade hub.

since obtained his freedom. I sailed with them down the river as far as Braam's Point[54] and wished them a successful voyage.

On the 8th of March, we celebrated the Prince of Orange's birthday at the headquarters. There…hearing Captain Bolts in an undeserved manner censured by the colonel's adjutant for recommending one of the young volunteers of an excellent character, but who had no friends to support him,[55] I broke through the ring that surrounded them in a passion and not being able to restrain myself publicly reproved the aggressor, even in Fourgeoud's presence. A furious altercation and very high words immediately ensued. The consequence of which was, that next morning at sunrise we walked to the savannah without seconds, where, near the gallows, we drew our small swords and after making a few passes at each other, Captain Van Guerick's point met my shell,[56] which having nearly pierced, his blade snapped in two pieces and the fortune of war put him entirely in my power. Disdaining, however, to take a mean advantage, I instantly dropped my small sword and desired him to step home and replace his own in order to renew the battle. This proposal he was pleased to call so generous that, taking me by the hand, he requested a renewal of friendship. Thus acknowledging we had been too hasty on both sides, we went to visit poor Bolts, who knew nothing of our morning walk, and was (though not without difficulty) persuaded also to enter into the amicable treaty. Through this, a second encounter was happily prevented and a general reconciliation took place.…

The following day I was shocked and surprised beyond the power of expression, at seeing a Miss Jettee de la Marre, daughter to the lately deceased gentleman of that name, a lovely mulatto girl aged fourteen, who had been christened in 1775 and educated as a young lady, dragged to court in chains along with her mother and a few more of her relations, the whole surrounded by a military guard. I had almost attempted a rescue, when, having enquired the cause, she called out to me herself, weeping most bitterly and informed me, that she was going to be tried by Mr. Schouten, her mother's master, for refusing to perform the work of a common slave. She was utterly unable to perform and could never have expected that type of work because of the footing upon which she had been educated until that unhappy moment.

By the laws of the country, however, she was not only obliged to submit, but also at his desire was condemned for disobedience, together with her poor mother and all her relations, who had presumed to support her claim to liberty, to be privately whipped. Had it not been for the humanity of Mr. Wickers, who was at that time the town clerk and since was governor, this infamous sentence would most certainly have been put in execution. The unfortunate

---
54. A spit of land where the Suriname River meets the Atlantic Ocean.
55. Original footnote: A Mr. *Sheffer*, already named, who has served with honor from first to last, on the pay of a private soldier, during this painful expedition.
56. The handguard of Stedman's sword.

Miss Jettee de la Marre was, from this period, nevertheless forced to submit to the tyranny of her unmanly master, while pitied by all her acquaintance and lamented by every stranger that was a witness to the inhuman transaction.

Such were the fatal consequences of not having been timely emancipated. Such were they indeed that they made me tremble for my little boy. Happily my uneasiness was not of long duration for, however improbable and unexpected, I was surprised on the very same day with a polite message from the governor and the court, acquainting me that, "having taken my former services into consideration, together with my humanity and gallantry, in offering my honor as bail to see my child, before I left him, made a free citizen of the world," they had unanimously decreed, without further ceremony or expense, to compliment me with a letter. At the same time it was officially presented to me, it contained HIS EMANCIPATION FROM THAT DAY, FOREVER AFTER.

No man could be more suddenly transported from woe to happiness than I was at this moment. His poor mother shed tears for joy and gratitude as we had lost all hopes and the favor came perfectly unexpected. All the while, near forty beautiful boys and girls were left to perpetual slavery by their parents of my acquaintance and many of them without being so much as once enquired after at all.

What is most extraordinary indeed is that while the well-thinking few highly applauded my sensibility, many not only blamed but publicly derided me for my paternal affection, which was called a weakness, a whim. So extravagant was my joy on this day, however, at having acted the reverse part of Inkle to Yarico that I became like one frantic with pleasure. I not only made my will in his favor (though, God knows, I had little to dispose of), I also appointed my friends Mr. Robert Gordon and Mr. James Gourlay to be my executors and his guardians during my absence. In their hands, I left all my papers sealed until I should demand them again or they should be informed of my death. I then ordered all my sheep, poultry, etc., which had prodigiously increased, to be transported and put under their care. And making a new suit of clothes for the occasion, which cost me twenty guineas, I waited on a Mr. Snyderhans, one of the clergymen at Paramaribo, to appoint a day when my boy, my Johnny Stedman, should be made a Christian.[57]

---

57. Original footnote: I should not here omit to mention, that in the colony of Suriname all emancipated slaves are under the following restrictions, viz.

> They are (if males) bound to help in defending the settlement against all home and foreign enemies.
>
> No emancipated slave, male or female, can ever go to law at all against their former master or mistress.
>
> And, finally, if any emancipated slave, male or female, dies in the colony, and leaves behind any possessions whatever, in that case one quarter of the property also goes to his former owners, either male or female.

On the 18th, Colonel Fourgeoud's remaining troops at last came down from the encampments at Cassipora Creek and every preparation was made for our departure. At the same time, the ecstasy of the few surviving marines at their quitting this country was so great, having now also received part of their clearance, that such intemperance, riot, and disorder ensued as produced the most formidable quarrels between them and the troops of the Society, until some being wounded and some being flogged, peace was finally, though with difficulty, re-established....

The day of our departure now approached fast, and I gave up my house. At Mrs. Godefroy's pressing invitation, I spent the few remaining moments with Joanna and her boy in her beautiful garden, charmingly situated under the shade of tamarind and orange trees. That house she also had neatly furnished with every accommodation that could be desired, besides allowing Joanna a negro woman and a girl to attend on her for life. Thus situated, how blessed should I have been in this spot to end my days! But fate ordained it otherwise.

On the 22nd, I made it my business with Captain Small...to wait on the Reverend Mr. Snyderhans according to appointment. The minister, to both our great surprise, peremptorily refused to christen the boy, alleging for his reason that as I was going to Holland, I could not answer for his Christian education. We replied that he was under two very proper guardians. The blacksmith's son[58] (for such was this divine) persisted and we remonstrated, but to no purpose. He was just as deaf as his father's anvil and, I believe upon my soul, quite as empty as his bellows. Until at length, I wearied out with his fanatical impertinence, I swore that I would sooner see the boy die a heathen than be christened by such a blockhead. My friend Small could not help bestowing on him a hearty curse and, slapping the door with a vengeance, we departed.

Feasting and conviviality now prevailed once more at Paramaribo as on our first arrival. Grand dinners, suppers, and balls were heard of in every quarter. But I only visited a few of my select friends, among which number had constantly been Governor Nepveu. At his home and for the last time, I made one of the company at a truly magnificent entertainment, which ended the scene of liberality and hospitality for which the inhabitants of Suriname are so justly conspicuous. On the 25th, the baggage was shipped on board the vessels.

Numberless, indeed, were the presents for the voyage with which I in particular was now overstocked from every quarter. My provisions of live cattle, poultry, wine, rum, etc., were almost sufficient to carry me round the globe....

On the 26th, we took our last leave of his excellency the governor, *en corps*, as assuredly was his due. After which, all the officers of the Society troops

---

58. It is unclear if Snyderhans was actually a blacksmith's son or not. In the eighteenth century, "blacksmith's son" was also used to describe an ignorant upstart who had risen above their station.

waited on Colonel Fourgeoud at the headquarters to wish us a prosperous voyage to Holland and the day was spent by a regale and a dinner, as usual, of salt provisions. I must acknowledge, however, that it was accompanied with as much good liquor of every kind as Suriname could furnish and a very hearty welcome.

I believe that now a hundred times Fourgeoud shook me by the hand, declaring that there was not a young man he loved better in the world and that had he commanded me to march through fire as well as water, he was convinced I should never have left it without accomplishing his orders in addition to many other fine compliments. But I must candidly acknowledge that though I had a heart to forgive, my mind would never permit me to forget the many and unnecessary difficulties and miseries to which I had been too wantonly exposed. At the same time he informed me that he did not propose to depart with us, but intended to follow the regiment very soon with the remains of the recently-arrived relief and he would render me every service in his power. Suffice it to say, whatever were his real motives for such a sudden change in his disposition towards me that few people at this time were better friends, than were the old Colonel Fourgeoud and Captain Stedman.

In the evening, I went to take a short farewell of my most valuable acquaintances…but my soul was too full of a *friend*[59] that was still dearer to be impressed with that sensibility on separating from them that it must have felt on another occasion. And here I cannot in justice omit remarking that while I gave the most impetuous vent to my feelings, not the smallest expression of poignant sorrow or even of dejection, escaped from Joanna's lips. While her good sense and fortitude even restrained the tear from starting in my afflicted presence, I now once more earnestly pressed her to accompany me—in which I was seconded by the inestimable Mrs. Godefroy and all her friends—but she remained equally inflexible, and her steady answer was as before. She proclaimed that, "dreadful as appeared the fatal separation, perhaps never more to meet, yet she could not but prefer remaining in Suriname. First from a consciousness that, with propriety, she had not the disposal of herself and, secondly, from pride, wishing in her present condition rather to be one of the first among her own class in America than a reflection or burden on me in Europe as she was convinced must be the case unless our circumstances became one day more independent." Here Joanna showed great emotion, but immediately retired to weep in private. What could I say or do? Not knowing how to answer or sufficiently to admire her firmness and resignation, which so greatly exceeded my own, I determined, if possible, to imitate her conduct and calmly to resign myself to my fate, preparing for the fatal moment, when my heart forebode me we were to pronounce the LAST ADIEU, and separate forever.…

---

59. I.e., Joanna.

The whole corps being ordered at seven o'clock on the morning of the 27th to wait on Colonel Fourgeoud at the headquarters, I tore myself away from all that was dear to me in this world without disturbing them in order to prevent the tender scene of parting. He then conducted us to the waterside where the boats lay in waiting and we were immediately embarked under a general salute and colors flying from the fortress and the vessels in the roads. After the whole corps dined on board the staff ship with Lieutenant Colonel de Borgnes, Colonel Fourgeoud politely invited me to accompany him back to town until next morning, but, with a broken heart, I thought best to decline. He then took his final leave and, wishing us all a safe and prosperous voyage to Europe, he returned under a salute of nine guns and three cheers with Captain Van Guerick, his adjutant, back to Paramaribo.

On the 29th of March at midnight, the signal-gun being fired, the two ships got under way and dropped down until before Fort New Amsterdam where they once more came to an anchor.

Here, my friends Gordon and Gourlay, the guardians of my boy…affectionately visited me and they did no less than actually prevail on me to accompany them back to Paramaribo. My soul could not resist this second invitation of once more beholding what was so dear to me. I went and—must I say it?—found Joanna, who had displayed so much fortitude in my presence now bathing in tears and scarcely alive so much was she become the victim of melancholy and despair. She had not partaken of food or sleep since my departure nor spoke to any living creature. Indeed, she had not stirred from the spot where I had left her on the morning of the 27th.

Since the ships were not ready to go to sea until two days later, I was prevailed upon to stay on shore a little longer with poor Joanna and her boy, which seemed to cheer her. But, alas! Too dear we paid for this too short reprieve! A few hours had elapsed when a sailor abruptly came in with the message that the ship's boat lay in waiting that minute to carry me on board. At that instant—Heavens! what were my feelings!—Joanna's mother took the infant from her arms and her brothers and sisters hung around me, crying, and invoking Heaven aloud for my safety. The unfortunate Joanna, now but nineteen years old, gazing on me and holding me by the hand was unable to utter one word!!! I perceived she was distracted and the hour was come. I exchanged a ringlet of their hair and fondly pressed them both to my bosom. The power of speech also forsook me and my heart tacitly invoked the protection of Providence to befriend them. Joanna now shut her beauteous eyes, her lips turned the pale color of death, she bowed her head, and motionless sunk in the arms of HER ADOPTED MOTHER.[60] Here I roused all my remaining fortitude

---

60. I.e., Mrs. Godefroy.

and leaving them surrounded by every care and attention departed, and bid GOD BLESS THEM!!!

The boat still delaying a few moments, I now stepped up to poor Fourgeoud, surrounded by my friends, and grasping his veteran hand. I could not, for my soul, but forgive him all the hardships he had ever occasioned me. He was *affected*. This was a debt he owed me. I wished him every good, and finally rowed down the river Suriname....

Appendix
The Diary and the Narrative

This appendix offers four examples to illustrate how Stedman and/or his editor and publisher transformed Stedman's experiences in Suriname from the initial impressions recorded in his diary into purposeful prose in the *Narrative*. In the process of narrativizing his account, Stedman downplayed, changed, or ignored any of his more ethically questionable activities. He and his editors likewise sought to make his Suriname experience into a morality tale, illustrating for readers the moral dangers of slavery. And, like many writers of his day, Stedman embraced popular eighteenth-century intellectual movements, including sentimentalism and humanitarianism. These ideals, popular with Enlightenment thinkers and literary figures alike, were meant to generate empathy with other human beings, especially those considered less fortunate, such as enslaved people. In Stedman's case, however, embracing these ideals meant rewriting and reframing his experiences in Suriname. In many cases, Stedman distorted the reality of his expedition to fit these tropes to such an extreme degree that it has led one literary scholar to call the *Narrative* "humanitarian pornography."[1] Another scholar, comparing the diary and *Narrative*, shows how Stedman used scientific rhetoric to "desexualize" his experiences in Suriname.[2] Confronting these changes and examining the difference between the diary and *Narrative* help us to understand better Stedman, his world, and why it is imperative to read his *Narrative* critically.

---

1. Mario Klarer, "Humanitarian Pornography: John Gabriel Stedman's *Narrative of a Five Years Expedition against the Revolted Negroes of Surinam* (1796)," *New Literary History* 36, no. 4 (Autumn 2005): 559–87.
2. Elizabeth Polcha, "Voyeur in the Torrid Zone: John Gabriel Stedman's *Narrative of a Five Years Expedition against the Revolted Negroes of Surinam*, 1773–1838," *Early American Literature* 54, no. 3 (2019): 673–710.

Example I: Mr. Lolkens's Maid

This example of Stedman's sexual encounter with an enslaved maid belonging to Mr. Lolkens, a Suriname planter and Stedman's patron, almost immediately upon his arrival in the colony has been documented by many anthropologists, historians, literary scholars, and previous editors of his work.[3] It is a short example that shows the way Stedman transformed sexual encounters he more than likely initiated into morality tales.

Diary

February 9, 1772: Our troops were disembarked at Paramaribo. A few soldiers faint. The whole corps of officers dine at the governor's table. I get fuddled[4] at a tavern. Go to sleep at Mr. Lolkens's, who was in the country. I fuck one of his negro maids.

1796 Narrative

CHAPTER I

...After partaking of this superb entertainment till about seven o'clock, I set out in search of the house of Mr. Lolkens, the hospitable gentleman who had invited me to make it my own. I soon discovered the place, but my reception was so ludicrous that I must relate the particulars. On knocking at the door, it was opened by a young female negro, of a masculine appearance, whose whole dress consisted of a single petticoat. She held a lighted tobacco-pipe in one hand and a burning candle in the other, which she brought close to my face, in order to examine me. I asked if her master was home, but she replied in a language totally unintelligible to me. I then mentioned his name, on which she burst into an immoderate fit of laughter, displaying two rows of very beautiful teeth. At the same time, grabbing the breast-buttons of my coat, she made me a signal to follow her. I was much at a loss how to act, but went in and was ushered by the girl into a very neat apartment. She brought some excellent fruit and a bottle of Madeira wine, which she placed upon the table. She then, in the best manner she was able, informed me that her *masera* [master], with the

---

3. See, for example, Polcha, "Voyeur in the Torrid Zone," 673–74; and Richard Price and Sally Price, eds., *Stedman's Surinam: Life in an Eighteenth-Century Slave Society* (Baltimore, MD: Johns Hopkins University Press, 1992), xxviii–xxx.

4. I.e., drunk.

rest of his family, left to spend a few days at his plantation. She was left behind to receive an English captain, whom she supposed to be me. I signified that I was and filled her out a tumbler of wine, which I had the utmost difficulty to persuade her to accept. That is the degrading light in which these unhappy beings are considered, and it is believed presumptuous for them to eat or drink in the presence of a European. I contrived for some time to carry on something like a conversation with this woman but was soon glad to put an end to it by recurring to my bottle.

Tired with the employments of the day, I longed for some rest and made a signal to my attendant that I wanted to sleep. My motion was strangely misconstrued. She immediately seized me by the neck and imprinted on my lips a most ardent kiss. Heartily provoked at this unexpected, and (from one of her color) unwelcome salutation, I disentangled myself from her embraces, and angrily flung into the apartment allotted for my place of rest. But here I was again pursued by my Black tormentor, who, in opposition to all I could say, insisted upon pulling off my shoes and stockings, and in a moment disencumbered me of that part of my apparel. I was extremely chagrined at her conduct, though this is commonly performed by the slaves in Suriname to all ranks and sexes without exception. No one should conceive that this apparently extraordinary conduct resulted from any peculiarity of the girl. Her behavior was only such as would have been practiced by the generality of female negro slaves, and what will be found, by all who visit the West India settlements, to be characteristic of the whole dark sisterhood.

Finding in the morning that my friend the planter had not returned, I took leave of his mansion and very hospitable servant....

Example II: Courting Joanna

In the 1796 Narrative, *Stedman made Joanna into a paragon of virtue, using her to show how even downtrodden, enslaved women of African descent could be honorable and fulfill the duties of European womanhood. From the start of their courtship, she was ladylike, behaved with the utmost courtesy, and was dutiful and loyal to Stedman. He even provided her own words for the reader. Yet, the diary tells a different story. Joanna was one of three enslaved girls Stedman vetted as a potential sexual partner. They were Joanna and two others whose names Stedman only recorded as "B——e" and "Q——."[5] Ultimately, Joanna won out after her mother made a deal with Stedman. The diary reveals a courtship that was less a romance and*

---

5. For more on this "courtship," see Polcha, "Voyeur in the Torrid Zone," 677, 683–85.

more of a business transaction. Finally, in both the diary and Narrative, Stedman acknowledges Joanna's age but does not dwell on their age difference. When he met her, she was fifteen, while he was twenty-eight. Between Joanna's enslaved status, African heritage, their brokered relationship, and the thirteen-year age gap, this serious power differential raises questions about Joanna's consent and agency, which the Narrative obfuscates.

Diary (all dates from 1773)

February

February 22:…A negro woman offers me the use of her daughter while here for a certain sum. We don't agree about the price.

February 25: Dine at the mess house and sup in my room with two mulatto girls[6] on bread, cheese, and a bottle of claret.

March

March 1:…Receive a cordial and two fine oranges from a mulatto girl.[7]

March 4:…B——e, a curious pasquil.[8]

March 12:…Three girls pass the night in my room.[9]

March 26:…B——e comes to me and stays the whole night.

April

April 7:…A discovery concerning B——e.

April 8:…I have a remarkable discourse with B——e.[10]

---

6. It is possible that one of these two girls was Joanna.
7. In the *Narrative*, Stedman later acknowledged it was Joanna who sent him the oranges.
8. It is unclear who "B——e" was, but she occasionally appeared in Stedman's diary. Most likely, she was one of the "three girls" who stayed with Stedman on March 12, and he may have courted. Likewise, what Stedman meant by "curious pasquil" is not clear. Nevertheless, a "pasquil" was another word for a satire or a lampoon. Perhaps Stedman considered "B——e" funny or some sort of vexing problem.
9. Stedman's use of the term "girls" here was not only derogative but also literal. One of them was probably Joanna, who would have been fifteen at the time and thus not legally an adult or "woman," but rather a "girl" in the eyes of the law.
10. While Stedman could be recounting his conversation with B——e, it may also be a sexual innuendo.

April 10:...Succor to Joanna.[11]

April 11: Dine at Demelly's. Joanna, her mother, and Q-'s mother come to close a bargain with me. We put it off for reasons I gave them...

April 13: B——e and Joanna both breakfast with me...

April 23: Joanna comes to stay with me. I give her presents worth about 10 pounds sterling and am perfectly happy.

MAY

May 8: Dine at Mr. Gordon's. Give my wedding.[12]

1796 Narrative

CHAPTER V

...I will offer a description of the beautiful mulatto maid Joanna. This charming young woman I first saw at the house of a Mr. Demelly, secretary to the court of policy, where I daily breakfasted.[13] His lady Joanna, but fifteen years of age, was a very remarkable favorite. Taller than average, she was possessed of the most elegant shape that nature can exhibit, moving her well-formed limbs with more than common gracefulness. Her face was full of modesty and the most distinguished sweetness. Her eyes, as black as ebony, were large and full of expression, bespeaking the goodness of her heart. She had cheeks, through which glowed, in spite of the darkness of her complexion, a beautiful tinge of vermillion, when gazed upon. Her nose was perfectly well formed and rather small. Her lips a little prominent, which, when she spoke, discovered two regular rows of teeth, as white as mountain snow. Her hair was a dark brown inclining to black, forming a beautiful globe of small ringlets and ornamented with flowers and gold spangles. Around her neck, her arms, and her ankles, she wore gold chains, rings, and medals. A shawl of India muslin, the end of which was negligently thrown over her polished shoulders, gracefully covered part of her lovely bosom. A petticoat of rich chintz alone completed her apparel. Bare-headed and bare-footed, she shone with double luster. She carried in her delicate hand a beaver hat, the crown trimmed round with silver.

---

11. I.e., Stedman provided some sort of aid and comfort to her. This is the likeliest interpretation of the original: "secrer to J——n" given what comes next in the diary, that is, he started to woo her and provide financial support.

12. Stedman proposed to Joanna, offering to free her, educate her, and make her his wife.

13. Demelly was the clerk for the Court of Policy and Justice, the primary court for adjudicating civil and criminal matters in Suriname.

The figure and appearance of this charming creature could not but attract my particular attention as they did indeed that of all who beheld her. It induced me to enquire from Mrs. Demelly, with much surprise, who she was as she appeared to be so much distinguished above all others of her species in the colony.

"She is, sir," replied his lady, "the daughter of a respectable gentleman, named Kruythoff, who had, besides this girl, four children by a Black woman, called Cery [Seerie], the property of a Mr. D. B. on his estate called Fauconberg, in the upper part of the river Commewijne.

"Some few years since Mr. Kruythoff made the offer of above one thousand pounds sterling to Mr. D. B. to obtain manumission for his offspring, which, being inhumanly refused, it had such an effect on his spirits, that he became frantic and died in that melancholy state soon after. That left in slavery, at the discretion of a tyrant, two boys and three fine girls, of which the one now before us is the eldest.[14]

"The gold jewelry, which seems to surprise you, are the gifts her faithful mother, who is a most deserving woman towards her children, and of some consequence amongst her caste, received from her father (whom she ever attended with exemplary affection) just before he expired.

"Mr. D. B., however, met with his just reward. Having since driven all his best carpenter negroes to the woods by his injustice and severity, he was ruined, obliged to flee the colony, and leave his estate and stock to the disposal of his creditors. One of the above unhappy deserters, a *sambo*,[15] has by his industry been the protector of Cery and her children. His name is Jolycoeur, and he is now the first of Baron's captains, whom you may have a chance of meeting in the rebel camp, breathing revenge against the Christians.[16]

"Mrs. D. B. is still in Suriname having been arrested for her husband's debts. She cannot leave until Fauconberg can be sold by execution to pay creditors.

---

14. Original footnote: In Suriname all such children go with their mothers; that is, if she is in slavery, her offspring are her master's property, should their father be a prince, unless he obtains them by purchase. [Slave societies in the Americas followed the legal principle of *partus sequitur ventrem* or just *partus*, meaning that children followed the status of their mothers. Thus, Joanna and her siblings were, like their mother, enslaved despite their father being white and free.]

15. Original footnote: A sambo is between a mulatto and a negro.

16. The relationship between Seerie and Jolycoeur speaks to how small and intimate of a society Suriname was. Jolycoeur was a leader of the rebels, while Seerie's daughter Joanna became close with Stedman, one of the officers sent to quell the rebellion.

This lady now lodges at my house, where the unfortunate Joanna attends her, whom she treats with peculiar tenderness and distinction."[17]

Having thanked Mrs. Demelly for her account of Joanna, in whose eye glittered the precious pearl of sympathy, I took my leave, and went to my lodging in a state of sadness and stupefaction. However trifling and romantic this relation may appear to some, it is nevertheless a genuine account. On that score, I flatter myself that it may not entirely be uninteresting to others....

I now took an early opportunity to enquire of Mrs. Demelly what had become of the amiable Joanna. I was informed that her lady, Mrs. D. B. had escaped to Holland on board the *Boreas* man-of-war under the protection of Captain Van de Velde and that her young mulatto was now at the house of her aunt, a free woman. She expected hourly to be sent up to the estate Fauconberg, friendless and at the mercy of some unprincipled overseer appointed by the creditors, who had now taken possession of the plantation and stock until the whole should be sold to pay the several sums due to them by Mr. D. B. Good God! I flew to the spot in search of poor Joanna and found her bathed in tears. She gave me such a look—ah! such a look! From that moment I determined to be her protector against every insult and eventually persevered. Here, reader, let my youth, blended with extreme sensibility, plead my excuse. Yet assuredly my feelings will be forgiven me—by those few only excepted—who delight in the *prudent* conduct of Mr. *Incle*, to the hapless and much-injured *Yarico* at Barbados.[18]

I next ran to the house of my friend Lolkens, who happened to be the administrator of Fauconberg estate. Asking his assistance, I intimated to him my strange determination of purchasing and educating Joanna.

---

17. Plantation owners everywhere in the Americas, especially in Suriname, were deeply in debt. Plantations were expensive to run, requiring constant upkeep of machinery and infrastructure and purchasing of enslaved laborers and provisions. Planters likewise led lavish lifestyles and borrowed heavily to acquire the latest fashions and luxury goods. These debts usually exceeded the value of their estates, meaning they were always on the cusp of financial ruin. One bad harvest, untimely death, revolt, or zealous creditor could create havoc for planters and, as one of the few forms of readily salable property they owned, enslaved people alike.

18. "Mr. Incle" and "Yarico" were the two lead characters in the popular 1787 comic opera *Inkle and Yarico*, about an English merchant, Inkle, shipwrecked in the West Indies, who is aided and falls in love with an Amerindian woman named Yarico. Musician Samuel Arnold composed the music, while dramatist George Colman wrote the libretto or text of the opera. The story is, in part at least, based on actual events. Richard Ligon, an English merchant and speculator most famous for writing an early history of Barbados, recounted the life and experiences of an enslaved Amerindian woman named Yarico, who lived in his household and was most likely his concubine. See Richard Ligon, *A True and Exact History of the Island of Barbados*, ed. Karen Ordahl Kupperman (Indianapolis: Hackett Publishing, 2011), 107.

Having recovered from his surprise, after gazing at me silently for some time, an interview at once was proposed. The beauteous slave, accompanied by a female relation, was produced trembling in my presence.

Reader, if you have perused the tale of Lavinia with pleasure, though the scene admits of no comparison, reject not the history of Joanna with contempt.[19] It now proved to be she who had privately sent me the cordial and the oranges in March when I was nearly expiring. She now modestly acknowledged she "was in gratitude for my expressions of compassion respecting her sad situation."[20] With singular delicacy, however, she rejected every proposal of becoming mine upon any terms. She was conscious, she said:

> "That in such a state should I soon return to Europe, she must either be parted from me forever or accompany me to a part of the world where the inferiority of her condition must prove greatly to the disadvantage of both herself and her benefactor and thus in either case be miserable."[21]

In these sentiments Joanna firmly persisting, she was immediately permitted to withdraw and return to the house of her aunt. I could only intreat of Mr. Lolkens his generous protection for her, that she might at least for some time be separated from the other slaves, and continue to reside in Paramaribo. In this request, his humanity was induced to indulge me.

…I was seized suddenly with a dreadful fever. Such was its violence that in a few days I was no more expected to recover.…Had it not been for the happy intervention of poor Joanna, who one morning entered my apartment to my unspeakable joy and surprise, accompanied by one of her sisters. She informed me that she was acquainted with my forlorn situation and that if I still entertained for her the same good opinion, her only request was that she might wait upon me until I recovered. I indeed gratefully accepted her offer. By her unremitting care and attention, I had the good fortune so far to regain my health.…

Until this time, I had chiefly been Joanna's friend. Now I began to feel I was her captive. I renewed my wild proposals of purchasing, educating, and transporting her to Europe, which, though offered with the most perfect sincerity, were rejected once more, with this humble declaration:

---

19. Lavinia was the wife of Aeneas, the hero of the ancient epic recounting the birth of Rome, the *Aeneid*. In the poem, she had many suitors from Italy but knew she was destined to marry a stranger and for greatness. Stedman's allusion to Lavinia suggested that Joanna was likewise destined to reside with a foreigner.
20. Readers should be skeptical of Stedman's direct quotations. He rarely recorded them in his diary and often relied on his faulty memory to compose them.
21. This is the first time that Joanna rejected Stedman's advances, especially any suggestion that she would leave Suriname and reside with him in Europe.

> "I am born a low contemptible slave. Were you to treat me with too much attention, you must degrade yourself with all your friends and relations. The purchase of my freedom you will find expensive, difficult, and apparently impossible. Yet though a slave, I have a soul, I hope, not inferior to that of an European and blush not to avow the regard I retain for you, who have distinguished me so much above all others of my unhappy birth. You have, Sir, pitied me. Now, independent of every other thought, I shall have pride in throwing myself at your feet until fate shall part us or my conduct become such as to give you cause to banish me from your presence."

This she uttered with a down-cast look and tears dropping on her heaving bosom while she held her companion by the hand.

From that instant, this excellent creature was mine. Nor had I ever after cause to repent of the step I had taken as will more particularly appear in the course of this narrative.

I cannot omit to record, that having purchased for her presents to the value of twenty guineas, I was the next day greatly astonished to see all my gold returned upon my table.[22] The charming Joanna having carried every article back to the merchants, who cheerfully returned her the money.

> "Your generous intentions alone, sir, (she said) were sufficient. Allow me to tell you, that I cannot help considering any superfluous expense on my account as a diminution of that good opinion which I hope you have and will ever entertain, of my disinterested disposition."

Such was the language of a slave, who had simple nature only for her instructor, the purity of whose sentiments stood in need of no comment, and these I was now determined to improve by every care.

I shall now only add, that a regard for her superior virtues, so singular amongst her cast, gratitude for her particular attention to me, and the pleasure of producing to the world such an accomplished character under the appearance of a slave could alone embolden me to risk the censure of my readers, by intruding on them this subject. Let this be my apology, and if it be accepted but by few, I shall not be inclined to complain.[23]

---

22. Stedman's reference to purchasing Joanna, the first mention of it in the *Narrative*, shows how he aggressively courted Joanna. Twenty guineas, or twenty-one pounds sterling, was a substantial sum of money in the eighteenth century.

23. Stedman worried about how his relationship with Joanna, a mixed-race woman, would be perceived by his readers. By transforming her into a paragon of virtue and innocence, he attempted to alleviate the audience's concerns.

In the evening I visited Mr. Demelly, who, with his lady, congratulated me on my recovery from sickness. At the same time, however strange it may appear to many readers, they, with a smile, wished me joy of what, with their usual good-humor, they were pleased to call my conquest. One of the ladies in company assured me, while it was perhaps censured by some, was applauded by many and, she believed in her heart, envied by all. A decent wedding, at which many of our respectable friends made their appearance, and at which I was as happy as any bridegroom ever was, concluded the ceremony....[24]

Example III: The Disappearing Lieutenant

Lieutenant Cabanus served under Stedman from their arrival in Suriname in February 1772 until Cabanus's death on June 3, 1776. Cabanus, however, remains something of an enigma, and we do not even know his first name. He started as a sergeant and, because of the deaths of commissioned officers, eventually worked his way up to lieutenant. Cabanus was a constant presence in Stedman's diary, largely because Stedman trusted and considered him a good soldier. He also possibly saved Stedman from drowning, although Stedman later challenged him to a duel and slept with his "girl." Despite their quarrels, however, Stedman did care about the man and seemed pained by his illness and death. Nevertheless, unlike the other two examples, where the Narrative *provides much more detail (even if embellished or outright false) than the diary, Cabanus rarely makes an appearance in the book. Indeed, he's only mentioned four times—three times performing his duties and the fourth being a record of his death. The original 1796 edition even misspelled Cabanus's name in both volumes and had to issue a correction in the "errata" section. It was corrected in later editions. The question remains why such a constant fixture of Stedman's experience in Suriname was written out of the* Narrative. *While that can never be fully answered, perhaps he felt guilt about their constant quarrels and the way he had treated Cabanus. Or, as in other parts of the* Narrative, *Stedman personalized the military matters, placing himself at the center of an expedition that was in reality a group effort.*

---

24. Stedman referenced his "wedding" in his diary on May 8, 1773. Under the law, enslaved people were not allowed to marry, meaning the ceremony's purpose is unclear besides formalizing the concubinage between Stedman and Joanna. The mention of the wedding here is once more trying to assuage his readers, who, as the last sentence implies, Stedman believed would judge him for his relationship with Joanna.

Diary

1773

September 3:…My sergeant Cabanus is made ensign.…

October 11:…Mewis is now 2nd lieutenant and Sergeant Cabanus is his ensign.…

1774

March 7:…Mr. Cabanus comes with a director, plaintiff, and free negro delinquent.[25]…Two directors dine here along with Mr. Cabanus.…

March 29: Mr. Cabanus dines here.…

April 14: I send him away. A punt comes from Tempatee loaded with about 150 men, Black and white, along with Major Abercrombie, Meyland, De Graaff, and Cabanus. I break my sword on the strongman.[26] Send negroes to Pathuysen and militia to Perica Creek. Send Cabanus and some men to Klarenbeek.…

April 28:…Cabanus comes to see us.…

1775

December 3: The command comes at last. They caught a pregnant woman and her little boy.…Mr. Cabanus, who took the above-mentioned woman, and two men carry her and the boy to Paramaribo.…

December 16:…Cabanus and Meijer come from Paramaribo.…

1776

January 1:…Hamell, Cranbe, Cabanus, and myself set off.…

February 8:…Hamell, Luik, Cabanus, and Rulagh to Maagdenburg.…

---

25. The "plaintiff" had a complaint against the Ranger ("free negro") who caused some offense. It is unclear if the plaintiff was free or enslaved, but the presence of a "director" or overseer suggests the latter.

26. This word is nearly illegible in the diary. Based on the draft, however, Stedman described how all these poorly disciplined soldiers arriving at the post caused pandemonium, and he had to restore order. He referenced breaking his sword while subduing one of the "ringleaders" in an attempt to restore peace. FD, 262.

April 4: …Monsieur Matthew comes here under my command. I continue to mess with Mr. Cabanus, being resolved not to eat at one table with the one just mentioned….[27]

April 6: I escape being drowned by Mr. Cabanus.[28]…

April 10: Send patrol and Mr. Cabanus to Klarenbeek.

April 13: …I challenge Cabanus for not being civil. He asks pardon and promises to mend. I roger his girl.

April 16: …Mr. Cabanus patrol to Klarenbeek….

April 22: Mr. Cabanus dines at Tomasberg.

May 1: …Cabanus goes to Abecable.

May 3: Mr. Cabanus comes back and with him is Mr. Francen, who dines with us and returns….

May 8: …Mr. Cabanus goes and dines at Knoppemombo….

May 13: I form a regular list for the mess, in which I have received Mr. Cabanus…. Mr. Cabanus goes on the rammle.[29]…

May 17: Mr. Cabanus comes home sick with fever….

May 19: …I order a waiter for Mr. Cabanus. He's very sick.

May 25: …I write to Appe-Cappe and beg Mr. Thys to send me the Society surgeon to consult with the one I have here, which was done accordingly. Both agree that poor Cabanus stands a bad chance of not recovering from his illness….

May 26: …I ask Doctor Romelyn how poor Cabanus fares and he told me with a self-sufficient grin that Cabanus would step off with the ebb….

May 27: Joanna makes Cabanus a ladle.[30] He is not worse….

June 3: …Poor Cabanus who relapsed last evening, this evening died at six o'clock….Mr. Francen comes from Klarenbeek to serve, to make Cabanus's inventory, and bury him.

---

27. i.e., Matthew.

28. This passage is awkwardly worded, and it is unclear if Cabanus attempted to drown Stedman or saved him from drowning. Stedman does not mention this episode elsewhere. Given Stedman's animus toward Cabanus below, he may have attempted the former.

29. "On the rammle" was a Scots slang term meaning to engage in noisy or boisterous behavior, especially under the influence of alcohol.

30. I.e., some sort of broth or soup.

June 4: Mr. Moryn gives Cabanus a black chest[31] and the poor lad was buried with all the decency that lay in my power....

June 8: Send Cabanus's goods to Paramaribo....

1796 Narrative

Chapter VIII

On my recommendation, my sergeant, Mr. Cubanns was appointed an ensign, which gave me pleasure....

Chapter XX

...Mr. Decabanes, my lieutenant, had the sling of his fusee[32] shot away....

Chapter XXIII[33]

...this poor woman and her boy were sent to Paramaribo, with Ensign de Cabaines, who had taken them: he had at the same time nearly seized a young girl about fifteen, who by her great agility, and being stark naked, slipped out of his hands....

Chapter XXV[34]

On the 3d, the surgeon made me the following report: "That my Ensign, Mr. Decabanes, had his anchor-apeek, and would certainly set sail for the other world with the ebbtide," which was really the case, for he died that very evening. This grieved me the more, as he had obtained his commission through my interest, and bore an excellent character.

---

31. I.e., coffin.
32. "Fusee" was a slang term for a flintlock rifle or pistol.
33. This chapter is not included in this edition. For the original quote, see John Gabriel Stedman, *The Narrative of a Five Years Expedition against the Revolted Negroes of Surinam: In Guiana, on the Wild Coast of South America; from the Year 1772 to 1777* (London: J. Johnson and J. Edwards, 1796), 2:174.
34. See John Gabriel Stedman, *The Narrative of a Five Years Expedition against the Revolted Negroes of Surinam: In Guiana, on the Wild Coast of South America; from the Year 1772 to 1777* (London: J. Johnson and J. Edwards, 1796), 2:232 for this quote.

Example IV: "Manner of Sleeping &c. in the Forest"

As part of recording his time in Suriname, Stedman painted many watercolors of the plants, animals, people, landscapes, and scenes he encountered. Throughout his life, Stedman dabbled in painting and visualized his experiences, especially in Suriname. These watercolors should be considered part of the diary. They were also the basis for the eighty engravings that appeared in the 1796 Narrative. *Nevertheless, as Stedman and his editors narrativized his experiences in Suriname to change its tone and message, the engravers also transformed Stedman's watercolors in significant and subtle ways. In the middle of this book are two images, Images 8 and 9. One is an original watercolor that was the basis for the other, an engraving entitled* Manner of Sleeping &c. in the Forest *that appeared in the* Narrative. *Examine how the engraver, Inigo Barlow (1759–?), changed Stedman's watercolor, especially the place and position of the enslaved people. How might these changes help to sanitize the* Narrative?

Further Reading

Editions of Stedman

Child, Lydia Maria. "Joanna." In *The Oasis*, edited by Lydia Marie Child, 65–105. Boston: Allen and Ticknor, 1834.

Joanna; or, the Female Slave. A West Indian Tale, Founded on Stedman's Narrative of an Expedition against the Revolted Negroes of Surinam. London: Lupton Relfe, 1824.

Stedman, John Gabriel. *The Narrative of a Five Years Expedition against the Revolted Negroes of Surinam: In Guiana, on the Wild Coast of South America; from the Year 1772 to 1777.* London: J. Johnson and J. Edwards, 1796.

———. *Narrative of a Five Years Expedition against the Revolted Negroes of Surinam: Transcribed for the First Time from the Original 1790 Manuscript.* Edited by Richard Price and Sally Price. Baltimore, MD: Johns Hopkins University Press, 1988.

Thompson, Stanbury, ed. *The Journal of John Gabriel Stedman, 1744–1797, Soldier and Author: Including an Authentic Account of His Expedition to Surinam in 1772.* London: The Mitre Press, 1962.

Biographies

Collins, Louise. *Soldier in Paradise: The Life of John Stedman, 1744–1797.* New York: Harcourt, Brace, and World, 1966.

Davis, Natalie Zemon. "Joanna." In *Dictionary of Caribbean and Afro–Latin American Biography*, edited by Franklin W. Knight and Henry Louis Gates, Jr., 3:416–18. New York: Oxford University Press, 2016.

Gelder, Roelof van. *Dichter in de Jungle: John Gabriel Stedman (1744–1797).* Amsterdam: Atlas Contact, 2018.

Thompson, Stanbury. *John Gabriel Stedman: A Study of His Life and Times*. London: Thompson and Company, 1966.

Secondary Sources

Brienen, Rebecca. "Joanna and Her Sisters: Mulatto Women in Print and Image, 1602–1796." *Early Modern Women: An Interdisciplinary Journal* 10, no. 2 (2016): 65–94.

Davis, Natalie Zemon. "Judges, Masters, Diviners: Slaves' Experience of Criminal Justice in Colonial Suriname." *Law and History Review* 29, no. 4 (October 2011): 925–84.

Fatah-Black, Karwan. *White Lies and Black Markets: Evading Metropolitan Authority in Colonial Suriname, 1650–1800*. Leiden: Brill, 2015.

Gwilliam, Tassie. "'Scenes of Horror,' Scenes of Sensibility: Sentimentality and Slavery in John Gabriel Stedman's *Narrative of a Five Years Expedition against the Revolted Negroes of Surinam*." *ELH* 65, no. 3 (1998): 653–73.

Hoogbergen, Wim. *The Boni Maroon Wars in Suriname*. Leiden: Brill, 1990.

Klarer, Mario. "Humanitarian Pornography: John Gabriel Stedman's *Narrative of a Five Years Expedition against the Revolted Negroes of Surinam* (1796)." *New Literary History* 36, no. 4 (Autumn 2005): 559–87.

Klooster, Wim, and Gert Oostindie. *Realm between Empires: The Second Dutch Atlantic, 1680–1815*. Ithaca, NY: Cornell University Press, 2018.

Polcha, Elizabeth. "Voyeur in the Torrid Zone: John Gabriel Stedman's *Narrative of a Five Years Expedition against the Revolted Negroes of Surinam*, 1773–1838." *Early American Literature* 54, no. 3 (2019): 673–710.

Pratt, Mary Louise. *Imperial Eyes: Travel Writing and Transculturation*. New York: Routledge, 1992.

Senior, Emily. "'Perfectly Whole': Skin and Text in John Gabriel Stedman's *Narrative of a Five Years Expedition against the Revolted Negroes of Surinam*." *Eighteenth-Century Studies* 44, no. 1 (2010): 39–56.

Index

Bold page numbers indicate an image or image caption.

abolitionism, xxii–xxxv
Accara, xix, 36, 36n189, 67, 69
Adricham, 74
Adventures of Roderick Random, The (Smollett), xii, xxxi
Aluku, xx
amelioration, xxxiv–xxxv
American Revenue, 171
Amerindian peoples, xv, xvii, xx, 51n29, 87n183, 97, 117n44, 154, 155n15, 155n17, 157n27
Anna Elizabeth, 75
Anna Elizabeth en Anna, 90
Anna Geertruy, 75–76
anti-Semitism, 96, 96n5, 176
Arawak (Arrowouka), 155, 155n15, 156–57
Arico, Captain, 49, 145
Arnold, Samuel, 117n44

banjos, 48, 48n18
Barbacoeba, 14–15, 17, 46, 89, 141
Barbacoeba Creek, 125
Barbados, xv–xvi, 117, 117n44, 189, 189n18
Barlow, Inigo, 196, pl. 9
Baron (rebel), 9, 111, 138, 145, 188
Baron (slave), 173
Bartolozzi, Francesco, pl. 2, pl. 3
Becquer, Captain, 3, 9, 12, 21, 34, 53
Beeltsuijders, Mr., 6
Berbice Slave Rebellion, xix, xxii, 29n142
Beugel, Mr., 5, 76
Beugel, Mrs., 58, 79

Blacks. *See* enslaved people; free Blacks; maroons
Blake, William, xxxv, pl. 6, pl. 7
Blenderman, Mr., 60–62, 64–65, 69, 69n109, 70, 70n112, 71–73, 136
Boni, Bokilifu, xx–xxi, xxiii–xxiv, 36n189, 145, 147
Boni/Aluku maroons, xv, xviii, xx–xxiv, 58, 58n66
Boni Maroon War, xv, xx, xxiv, xxxiii, pl. 2
Boreas, 6, 114, 116, 189
Boucou maroons, xx–xxi, 118, 118n49
Brandt, Mr., 23–24, 35, 43, 82

Cabanus, Lieutenant: death of, 69–70, 195; drowning incident, 61, 61n76, 194, 194n28; illness of, 66 -67; promotion of, 20, 24; relationship with Stedman, 37, 39, 41, 43, 49, 51, 53, 56, 60, 62–65, 192–94
Campbell, James, 23–24, 46, 54
Campbell, Robert, 9, 9n32, 26, 31
Carew, Bampfylde Moore, xxxi–xxxii
Caribbean, xv–xvi, 96, 96n4. *See also* West Indies
Caribs, 96
cassava, 36, 42, 42n220, 45, 49, 49n20
Cassipora Creek, 15–17, 45, 88, 170, 176, 179
Cats, Jacob, xxxviii, 45, 45n5
Cerberus, 121n53
Ceulen, Antoinetta Christina van, xi
Charon, 121, 121n53
Claas Creek, 51

199

Cling, Otto, 64, 70–71, 73
Coene, Johann, 21, 24, 52, 65, 71
Coermoetibo Creek, 14–15, 25–26, 29, 31, 50, 52
Cojo, 36, 36n195, 71, 71n118, 73, 138–39, 145
Coke, Captain, 10
Colman, George, 117n44
Commewijne River, 7, 30, 35, 114, 116, 162, 167
Cook, James, 97, 97n7
Coopman's Creek, 14
Coromantyn, Captain, 145
Cottenburgh, Mr., 16, 18, 18n92, 20, 24
Cottica River, 13–14, 16, 114, 116, 170
Crass, Captain, 8–9, 118
Cunningham, Alexander, 45–46

de Borgnes, Colonel, 59, 62, 73, 181
Dederlin, Ensign, 10, 53, 53n39
De Graaff, Mr., 27, 37, 41, 46–48, 48n17, 49, 52–56, 56n55, 58, 59, 62, 64–65, 77–84, 86, 87, 90, 154, 163, 176, 193
Demelly, Mr., 5, 7–8, 10–11, 34, 59, 110, 192
Demelly, Mrs., 8–9, 73, 111–12, 116, 189
Der Goede Vrienden, 58
Devil's Harwar, xxxviii, 14, 14n69, 15–17, 121, 124–28, 160. *See also* 's-Lands Welvaren
Du Peron, Sous-Lieutenant, 9, 36, 43
Dutch West India Company, xvi, 102, 102n15

enslaved people: emancipation of Rangers, xx–xxi; impact of tropical disease, xvii–xviii; prohibition on marriage, 106, 120n52; resistance by, xviii–xx, 10, 29n142, 36n189, 99, 99n9, 111n31, 141, 169; status of mother, 111n29; violence against, xvii–xviii, xxxi, 6, 9, 12–13, 42, 42n225, 65, 83–84, 110, 112–16, 128, 131, 134–36, 159–60, 162–66, 166n40, 167–69, 174, pl. 3. *See also* slavery
enslaved women: captured by maroons, xix–xx, 16, 163, 163n34, 169; hired as concubines, 33, 33n177; relations with Europeans, 103–4, 106, 108; sexual exploitation of, xxv, xxxix; as victims of rape, xxi–xxii, xxx, 137, 137n76; violence against, 55, 78, 82, 82n162, 83, 101, 163, 167, 177
Essay on Man (Pope), 98n8
Europe Supported by Africa and America (Blake), pl. 7

First Boni War, xv, xx, xxiv, xxxiii
Fort New Amsterdam, 3–4, 13, 25, 74, 100, 100n14, 101
Fortune Dago-So, 75
Fort Zeelandia, 48, 54, 77, 102, 102n17, 114, 118
Fourgeoud, Louis Henri: campaign against maroons, xxiv, 4, 4n6, 6–9, 14–16, 21, 25, 27–28, 118, 127, 137, 141–42, 151–52, 154–55, 170, 173; as commanding officer, xix, xxii, 47, 100; at Maagdenburg, 133–34; in New Rosenback, 136–37; political differences, xxii–xxiii, 108, 108n27, 109, 114; preparations for departure, 74–77; protection of Accara, 36n189; protection of Gausarie, 29n142; relations with maroons, 76, 133, 161, 169; Stedman critique of, 121, 123–24, 126, 128, 142; Stedman relations with, xxii–xxiii, 17–20, 22, 22n109, 23–24, 26–27, 29, 29n144, 30, 30n150, 32, 40, 42–44, 56–57, 114, 114n38, 121, 127–28, 173, 180–81; Wana Creek camp, 133–34
Fourth Anglo-Dutch War (1780–1784), xxviii
Fowler, James, xxxviii, 28, 41, 76n132, 77, 127, 147–48, 151
Fowler, John, 58, 70
Fredericy, Captain, 30–31, 34–35, 47–48, 50–53, 72, 79, 136
free Blacks: battles against rebels, 9, 16, 27; defense of Suriname, 173; destruction of rebel properties, 9, 71; discharged by Fourgeoud, 28; and Dutch forces, 9, 29, 29n142, 40, 64, 68, 154, 161; military skills of, 144. *See also* Rangers
French Guiana, xx, xxiv, 155, 155n14

Gado-Saby, 141, 146–47, pl. 2
Gausarie, xix, 29, 29n142, 30, 62, 88
George III, King, xiii, xxviii, 66n97
Gersdorph, Colonel, 12, 28
Gibhart, Judas, 48, 48n17, 49, 49n23, 51–52
Godefroy, Elizabeth: care of Joanna and Jack/Johnny, xxvii, 158, 162, 170, 179; friendship with, 24, 35, 37–39, 46, 49–50, 53–59, 74, 84–87; humanity toward enslaved, 175; plantation ownership, 113, 159; promise to free Joanna, 81, 81n154, 166; purchase of Joanna and Jack/Johnny, xxvii, 56, 56n55; refusal to post bond for Joanna and Jack/Johnny, 76, 78, 80–81
Gordon, Jamie, 46
Gordon, Robert, 5, 8–9, 12, 34, 52, 73, 75, 84, 87, 178, 181
Gourlay, James, 62–64, 68–69, 72–73, 75–77, 178, 181
Guianas, xv–xvi, xxii, 87n183, 155n14, 155n17

Halfhide, Mr., 50, 52, 60, 62, 90
Hamell, Captain, 39, 49, 53–54, 56, 60–62, 72, 76, 152, 161, 193
Hannibal, Captain, 32, 32n168, 145–46, 172
Harmony, 23
Hastings, Warren, xxxii
Henry (Joanna's brother), 176
Hind, 81
Hogarth, William, 149, 149n6
Hollandia, 90
Howe, William, 86n180
Huijsman, Mr., 5, 41, 42, 66
Hultman, Charlotta, 51n31

Incle, 117, 117n44, 189, 189n18

Jacoba Geertruyda, 90
Jamaica, xix, xxix–xxx, 96
James Ford Bell Library (University of Minnesota), xxxvii
Java Creek, 52, 72, 159
Jewish people: anti-Semitism, 96, 96n5, 176; banishment to Jew's Savannah, 13, 13n60; brutality toward enslaved, 12–13, 16n76; moneylenders, 176n52; Simchat Beit HaShoeivah celebrations, 84, 84n170; in Suriname, x, xvii, 9; violence against, 13, 13n61
Jew's Savannah, 13, 13n60, 16, 53–54, 78n142
Joanna, pl. 4, pl. 5; death of, xxix; description of, 110–11; gifts of oranges from, 6, 6n13, 112, 117, 186, 186n7; Godefroy and, xxvii, 56n55, 76, 76n134, 78, 81, 81n154, 87, 158, 166, 170; illness of, 47, 50, 53, 59, 71–73, 75, 137; Kruythoff manumission attempt, 111, 188; at L'Espérance, 64–65, 129, 133, 133n68, 134, 138; as paragon of virtue and innocence, xxvi, 95, 120, 120n51, 185, 187–91, 191n23; and Plantation Fauconberg, 37n199, 42, 65, 133, 133n68, 137; pregnancy of, 42, 42n221; refusal to leave Suriname, 117n47, 154, 158, 171, 180–81, 190n21; rejection of Stedman's advances, 117, 117n47, 118, 190, 190n21; relationship with Stedman, xxiv–xxvii, xxix, xxxii, 7n21, 8, 8n26, 10, 10n35, 12, 17–18, 22, 24–26, 30, 33–34, 37–39, 44, 53–54, 57, 64–66, 71, 71n118, 75, 109–11, 111n31, 112, 112n33, 116–17, 119–20, 120n50, 128, 154, 179–81, 185–87, 191; son Jack/Johnny, xxvii, 48–49, 49n19, 154, 154n12; Stedman's attempt to purchase, xxvii, 39n207, 81, 117–18, 120n50, 129–30, 139, 158, 189–90; victim of rape by Stedman, xi, xxi–xxii; wedding with Stedman, 9, 9n34, 120, 120n52, 192, 192n24
Johannes and Elizabeth, 10
Johnson, Joseph, xxxiii–xxxiv, xxxvi
Jolycoeur, Captain, 111, 111n31, 138–39, 145
Journal of John Gabriel Stedman (1962), xxxvii

Kennedy, Walter, 5–11, 13, 33, 35, 39, 64, 107, 119
Kiefhaber, Jan, 90
Kruythoff, Anthony Tielenius, xxv, 111, 188
Kwinti maroons, xviii

La Marre, Jettee de, 177–78
La Marre, Mr., 22, 34, 34n183, 35, 49, 56, 56n56, 128
Lantman, Colonel, 8–10

Laurant, Mr., 32, 32n168, 48, 85
Lepper, Lieutenant, 11, 11n48, 26n125
L'Espérance: command of, 35–43, 59–73; Joanna at, 64–65, 129, 133, 133n68, 134, 137–38; maroon raids in, 122; Stedman's cabin at, 49, 64, 129, 132–33, 137, pl. 5; sugar plantation at, 129–32
Life and Adventures of Bampfylde Moore Carew, The, xxxi
Life and Opinions of Tristram Shandy, Gentleman, The (Sterne), xxxi
Ligon, Richard, 117n44, 189n18
lockoman (sorcerer), 171–72
Lolkens, Mr., 3, 3n2, 4–10, 13, 34–35, 102–3, 115, 117–18, 129–30, 184, 189–90
Luck, Sergeant, 10
Lucretia, 39, 133

Maagdenburg, 56, 60–70, 72–73, 133–34
MacDonald, Charles, 50n27
MacNeil, Captain, 6, 6n16, 54–55, 59, 63, 75–76, 80, 112–14
MacNeil, Donald, 54, 155
Malthus, Thomas, xxxiii
Manner of Sleeping &c. in the Forest (Barlow), 196, pl. 9
maroonage, xviii
maroons: appearance of, 142; capture of enslaved women, xix–xx, 16, 163, 163n34, 169; culture of, 152–53; Jolycoeur leadership of rebels, 111, 111n31, 138, 145; military tactics of, xxiii–xxiv, 142, 145, 145n1, 148–49, 153; peace treaties with, xix; principal settlements of, xviii–xix, 145–46; raids on plantations, xviii–xxi, xxiii, 19, 22, 25, 25n122, 50, 122, 124, 127, 133, 138, 142, 163, 169; war against, xv, xix–xxi, xxiii–xxiv, 19–21, 126–28, 141–53
Matapacca Creek, 6, 14, 112
Matthew, Mr., 12, 22, 24, 52, 60–62, 194
Medlaer, Major, 13, 16, 35–41, 43, 48–49, 51, 54–55, 60, 65–67, 77, 147
Mewis, Mr., 10, 24, 31, 43, 48, 56, 70–74, 78, 193
Mewis, Mrs., 78
Meyer, Mr., 12–13, 43, 48, 69–70, 73, 76

Meyland, Captain, 41, 45–48, 52, 141, 144–45, 147
Mijnershaaven, Mrs., 74, 80, 83, 87
Minott, Captain, 10
Moryn, Mr., 53, 68–70, 70n112, 195

Narrative of a Five Years Expedition against the Revolted Negroes of Surinam, The (Stedman): antislavery message, xxxiii–xxxiv, xxxviii; barge travel in, 112–13, 116, 121, 121n53, 123; brutality of slavery in, 101, 110, 112–16, 128, 131, 134–36, 159–60, 162–66, 166n40, 167–69, 174–75; command of Devil's Harwar, 121–28; command of the Commewijne River, 162, 167; critical reading of, xxvi, 183; departure from Suriname, 158–59; dissipation in, xxi–xxxii, 107, 110, 118–19, 137; editing of text in, xxxiii–xxxv, xxxix; final campaign in, 170–73, 179; illustrations in, xxxv–xxxvi; jungle fighting and tracking, 121, 125–26, 142–53, 170; literary influences on, xxxi–xxxii; maroon raids in, 121–22, 127, 133, 141–42; as morality tale, 183–85; natural history in, xxxii–xxxviii, 101, 105, 105n22, 106, 108–9, 114, 124–26, 144, 149, 172; nature of expeditions in, 125–26; political dysfunction and, 108, 108n27, 109; preface to, 95–96; preparations for departure, 179–82; publication of, xi, xxix–xxx, xxxii–xxxvi; Rangers in, 102, 102n16, 118, 118n48; reformist vision of slavery in, xxxii, 96, 96n3, 159, 162–63, 170–71, 174–75; relationship with Joanna, xxiv–xxvii, xxxi, 95, 95n1, 109–12, 112n33, 116–17, 119–20, 120n50, 120n51, 154; soldier sickness and death, 116, 121–24, 136, 176; as Stedman ego-diary, xxx–xxxi; sugar plantations in, 129–32; tropical climate and disease in, 101, 107–8, 114, 116, 119, 121–22, 124–25, 125n58, 126; use of language in, xxxviii–xxxix, 103n18, 107n24; use of *Suriname Diary* for, xxxii, 1
natural history: bats, 28, 47, 56, 159; European plants, 161; illustrations of, xxxv; insect life, 21, 32, 101, 105–6, 108, 114, 124–25, 125n58, 126, 143, 149, 149n7; in

Narrative, xxxii; Stedman interest in, ix, xxxi–xxxii, xxxviii, 77, 109; trees and shrubs, 32, 32n165, 105, 105n21, 161, 172, 172n47

Ndyuka. *See* Okanisi maroons

Nepveu, Jan, xxii–xxiii, 38n206, 85, 162, 179

Netherlands: control of Suriname, xvi, 102, 102n15; German army recruits, 26, 26n126, 125, 125n60; as oligarchic republic, 99n9; Scots Brigade, xi–xiii, 99–100; Suriname expeditionary forces, 97–100; war on Britain, xvi, xxviii. *See also* Society of Suriname

New Rosenback, 136–39

Okanisi maroons, xviii–xix

Olive Branch, 24

Orzinga, Captain, 18–19, 47, 50, 121–22

Owca maroons, 58, 58n66, 96, 154, 161, 169

Palmer, Thomas, xxxii, 63–65, 68, 79, 85, 175

Paramaribo: Dutch departure from, 179–82; Dutch expeditionary forces in, 4, 6–7, 13, 34, 74, 100–109, 114; English colony in, xvi; enslaved people in, xvii, xxv; social clubs in, 54, 54n47; Stedman arrival in, 3–4, 102–3; Stedman recuperation in, 22–23, 128, 159

Paramaribo (ship), 74, 76

Passalage, Mr., 38–39, 39n207, 129

Patamacca, 14, 18, 22, 31, 122–23

Patamacca Creek, 13, 17, 31

Peggy, 171

Perica Creek, 14–15, 21n101, 40, 62, 124, 126, 133

Perret, Captain, 47, 49, 51–52, 79

Plantation Fauconberg, xxv, 37, 37n199, 38–39, 42, 64–65, 111, 116–17, 129, 137, 189

plantations: in Barbados, xv–xvi; *bassia* on, 27, 27n130, 115, 115n40; brutality toward enslaved, xvii, xxx, 6, 42–43, 79–80, 112–16, 128, 134–36, 167, 174; cacao, xv, xvii, 113, 159; coffee, xv, xvii, 6–7, 112, 114, 116, 159; depictions in the *Narrative*, xi, xxxi; enslaved resistance, xviii–xix, 10; indigo, 80–81, 166; *lockoman* (sorcerer), 171–72; maroon raids, xviii–xxi, xxiii, 19, 22, 25, 25n122, 50, 121–22, 127, 133, 138, 142, 163, 169; owner debt, xxv, 111n32, 189, 189n17; sugar plantations, xv, 114, 130–32; in Suriname, xi, xv–xx, 164n37; in Tobago, 11n46

Pope, Alexander, 98n8

Price, Richard, xxxiii

Price, Sally, xxxiii

Prince William VI, 13

Quaco: attendance on Stedman, 4, 4n4, 33, 39, 49–50, 64, 128, 150; gifted to Stedman, xxii, 107, 107n23; gifted to the Countess of Rosendaal, xxviii, 107n23; manumission of, xxviii; Stedman's purchase of, 158

Quassi, Graman, 57, 81–82, 170–72

Quammy, 145–46

Raleigh, Walter, xv

Randwijk, Lieutenant, 33–34, 42

Rangers, xx–xxi, xxiii–xxiv, 9, 9n34, 102, 102n16, 118, 118n48, 148, 150, 160, pl. 6

Reygersman, Mr., 5, 7, 34, 58, 77

Rosendaal, Countess of, xxviii, 107n23

Roux, Mr., 12, 74, 80, 158

Rughcop, Mr., 5, 8–9, 12, 25–27, 35

Rulagh, Mr., 24, 37, 39, 56, 60, 62, 65–66, 70–71, 73

Rynsdorp, Andrew, 172

Rynsdorp, Charles, 84, 114, 169

Rynsdorp, Mr., 6–7, 79, 102, 159–60

Rynsdorp, Mrs., 63, 67, 87

's-Lands Welvaren, xxxviii, 14–19, 19n95, 21, 58. *See also* Devil's Harwar

Saamaka maroons, xviii–xix, 58, 58n66, 96, 154, 161, 169

Sampson, Zubly, 53, 53n38

Sancho, 28, 28n139, 31

Sara, 71, 73

Saramacca. *See* Saamaka maroons

Saramaka. *See* Saamaka maroons

Scots Brigade: in Dutch army, xi–xiii, xxviii–xxix, 99–100; loyalty to Britain, xiii, xxviii–xxix; refusal to fight in the American revolution, 66n97, 86n180; Stedman service in, xii–xiv, xxviii, 99, 99n10, 100–101; Suriname expeditionary forces, ix, xiv, xxi–xxiv, 97, 99–101

Second Anglo-Dutch War (1665–1667), xvi
Seerie (Cery), xxv–xxvi, 111, 111n31, 188
September (prisoner), 41, 133, 133n70
Seven Provinces, 13–14, 16–19
Seyburg, Colonel, 46–48, 48n17, 49n23, 50–52, 54, 66–67, 75, 91
slavery: ameliorationist policy, xxxiv–xxxv; anti-Semitism, 96, 96n5; emancipation, 169, 178, 178n57, 188; images of, xxxvi, pl. 3; moral dangers of, ix, xxxi–xxxii, 163, 183; public opinion on, xxxiii–xxxiv; reformist vision of, ix, xiv, xxxi–xxxiv, 96n3, 162–63, 170–71, 174–75; resistance to, xviii, 98. See also enslaved people; plantations
slave societies: brutality in, 110, 112–16, 129, 162–63, 174–75; diaries by whites in, xxx–xxxi, xxxix; enslaved resistance in, 98–99; white privileges in, xvii, xxi–xxii, xxv, xxxi, 104. See also plantations
Smollett, Tobias, xii, xxxi
Society of Suriname: administration of colony, xvi, 102, 102n15; Amsterdam investment in, 55, 55n50; control of 's-Lands Welvaren, 19, 19n95; Rangers, xxi, xxiii–xxiv; Soribo military post, 21, 21n101; war on maroons, xxi, xxiii–xxiv, 41, 121–22, 124
Soribo, 21, 21n101
Stedman, Adrian, xxviii
Stedman, Charles, 86n179
Stedman, George William, xxviii
Stedman, John Cambridge, xxviii
Stedman, John Gabriel, pl. 2; admiration for Rangers, xxiii, 144, 148; as ameliorationist, xxxiv–xxxv; anti-Semitism, 96, 96n5, 176; arrival in Paramaribo, 102–5; attempt to free Jack/Johnny from slavery, xxvii, 81, 84, 162, 166, 169, 176; attempt to purchase Joanna, xxvii, 39n207, 81, 117–18, 120n50, 129–30, 139, 162, 189–90; biography of, xi–xii, xxxvii–xxxviii; classism, 96n3, 96n5; criticism of Fourgeoud, 121, 123–24, 126, 128, 142; critiques of slavery, xxxiv–xxxv, xxxix, 96, 96n3; death of, xxx, xxxii; departure from Suriname, xxvii–xxviii, 179–82; diary writing, xxx–xxxi; excessive drinking, xi, xxi, 4, 8, 33, 33n176; exile to England, xxix; family with Adriana, xxviii; interest in American Revolution, 86n180; interest in natural history, ix, xxxi–xxxii, 32n165, 105, 105n22, 106, 109, 114, 149, 149n7, 159, 172; racist discourse, xxviii, xxxi, 96, 96n3, 96n5, 153–57; relationship with Joanna, xxiv–xxvii, xxix, 7n21, 8, 8n26, 9, 9n35, 10, 10n45, 12–13, 17–18, 20, 22, 24–26, 30, 33–34, 37–39, 44, 53–54, 57, 64–66, 71, 71n118, 75, 109–11, 111n31, 112, 112n33, 116, 119–20, 120n50, 120n51, 128, 154, 179–81, 185–87, 191, pl. 5; relations with Black and mixed-race women, xxi, xxiv–xxv, xxxii, 95n1, 104, 106, 120n51; Scots Brigade service, xii–xiv, xxviii, 99, 99n10, 100–101; sexual appetite, xi, xiii–xiv, xxi–xxii, xxvi, 4–5, 7–8, 57, 61, 185–86; sexualizing of women of color, 154–55, 155n16, 156, 161; sketches and watercolors by, xxxii, xxxv, 55, 55n49, 83, 87, 175, 196, pl. 8; slave ownership, xxii, xxvi, 129, 138, 138n77; son Jack/Johnny, xxvii, xxix, 48–49, 49n19, 154n12, 166; Suriname expeditionary forces, xiv–xv, xxi–xxiv, 97, 100–103; violence by, xiv, xxii, xxxi, 14, 121, 127; wedding to Joanna, 9, 9n35, 120, 120n52, 192, 192n24
Stedman, Jack/Johnny (son), pl. 5; birthday of, 48–49, 88; death of, xxix; emancipation of, 178; Godefroy refusal to post bond, 76, 76n124, 78; illness of, 47, 50, 53, 59, 68, 72–73; joining father in England, xxix; at L'Espérance, 64–65
Stedman, John (uncle), xii
Stedman, Maria Joanna, xxviii
Stedman, Robert, xi–xiii
Stedman, Sophia Charlotte, xxviii
Stedman, William George, xiii, xxix, 28, 28n138, 51, 51n31, 66, 85
Sterne, Laurence, xxxi
Stolker, Mr., 6, 84, 84n167
Stolker, Mrs., 42, 136, 136n75
Stromer, Lieutenant, 12–13, 16–18, 24
Stuart, John, 99
Summer (Thomson), 123n55
Suriname, vii; arrival of Dutch forces in, 99–109; enslaved people in, xvii, xix–xx;

exploration of, 97–98; longevity of women in, 107–8; military politics in, xxii–xxiii, 102, 102n15; mixed-race people in, 103n18; plantation agriculture in, xv–xx, 164n37; *polder* system in, xvi–xvii; slave rebellion/maroon war in, xv, xviii–xxi, xxiii–xxiv, 98–99, 99n9, 100; Sranan Tongo language in, 164n37; tropical climate and disease in, xvii, xxiii, 101, 107–8, 114, 116, 119, 125, 125n58. *See also* plantations

Suriname Diary of John Gabriel Stedman, **92**, pl. 1; American Revolution in, 86, 86n179, 86n180; arrival in Suriname, 3–4; biography in, xxxvii–xxxviii; command of Cottica River, 13–21; command of L'Espérance, 35–43, 59–73, pl. 5; court-martialing, 30, 30n152; creation of dams, 67, 69, 69n107, 70, 70n112; on the dance banjar, 48, 48n18; encounter with witch, 16, 16n76; excessive drinking in, 4, 8, 11–12, 12n57, 22, 25, 25n120, 33, 33n176, 43, 46, 73–74; German messmates, 26, 26n126; on Joanna's illness, 47, 50, 53, 59, 62, 71–73; on Jack/Johnny's illness, 47–50, 53–54, 59, 62, 68, 72–73; march to Cassipora Creek, 88–91; maroon raids in, 9–11, 19, 50, 88; miserable marching conditions, 21, 26–32, 32n161; preparations for departure, 73–82; promotions of soldiers, 9–10, 12, 28, 35, 50; provisioning in, 16–19, 23, 23n116, 24, 27, 39, 41, 51, 65, 68, 72; sexual exploits in, 4–5, 7–8, 57, 57n61, 61; shooting of monkeys, 17, 17n83, 18; soldier sickness and death, 14–20, 20n98, 21–22, 26–27, 32, 32n162, 37, 39–43, 46–52, 60–62, 66–67, 69–70, 72, 76, 90; as source for *Narrative*, xxxii, 1; theft of pork by Blacks, 27, 27n132; tracking maroon rebels, 20–21, 28–31, 45; use of language in, xxxvii–xxxviii, 16n78, 36n193; violence against enslaved in, 6, 9, 12–13, 42, 42n225, 65

Suriname River, xvi, 7–8, 16, 105, 116

Swildens, Mr., 13, 28, 35, 43–44, 52, 62, 76

Tamera, 138–39
Texier, Colonel, 5, 23–24, 54, 58, 61, 83, 86, 88, 107

Thistlewood, Thomas, xxx
Thompson, Stanbury, xxxvii
Thompson, William, xxxiii–xxxv
Thomson, James, 123, 123n55
Timme, Mr., 60–62, 64, 66–69
Timmons, Tom, 23
Tobago, 11, 11n46, 11n49
Tulling, Captain, 12, 48, 53, 76, 135, 155

Van Aerssen van Sommelsdijck family, xvi, 102n15
Van Coeverden, Lieutenant, 9, 30, 43, 54, 72, 84
Van der Meij, Mr., 7, 157
Van de Velde, Captain, 6, 11, 11n52, 23, 24n118, 114, 116, 189
Van Halm, Lieutenant, 12, 36–38, 42, 58, 60–61
Van Zende, Sous-Lieutenant, 10
Vernon, Edward, 123n55
Vigilance, 9, 100
Vrou Anna Geertruy, 74

Wana Creek, 25–26, 26n126, 28–29, 31, 41, 51–52, 58, 91, 133–34
Washington, George, 86n180, 159
Westellingwerf, 8, 118
Westerloo, Colonel, 9, 17–19, 21–24, 33, 127–28, 128n64
West Indies, xiv, xxxiv, 96, 96n4. *See also* Caribbean
whites (Europeans): debaucheries of, xvii, xxi; impact of tropical disease and climate, xvii, 107–8, 118, 124; indentured servants, xv, 128, 128n64; racist discourse, 156; rape of enslaved women, xxi–xxii, xxx; sexual exploitation by, xxi, xxii, xxv, 106; slave society diaries, xxx–xxxi; slave society privileges, xvii, xxi–xxii, xxv, xxxi, 104
Wierts van Coehorn, Adriana, xxviii–xxix
William V, 99, 100n11
Wollstonecraft, Mary, xxxiii

Yarico, 117, 117n44, 178, 189, 189n18

Zeebrandt, Cornelius, 9
Zeelust, 33